Cultivating
Communities
of Practice

A GUIDE TO MANAGING KNOWLEDGE

Cultivating Communities of Practice

Etienne Wenger

Richard McDermott

William M. Snyder

HARVARD BUSINESS SCHOOL PRESS

Boston, Massachusetts

Requests for permission to use or reproduce material from this book should be directed to permissions@hbsp.harvard.edu, or mailed to Permissions, Harvard Business School Publishing, 60 Harvard Way, Boston, Massachusetts 02163.

Library of Congress Cataloging-in-Publication Data

Wenger, Etienne, 1952-

   Cultivating communities of practice : a guide to managing knowledge / Etienne Wenger, Richard McDermott, William Snyder.

     p. cm.

   Includes bibliographical references and index.

   ISBN 1-57851-330-8

   1. Knowledge management. 2. Organizational learning. I. McDermott, Richard A. (Richard Arnold) II. Snyder, William, 1956- III. Title.

HD30.2 .W46 2002

658.4'038—dc21

2001051483

The paper used in this publication meets the requirements of the American National Standard for Permanence of Paper for Publications and Documents in Libraries and Archives Z39.48-1992.

from Etienne, to his wife, Paula
from Richard, to his dad, F. Arnold McDermott
from Bill, to his parents, Pat and Monte

Contents

Preface

Some connections are inevitable. Given enough time and networking, some people are bound to meet and find that they share a passion. For more than a decade, the three of us had been working with communities of practice in our own ways. Etienne had been involved in the original research at the Institute for Research on Learning as well as some early work at Xerox and National Semiconductor; he had also written a seminal book on communities of practice. Richard had been building "learning communities" for a dozen years at companies such as Ben & Jerry's, Shell Oil Company, and Hewlett-Packard, as well as writing articles and developing tools to help change agents build such communities. Bill had found the concept in Etienne's dissertation and used it as a key element in his own dissertation on the connection between learning and performance in organizations. He also used it to inform his work on knowledge and communities at Colgate-Palmolive, McKinsey & Company, and the federal government.

When Bill invited Richard to a colloquium he had organized at Boston College, with Etienne as a speaker, the planets—or at least the networks—were aligned. By then we were all consulting with organizations on issues related to learning and knowledge, and we started working together. We also started leading workshops and conferences together. Along with our growing friendship, we were developing a common practice. Etienne had a proposal with Harvard Business School Press to write a new book targeted at practitioners. It was a logical step to invite Bill and Richard to join forces.

Meanwhile, interest in communities of practice was exploding. The field of knowledge management had gone through a first wave of focus on technology. A second wave dealt with issues of behavior, culture, and tacit knowledge, but mostly in the abstract. A third wave now is discovering that communities of practice are a practical way to frame the task of managing knowledge. They provide a concrete organizational infrastructure for realizing the dream of a learning organization.

The number of companies launching initiatives on communities of practice is increasing so rapidly, we have no way of keeping track. In this book, we use a few pioneering firms as examples. Now, however, leading organizations in a wide range of industries and sectors, including many organizations you would not expect, are basing their knowledge initiatives on communities of practice, including Microsoft, Hallmark Cards, Procter & Gamble, Johnson & Johnson, federal agencies, military services, school systems, nonprofits, and citizen groups. In addition, there are now regular conferences on communities of practice, and many academics are turning their attention to the topic. We had anticipated that communities of practice would become an increasingly visible part of the management agenda. Still, we are all surprised to see how fast and how widely this trend has grown.

There was a need for a book to provide a common foundation for this spreading movement. Etienne's earlier book served this purpose to some extent, but it was targeted to an academic audience, and at the time it was written, applicable experience in organizations was limited. All three of us wanted to write a guide for practitioners, built on actual examples that described how communities of practice could be made an explicit part of how organizations work.

We knew that this book had to reach a number of different audiences to whom our concepts and methods were relevant—executives, managers, knowledge officers, and community developers. We believe that because these people need to work in coordination, there is much to be gained from sharing a basic text. Executives and managers need to appreciate the strategic value of communities of practice and the role of management, but they also need to trust that they can rely on a robust practice of community development. People in charge of knowledge resources need to know how to run a broad initiative, but they also need to understand in some detail what it takes to start communities and support their leaders. Community coordinators need to understand the developmental stages of communities and the specific actions they can take to help their communities evolve, but they also need to reflect on their work in the context of strategic objectives and organizational transformation.

So, we wrote a book that covers a lot of territory in a succinct fashion. We start with the conceptual foundations in chapters 1 and 2, including what communities of practice are and why they are important for organizations. In chapters 3, 4, and 5, we discuss the art of community development, from basic design principles to the process of supporting a community through its stages of development. In chapter 6 we consider the special case of distributed communities, and in chapter 7 we take a good look at the potential downside of communities. Then we turn to the challenges of measurement and management in chapter 8 and of running a company-wide knowledge initiative in chapter 9. Finally, in chapter 10 we muse on the broader potential of communities of practice for organizing knowledge beyond single organizations and in society more generally.

Cultivating Communities of Practice represents an important step in moving from theory to practice; one we hope will open new doors in the field. We see this book as just one foundational element in the emerging community of community-development practitioners. Eventually, we hope this book will spur a broader movement to apply the principles of community-based knowledge development to domains beyond business—including government, education, and even civic arenas. We share a vision that communities of practice will help shape society with pervasive knowledge-oriented structures. They will provide new points of stability and connection in an increasingly mobile, global, and changing world.

The ideas expressed in a book such as this one are never the creation solely of the authors. In our case, they find their origin in a vast web of relationships and conversations that include people we have worked with and who have directly influenced our thinking as well as people whose influence has been indirect, sometimes beyond our awareness. To all, we express our gratitude and our sense of belonging to a community in search of itself. Here we would like to acknowledge explicitly the intellectual and practical companionship and support of a few of our fellow travelers: Pat Amberg-Blyskal, Larry Baumgart, Mary Lynn Benninger, John Seely Brown, Michael Burtha, Roberto Chavez, Cindy Cisneros, Steve Denning, Stephan Egnolff, Nathaniel Foote, Paul Gustavson, Susan Hanley, Peter Hiller, Jeff Jackson, Pam Johnson, Sean Lave, Eric Lesser, Paul Lotts, Brook Manville, R. S. Moorthy, Michael Müller, Joshua Plaskoff, George Por, Larry Prusack, Melissie Rumizen, Hubert Saint-Onge, Michael Seelman, Lesley Shneier, John Smith, Estee Solomon-Gray, Jeff Stemke, Marc Swartz, Erick Thompson, Joe Thompson, Alex van den Berg, Eric Vogt, and Vivian Wright. We also want to thank our team at HBS Press, Hollis Heimbouch, Genoveva Llosa, Melinda Merino, Jill Connor, and Julie Devoll for their exceptional competence, support, patience, and substantive contribution to the manuscript.

Cultivating Communities of Practice

Communities of Practice and Their Value to Organizations

I N 1988, WHEN JAPANESE COMPETITION WAS THREAT-
ening to put the Chrysler Corporation out of business, no one
suspected that the resurgence of the company (now the Chrysler unit of
DaimlerChrysler) would depend in part on the creation of an innovative
knowledge system based on communities of practice. While some of its
competitors took as little as three years to get a new vehicle to market, a
typical new-product development cycle at Chrysler easily ran five years.
This was no way to compete. The first order of the day was to achieve a dramatic reduction in this product-development cycle.

   The story is well known, though the role that communities of practice
played is less widely understood. At the time, Chrysler was a traditional
organization typical of large manufacturing operations, with functional
units such as design, engineering, manufacturing, and sales. The design
department would send a new design to engineering, which would send it
back for redesign a few times. The design would then go to manufacturing

*and be returned for reengineering until the vehicle was deemed "manufac-
turable." The localized focus of the various functional units limited interaction between departments and thus gave rise to these unavoidable itera-
tions. Repeated hand-offs, duplication, and therefore slowness, were built
into the system.*

*The decision was made to radically reorganize the unit. Engineers would
now belong to "car platforms." These platforms were product-oriented,
cross-functional structures that focused on a type of vehicle: large cars,
small cars, minivans, trucks, and Jeeps. Each platform was responsible for
all phases of development associated with the whole vehicle. Engineers of
all specialties reported to supervisors within the platform on which they
worked. As a result, their primary focus was on the development of a specific vehicle. For instance, if you were a brakes engineer, your main alle-
giance, your reporting relationships, and your performance evaluation
were no longer with the brakes department, but with a platform, such as
small cars or minivans.*

*Eventually, the move to car platforms succeeded in reducing the product-
development cycle from five to two and a half years, with a corresponding
cut in research and development costs. But the restructuring did not come
without its own costs. A host of new problems started to appear: multiple
versions of the same part with slight variations, uncoordinated relationships with suppliers, innovations that did not travel, and repeated mistakes. The company had gained the advantage of product focus, but com-
promised its ability to learn from its own experiences. Something had to be
done to save the platform idea.*

*With a clear need for communication across platforms, former col-
leagues from functional areas started to meet informally. Managers recognized the value of these informal meetings in fostering learning processes
that cut across all platforms. Still, they wanted to keep the primary alle-
giance and formal reporting relationships of engineers within the platforms. Rather than formalizing these emerging knowledge-based groups
into a new matrix structure, they decided to keep them somewhat informal
but to sanction and support them. The Tech Clubs were born.*

*Tech Clubs began to take more active responsibility for their areas of
expertise. For instance, they started to conduct design reviews for their*

members before a design went through quality gates. In 1996, an engineering manager revived the old idea of creating an Engineering Book of Knowledge (EBoK), a database that would capture the relevant knowledge that engineers needed to do their job, including compliance standards, best practices, lessons learned, and supplier specifications. The EBoK vision could succeed only if the engineers themselves took responsibility for creating and maintaining the content. Some Tech Club leaders saw the project as an opportunity for consolidating Tech Club knowledge and taking stewardship of it. Documenting engineering knowledge had been tried several times before, but now it was part of the activities and identity of specific communities in charge of designated areas of engineering. This communal responsibility for producing the EBoK was key to its success.

Over time, Tech Clubs progressively established their value and they have become an integral part of engineering life at the Chrysler division. Engineers have discovered that participation helps them do their jobs better, and the time spent together is a good investment. It often saves them time later and increases their confidence in their own designs. It gives them a chance to get help with specific problems, to learn what others are discovering, and to explore new technologies. Today, there are more than one hundred officially recognized Tech Clubs, plus a few emerging ones. They are responsible for a host of knowledge-based activities such as documenting lessons learned, standardizing practices for their area, initiating newcomers, providing advice to car platforms, and exploring emerging technologies with suppliers. Through the Tech Clubs, Chrysler realized the value of what today people call "communities of practice." Theirs is among the pioneering stories, but it is no longer unique. It reflects a movement spreading all over the world.

Companies at the forefront of the knowledge economy are succeeding on the basis of communities of practice, whatever they call them. The World Bank delivers on its vision of fighting poverty with knowledge as well as money by relying on communities of practice that include employees, clients, and external partners. Shell Oil relies on communities of practice to preserve technical excellence across its multiple business units, geographical regions, and project teams. McKinsey & Company counts on its communities of practice to maintain its world-class expertise in topics important to clients who are themselves becoming smarter and more demanding. The list could go on and on. In all industries, companies are discovering that communities of practice are critical to mastering increasingly difficult knowledge challenges. They are learning to recognize and cultivate these communities. Moreover, once these communities find a legitimate place in the organization, they offer new possibilities—many yet undiscovered—for weaving the organization around knowledge, connecting people, solving problems, and creating business opportunities. And because communities of practice are not confined by institutional affiliation, their potential value extends beyond the boundaries of any single organization.

What Is a Community of Practice?

COMMUNITIES OF PRACTICE are groups of people who share a concern, a set of problems, or a passion about a topic, and who deepen their knowledge and expertise in this area by interacting on an ongoing basis. Engineers who design a certain kind of electronic circuit called phase-lock loops find it useful to compare designs regularly and to discuss the intricacies of their esoteric specialty. Soccer moms and dads take advantage of game times to share tips and insights about the subtle art of parenting. Artists congregate in cafés and studios to debate the merits of a new style or technique. Gang members learn to survive on the street and deal with an unfriendly world. Frontline managers running manufacturing operations get a chance to commiserate, to learn about upcoming technologies, and to foresee shifts in the winds of power.

These people don't necessarily work together every day, but they meet because they find value in their interactions. As they spend time together, they typically share information, insight, and advice. They help each other solve problems. They discuss their situations, their aspirations, and their needs. They ponder common issues, explore ideas, and act as sounding boards. They may create tools, standards, generic designs, manuals, and other documents—or they may simply develop a tacit understanding that they share. However they accumulate knowledge, they become informally bound by the value that they find in learning together. This value is not merely instrumental for their work. It also accrues in the personal satisfaction of knowing colleagues who understand each other's perspectives and of belonging to an interesting group of people. Over time, they develop a unique perspective on their topic as well as a body of common knowledge, practices, and approaches. They also develop personal relationships and established ways of interacting. They may even develop a common sense of identity. They become a community of practice.

Communities of practice are not a new idea. They were our first knowledge-based social structures, back when we lived in caves and gathered around the fire to discuss strategies for cornering prey, the shape of arrowheads, or which roots were edible. In ancient Rome, "corporations" of metalworkers, potters, masons, and other craftsmen had both a social aspect (members worshipped common deities and celebrated holidays together) and a business function (training apprentices and spreading innovations).[1] In the Middle Ages, guilds fulfilled similar roles for artisans throughout Europe. Guilds lost their influence during the Industrial Revolution, but communities of practice have continued to proliferate to this day in every aspect of human life.[2] Every organization and industry has its own history of practice-based communities, whether formally recognized or not. Why else are the surviving U.S. automakers all based in Detroit? What explains the high-tech fertility of Silicon Valley? And why can't you buy a world-class flute outside of three small manufacturers based in Boston?[3]

Communities of practice are everywhere. We all belong to a number of them—at work, at school, at home, in our hobbies. Some have a name, some don't. Some we recognize, some remain largely invisible. We are core members of some and occasional participants in others. Whatever form our participation takes, most of us are familiar with the experience of belonging to a community of practice.

A Key to Success in a Global Knowledge Economy

I F COMMUNITIES OF PRACTICE have been so pervasive for so long, why should organizations suddenly focus on them? It is not communities of practice themselves that are new, but the need for organizations to become more intentional and systematic about "managing" knowledge, and therefore to give these age-old structures a new, central role in the business.

Knowledge has become the key to success. It is simply too valuable a resource to be left to chance. Companies need to understand precisely what knowledge will give them a competitive advantage. They then need to keep this knowledge on the cutting edge, deploy it, leverage it in operations, and spread it across the organization.[4] Cultivating communities of practice in strategic areas is a practical way to manage knowledge as an asset, just as systematically as companies manage other critical assets. Indeed, the explosion in science and technology creates a difficult paradox. At the same time that the increasing complexity of knowledge requires greater specialization and collaboration, the half-life of knowledge is getting shorter. Without communities focused on critical areas, it is difficult to keep up with the rapid pace of change.

These changes are happening at a time when firms are restructuring many relationships internally and externally to respond to the demands of a shifting market. Internally, companies are disaggregating into smaller units focused on well-defined market opportunities, as illustrated by the DaimlerChrysler Tech Club story. Externally, they increasingly partner with other organizations in the context of their extended enterprise. Both types of relationships spread production and delivery of value over many distinct entities.[5] Communities of practice connect people from different organizations as well as across independent business units. In the process, they knit the whole system together around core knowledge requirements.

The knowledge economy presents an additional challenge. Knowledge markets are globalizing rapidly.[6] What someone knows in Turkey could make or break your business in London. What a competitor's team is learning in South America could be the undoing of your project in Massachusetts. Consider the example of the Siemens sales team in Malaysia that was able to get a large telecommunication contract because of the experience and material developed by their peers in Denmark. Success in global markets depends on communities sharing knowledge across the globe.

Besides contributing to the success of organizations in world markets, these communities have another benefit. In the globalizing knowledge economy, companies are not just competing for market share. They are also competing for talent—for people with the expertise and capabilities to generate and implement innovative ideas. One company found that employees belonging to world-class communities of practice exploring cutting-edge issues were much more likely to stick around.[7] Finding and keeping the right people can make a big difference in a company's ability to become a market leader and to gain access to venture capital. In some industries, recruiting, developing, and retaining talent is a greater challenge than competing in commercial markets.

All these trends of the knowledge economy point to the critical role that communities of practice are destined to play. Indeed, knowledge-driven markets make it imperative to develop a "knowledge strategy" along with a business strategy. Yet many organizations have no explicit, consolidated knowledge strategy. Rather, it exists implicitly at best, dispersed in strategic plans, human resource reports, or system-improvement proposals. A knowledge strategy details in operational terms how to develop and apply the capabilities required to execute the business strategy. Therefore, a knowledge strategy eventually depends on communities of practice. Amoco and the U.S. Navy, for example, each established a process for developing such a knowledge strategy. The process starts with strategic goals and required core competencies, business processes, and key activities. It analyzes these in terms of critical knowledge "domains." Finally, it identifies the people who need this knowledge for their work and explores how to connect them into communities of practice so that together they can "steward" this knowledge.[8]

The Nature of Knowledge: A Managerial Challenge

A LTHOUGH EXECUTIVES RECOGNIZE the value of knowledge and the need to develop an intentional knowledge strategy, exactly how to do that is less clear. Recently, new information technologies have inspired dreams of capturing all the knowledge of an organization into databases that would make it easily accessible to all employees. Early attempts at knowledge management, however, were beholden to their origin in information technology (IT) departments. They tended to confuse knowledge and information. Building the system alone devoured resources, but it turned out to be even more difficult to motivate people to use these early knowledge bases. Companies that had invested their entire knowledge strategies in such information systems sooner or later found out that they had created digital junkyards. For instance, one consulting firm audited its knowledge systems and found it had 1,100 databases. Only thirty of them were active, and of these, at least twenty were actually news feeds. Companies discovered the hard way that useful knowledge is not a "thing" that can be managed like other assets, as a self-contained entity. Nor does it just float free in cyberspace. If companies are going to compete on knowledge, and manage and design structures and technology for it, they need to base their strategy on an understanding of what the knowledge challenge is. The essence of this challenge comes down to a few key points about the nature of knowing.

Knowledge Lives in the Human Act of Knowing

If a friend told you that he had read many books about surgery and was ready to operate on your skull, you would be right to decline politely. When surgeons operate on a patient, they do not blindly apply knowledge they have gleaned from books or procedures they have stored in their heads. They consider the patient's medical history, monitor vital signs, look at tissues, make incisions, draw conclusions, and possibly revise the plan to make sure that the procedure is constantly responsive to the evolving situation. Engaging their expertise in this way is an active, inventive process that is just as critical as their store of knowledge itself.[9]

To develop such expertise, practitioners need opportunities to engage with others who face similar situations. Neurosurgeons, for instance, will travel long distances to operate with a colleague in order to refine their technique.[10] The knowledge of experts is an accumulation of experience—a kind of "residue" of their actions, thinking, and conversations—that remains a dynamic part of their ongoing experience.[11] This type of knowledge is much more a living process than a static body of information. Communities of practice do not reduce knowledge to an object. They make it an integral part of their activities and interactions, and they serve as a living repository for that knowledge.

Knowledge Is Tacit As Well As Explicit

We are all aware that "we know more than we can tell."[12] Not everything we know can be codified as documents or tools. From a business standpoint, the tacit aspects of knowledge are often the most valuable.[13] They consist of embodied expertise—a deep understanding of complex, interdependent systems that enables dynamic responses to context-specific problems. This type of knowledge is very difficult for competitors to replicate.[14]

Sharing tacit knowledge requires interaction and informal learning processes such as storytelling, conversation, coaching, and apprenticeship of the kind that communities of practice provide.[15] This is not to say that it is not useful to document knowledge in whatever manner serves the needs of practitioners. But even explicit knowledge is dependent on tacit knowledge to be applied.[16] Companies have found that the most used, and useful, knowledge bases were integrated into the work of one or more communities. The success of Daimler-Chrysler's EBoK is largely due to the fact that the Tech Clubs are in charge of the process and view it as part of what their community is about. Communities of practice are in the best position to codify knowledge, because they can combine its tacit and explicit aspects.[17]

They can produce useful documentation, tools, and procedures because they understand the needs of practitioners. Moreover, these products have increased in meaning because they are not just objects by themselves, but are part of the life of the community.

Knowledge Is Social As Well As Individual

You know that the earth is round and orbits the sun, but you did not create that knowledge yourself. It derives from centuries of understanding and practice developed by long-standing communities. Though our experience of knowing is individual, knowledge is not. What counts as scientific knowledge, for instance, is the prerogative of scientific communities, which interact to define what facts matter and what theories are valid. There may be disagreements, there may be mavericks, but it is through a process of communal involvement, including all the controversies, that a body of knowledge is developed. It is by participating in these communities—even when going against the mainstream—that members produce scientific knowledge.[18]

Appreciating the collective nature of knowledge is especially important in an age when almost every field changes too much, too fast for individuals to master.[19] Today's complex problem solving requires multiple perspectives. The days of Leonardo da Vinci are over. We need others to complement and develop our own expertise. This collective character of knowledge does not mean that individuals don't count. In fact, the best communities welcome strong personalities and encourage disagreements and debates. Controversy is part of what makes a community vital, effective, and productive.

Knowledge Is Dynamic

Knowledge is not static. It is continually in motion. In fact, our collective knowledge of any field is changing at an accelerating rate. What was true yesterday must be adapted to accommodate new factors, new data, new inventions, and new problems.[20] This dynamism does not mean that a domain of knowledge lacks a stable core. In all fields, there is a required baseline of knowledge. One of the primary tasks of a community of practice is to establish this common baseline and standardize what is well understood so that people can focus their creative energies on the more advanced issues. Meeting this baseline is essential even to be in the game; you must be on the leading edge to hold a competitive advantage. That is why knowledge, even explicit knowledge, must be constantly updated by people who understand the issues and appreciate the evolution of their field. But to keep up with the ever-advancing amount and rate of change of knowledge, these people must work as a community. In one community, for instance, members list the relevant conferences for a given year and each attends one, then reports back to the others. Such interaction helps members manage information overload, get knowledgeable feedback on new ideas, and keep abreast of leading thoughts, techniques, and tools.

In short, what makes managing knowledge a challenge is that it is not an object that can be stored, owned, and moved around like a piece of equipment or a document. It resides in the skills, understanding, and relationships of its members as well as in the tools, documents, and processes that embody aspects of this knowledge.[21] Companies must manage their knowledge in ways that do not merely reduce it to an object.

Social Structures As a Management Tool

What managers have been missing so far is an understanding of the kind of social structure that can take responsibility for fostering learning, developing competencies, and managing knowledge.[22] Managers have discovered specific structures for other purposes. For instance, in the last three decades many firms were able to move to customer-focused, project-based organizations because they had discovered teams—the ideal social structure to which managers can assign project responsibility.

But what about the ownership of knowledge? Conventional structures do not address knowledge-related problems as effectively as they do problems of performance and accountability. Even though a lot of learning happens in business units and teams, it is easily lost. Business units focus on immediate opportunities in the market in order to achieve their business goals, so learning usually takes the back seat. Project teams are temporary, so their knowledge is largely lost when they disband. Ongoing operational teams are focused on their own tasks, so their knowledge often remains local. Traditional knowledge-oriented structures such as corporate universities and centers of excellence have usually been located in headquarters, separated from the line employees who would put the knowledge to use.[23] Many companies are discovering that communities of practice are the ideal social structure for "stewarding" knowledge. By assigning responsibility to the practitioners themselves to generate and share the knowledge they need, these communities provide a social forum that supports the living nature of knowledge.

Cultivating Communities of Practice

C OMMUNITIES OF PRACTICE are a natural part of organizational life. They will develop on their own and many will flourish, whether or not the organization recognizes them. Their health depends primarily on the voluntary engagement of their members and on the emergence of internal leadership. Moreover, their ability to steward knowledge as a living process depends on some measure of informality and autonomy. Once designated as the keepers of expertise, communities should not be second-guessed or overmanaged.[24] These observations may lead some to argue that there is nothing one can do to cultivate communities of practice, or worse, that anything organizations do will merely get in the way. We disagree. In fact, this book is born of our experience that organizations need to cultivate communities of practice actively and systematically, for their benefit as well as the benefit of the members and communities themselves.

Cultivation is an apt analogy. A plant does its own growing, whether its seed was carefully planted or blown into place by the wind. You cannot pull the stem, leaves, or petals to make a plant grow faster or taller.

However, you can do much to encourage healthy plants: till the soil, ensure they have enough nutrients, supply water, secure the right amount of sun exposure, and protect them from pests and weeds. There are also a few things we know not to do, like pulling up a plant to check if it has good roots.

Similarly, some communities of practice grow spontaneously while others may require careful seeding. Yet in both cases, organizations can do a lot to create an environment in which they can prosper: valuing the learning they do, making time and other resources available for their work, encouraging participation, and removing barriers. Creating such a context also entails integrating communities in the organization—giving them a voice in decisions and legitimacy in influencing operating units, and developing internal processes for managing the value they create.

If organizations fail to take active steps in this direction, communities of practice will still exist, but they are unlikely to achieve their full potential. They will tend to organize along friendship lines or within local geographical or organizational contexts rather than cover the whole organization. Some communities may not develop at all, either because people do not know about each other or because they do not have the time and energy to devote to community development. It is also difficult to channel resources (both time and financial) in the absence of active engagement with the organization. Without intentional cultivation, the communities that do develop will depend on the spare time of members, and participation is more likely to be spotty, especially when resources are lean. As a result, communities are apt to have less impact. They may not be fully aligned with the organization and therefore fail to contribute all they could. Just as important, the organization may not be well aligned with them, and therefore fail to recognize and leverage their contributions.

Still, there is some truth to the claim that there is nothing that organizations can or should do. You cannot cultivate communities of practice in the same way you develop traditional organizational structures. Design and development are more about eliciting and fostering participation than planning, directing, and organizing their activities.

The process has to be one of negotiation. You cannot act unilaterally. With a team of employees you can choose the goal, because you hired them to meet that goal. But with a community, your power is always mediated by the community's own pursuit of its interest. You cannot violate the natural developmental processes and dynamics that make a community function as a source of knowledge and arbiter of expertise, including members' passion about the topic, the sense of spirit and identity of the community, and its definition of what constitutes expert performance. Rather, you must learn to understand and work with these processes and dynamics. Cultivating communities of practice in an organizational context is an art, and the following chapters offer a guide to the subtleties of this art.

Creating Multiple Types of Value

ORGANIZATIONS that have taken steps to cultivate communities of practice have found that these communities are unique among organizational structures in their ability to deal with a broad variety of knowledge-related issues. For instance, they can

- connect local pockets of expertise and isolated professionals,
- diagnose and address recurring business problems whose root causes cross team boundaries,
- analyze the knowledge-related sources of uneven performance across units performing similar tasks and work to bring everyone up to the highest standard, and
- link and coordinate unconnected activities and initiatives addressing a similar knowledge domain.

Appreciating the value communities of practice create depends on setting the right expectations. Communities of practice are not a universal silver bullet. They are not meant to replace teams or business units as structures for serving markets and delivering products and services. But when their role in stewarding knowledge is well understood, they will be recognized as one of the primary contributors to success in the knowledge economy. Communities of practice do not merely manage knowledge assets. They create value in multiple and complex ways, both for their members and for the organization.

Short-Term and Long-Term Value. Participating in a community of practice has both short-term and long-term value, as summarized in table 1-1. In the near term, members can get help with immediate problems. They spend less time hunting for information or solutions. By including the perspectives of their peers, they devise better solutions and make better decisions.[25] They can be more daring in taking risks or trying new things, knowing they have a community to back them up. They can coordinate efforts and find synergies across organizational boundaries. As they address current problems, meanwhile, communities are also building sustained value by developing an ongoing practice that will serve the organization's long-term strategy. Members develop professionally; they keep abreast of new developments in their field and benchmark their expertise against that of colleagues in other organizations. This confluence of short-term and long-term value creation is well illustrated by DaimlerChrysler's Tech Clubs. They help each other solve immediate problems, but they also accumulate their experience in a knowledge base. They constantly discuss upcoming technologies with suppliers and prepare the organization to respond to these developments.

Tangible and Intangible Value. The value communities create includes tangible results such as a standards manual, improved skills, or reduced costs through faster access to information. It also includes less tangible outcomes such as a sense of trust or an increased ability to innovate. Tying community activities to tangible business outcomes is important lest business leaders make the mistake of dismissing communities as "soft" structures. Articulating the value of communities in terms of their tangible effects on performance provides them with the legitimacy they need to steward knowledge effectively. But it is still important to remember that some of their greatest value lies in intangible outcomes, such as the relationships they build among people, the sense of belonging they create, the spirit of inquiry they generate, and the professional confidence and identity they confer to their members.[26]

TABLE 1-1 SHORT- AND LONG-TERM VALUE TO ORGANIZATIONS AND COMMUNITY MEMBERS

Note: In each entry, examples of value are listed from more tangible to less tangible.

	SHORT-TERM VALUE	LONG-TERM VALUE
	IMPROVE BUSINESS OUTCOMES	DEVELOP ORGANIZATIONAL CAPABILITIES
Benefits to Organization	• Arena for problem solving • Quick answers to questions • Reduced time and costs • Improved quality of decisions • More perspectives on problems • Coordination, standardization, and synergies across units • Resources for implementing strategies • Strengthened quality assurance • Ability to take risks with backing of the community	• Ability to execute a strategic plan • Authority with clients • Increased retention of talent • Capacity for knowledge-development projects • Forum for "benchmarking" against rest of industry • Knowledge-based alliances • Emergence of unplanned capabilities • Capacity to develop new strategic options • Ability to foresee technological developments • Ability to take advantage of emerging market opportunities
	IMPROVE EXPERIENCE OF WORK	FOSTER PROFESSIONAL DEVELOPMENT
Benefits to Community Members	• Help with challenges • Access to expertise • Better able to contribute to team • Confidence in one's approach to problems • Fun of being with colleagues • More meaningful participation • Sense of belonging	• Forum for expanding skills and expertise • Network for keeping abreast of a field • Enhanced professional reputation • Increased marketability and employability • Strong sense of professional identity

Strategy-Implementing and Strategy-Making Value. Communities of practice provide value through their abilities to develop new strategies as well as implement existing ones. On the one hand, communities of practice are a way to realize a business strategy. Implementing strategy most often depends on the participation of highly competent frontline practitioners who understand the products, are aware of market trends, and know what it will take to beat the competition. At Procter & Gamble, for example, communities are a key component of the strategy to apply technological innovation across product lines. The process design community leverages the strategic value of deploying process innovations across various product lines by translating ideas and techniques across manufacturing operations. On the other hand, communities of practice can contribute to the formulation of new strategies. McKinsey is known as a premier strategy-consulting firm, and yet it relies largely on its communities of practice to drive the evolution of its own strategy. For example, a dramatic expansion in its retail-finance consulting was triggered when, in the late 1980s, a small group led by five to seven consultants started meeting at Chicago's O'Hare Airport to pool their knowledge about consumer marketing and financial institutions. Soon they had developed several effective approaches for clients, and over the next few years the practice grew to include hundreds of consultants serving clients in the United States and Europe in a fast-growing market niche. When highly developed, influential communities of practice keep abreast of market opportunities as well as their own practice development, they can inform or enact new strategic initiatives.

Connecting Professional Development and Corporate Strategy

Most important, communities of practice create value by connecting the personal development and professional identities of practitioners to the strategy of the organization. Successful ones deliver value to their members as well as to the organization. If it is not clear how members benefit directly from participation, the community will not thrive, because the members will not invest themselves in it. Similarly, if the community's value to the organization as a whole is not understood, it is

difficult to justify investing resources in the community and to legitimize its voice. The ability to combine the needs of organizations and
community members is crucial in the knowledge economy, where companies succeed by fully engaging the creativity of their employees. The
multiple and complex ways in which communities of practice deliver
value to both members and organizations is the reason they are fast
becoming a central part of the management agenda.

Ushering in the "Double-Knit" Knowledge Organization

FOR AN ORGANIZATION to learn from its own experience and
to fully leverage its knowledge, the communities that steward
knowledge and the business processes where knowledge is applied
must be tightly interwoven—creating what we call a "double-knit"
organization.[27] Practitioners themselves, in their dual roles as both
community practitioners and operational team members, help link the
capabilities of communities of practice to the knowledge requirements
of teams and business units.

In this regard, a community of practice is very different from a center of excellence where specialists develop knowledge without being
involved in line operations. At DaimlerChrysler, for instance, engineers
wear two hats. Their main affiliation with their car platform focuses on
working with other engineers to optimize the design of a model; as Tech
Club members, they keep up with their specialty, coordinate standards,
and share knowledge and lessons learned. This *multimembership* creates a learning loop, as illustrated in figure 1-1. As members of teams
and workgroups, people are accountable for performing tasks. When
they face familiar problems, they apply and refine their skills; when
they encounter new problems, they invent new solutions. But the same
people are also community members, and as such they are accountable
for developing a practice. They bring their team experience to their
communities and receive help with their problems. They can discuss

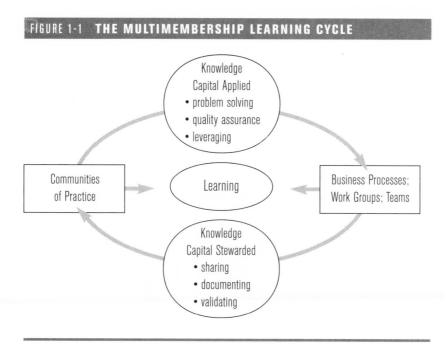

FIGURE 1-1   THE MULTIMEMBERSHIP LEARNING CYCLE

Knowledge Capital Applied
• problem solving
• quality assurance
• leveraging

Communities of Practice

Learning

Business Processes; Work Groups; Teams

Knowledge Capital Stewarded
• sharing
• documenting
• validating

their new solutions, generalize or document them, and integrate them into the community's practice. Then they return to their projects equipped with expanded capabilities, which again face the test of application to real problems. Through this multimembership the learning cycle continues indefinitely. That is why it is so important to have communities of actual active practitioners manage their own knowledge.

This double-knit structure of teams and communities is reminiscent of "matrix" organizations, in which people have multiple reporting relationships to serve different purposes. For instance, you might have a boss in your business unit and another in your functional or geographic area. In fact, a knowledge-management guru once asked us whether this was not "matrix management done on the cheap." We had to respond that this was in fact the original idea behind matrix management *done right*. Actually, communities of practice provide a fundamentally different approach toward the same goal. The matrix structure only focuses on the distribution of authority and the coordination of resources by multiplying reporting relationships. It does not create different structures for different purposes. Whereas a matrix has reporting relationships on both arms, communities of practice provide a different kind of structure for focusing on knowledge. They are based on collegial relationships, not reporting relationships. Even community leaders are not your bosses; they are your peers. This combination of formal and informal structures is fundamentally different from a matrix. It provides new degrees of freedom for designing organizations. Managers can design formal structures to focus on accountability for customer and business results, while relying more heavily on informal structures such as communities of practice to address issues related to knowledge, competence, and innovation.[28]

Relying explicitly on communities of practice fundamentally transforms the landscape of the organization. Domains of knowledge become focal points for connecting people in different units who are working on potentially related projects. The power associated with these knowledge domains becomes a more visible part of the organization. In fact, in a fast-moving knowledge economy, these domains are often more stable and enduring than specific projects, jobs, products, or even businesses. Business units are constantly being reorganized. Projects come and go. Teams are assembled and dispersed. Given such flux in the formal organization, communities of practice offer an underlying layer of stability. They provide a welcome "home for identity" where practitioners can connect across organizational and geographic boundaries and focus on professional development rather than merely the application of expertise to meet a specific goal.[29]

As one engineer reported, "You are redeployed so often, the only source of stability is your community of practice. It is great to have them. These are people you know you will be with the rest of your career." In an organization that is constantly changing, employees may not know who their boss is going to be tomorrow, which country they will be sent to, or which team they will join. But they know that they will still belong to their community of colleagues.

The focus on communities of practice thus points the way to a new wave of organizations where the formal structures—those organized around providing products and services—are constantly changing to meet shifting market needs, while the informal, voluntary structures—those organized around knowledge—are more stable. Indeed, one could argue that with the stability provided by communities of practice, organizations can be even more flexible in response to shifting market demands. As a consequence, leading knowledge organizations are increasingly likely to view communities of practice not merely as useful auxiliary structures, but as foundational structures on which to build the organization.

Communities of Practice and Their Structural Elements

PARTICIPATION IN THE MONTHLY TELECONFERENCE *calls of the high-availability software community at Hewlett-Packard Company (HP) is voluntary, but attendance remains fairly constant. The core group came together a few years ago with the help of facilitators from a knowledge-management support team. They had been largely isolated, and discovering how many problems they had in common and how much they could learn from each other generated a lot of energy for developing a shared practice. For instance, they succeeded in standardizing the software's sales and installation processes and establishing a consistent pricing scheme for HP salespeople. These areas had been a source of much frustration. Since then, the community has grown and has addressed many other problems.*

Today the call focuses on Maureen's experiences installing the product for a major customer. Before diving in, however, the consultants spend the first ten minutes chatting about the recent reorganization of their division—

whether it is a good thing, what it means for them, and so on. Maureen hasn't spent a lot of time preparing a formal presentation. She knows that only by talking directly and openly can she spur the back-and-forth that will make the call worthwhile for the group. People know each other and they know the kinds of problems they share. They don't need fancy explanations. As the call proceeds, community members interrupt Maureen constantly with questions and examples from their own experiences—all of which not only helps her understand how to work more effectively with her client but also helps everyone broaden their repertoire of cases. Chris will put the notes on the Web site.

The conversation then turns to a persistent bug in the software. Rob, a member of the software division that developed the product, has been invited to take part in these calls in order to create a stronger connection between the product-delivery consultants and the software developers. He's already worked out a way to eliminate the bug, but from the stories he hears in the teleconference, he learns how to make the fix even more effective. He will follow up during the next month's call.

Communities of Practice Take Many Forms

THE COMMUNITY OF PRACTICE in this story meets primarily via teleconference. At HP it is known as a "learning community." Communities of practice vary widely in both name and style in different organizations. In this chapter we will explore both the variety of forms communities of practice take and the fundamental characteristics they have in common. Knowing these variations is important because it helps people recognize communities of practice, despite different guises and names.[1] The first skill of community development is to be able to "see" communities of practice. They are as diverse as the situations that bring them into existence and the people who populate them.

> *Small or big.* Some communities of practice are small and intimate, involving only a few specialists, while others consist of hundreds of people. The largest ones we know of have more than

one thousand members. Size does matter, however, and very large communities are structured differently, usually subdivided by geographic region or by subtopic in order to encourage all members to take part actively.

Long-lived or short-lived. The development of practice takes time, but the life span of communities of practice varies widely. Some exist over centuries—for example, communities of artisans, such as violin makers, who pass their craft from generation to generation. Many are shorter-lived but still last a good number of years— a group of COBOL programmers, for instance, might be such a community.

Colocated or distributed. Sharing a practice requires regular interaction. Naturally, therefore, many communities start among people who work at the same place or live nearby. But colocation is not a necessity. Many communities of practice are distributed over wide areas. Scientists have long been forming communities of practice by communicating across the globe (once by letter and now by e-mail). Some communities meet regularly, say for breakfast every Wednesday. Others are connected primarily by e-mail and phone and may meet only once or twice a year. What allows members to share knowledge is not the choice of a specific form of communication (face-to-face as opposed to Web-based, for instance), but the existence of a shared practice—a common set of situations, problems, and perspectives. Whether some face-to-face interaction is absolutely required and how much is a minimum are open questions. However, new technologies and the need for globalization are quickly making distributed communities of practice the standard rather than the exception.[2]

Homogeneous or heterogeneous. Some communities are homogeneous, composed of people from the same discipline or function. Others bring together people with different backgrounds—for instance, all people from different functions who deal with a big customer or a certain country. It is often easier to start a community among people with similar backgrounds, but having a problem in common is also a strong motivation for building a shared practice, even among people who share little else. Over time people with different backgrounds may end up being as closely bonded as people who started with a lot in common.

Inside and across boundaries. Communities of practice can exist entirely within a business unit or stretch across divisional boundaries. Many even cross the boundaries between organizations.

- *Within businesses:* Communities of practice arise as people address recurring sets of problems together. Claims processors within an office might form a community of practice to expedite the constant flow of information they must process. By participating in such a "communal memory," they can do the job without having to remember everything themselves.

- *Across business units:* Important knowledge is often distributed throughout different business units. People who work in cross-functional teams often form communities of practice to keep in touch with their peers in various parts of the company and thus maintain their expertise. At a large chemical company, for example, safety managers from each business unit interact regularly to solve problems and develop common guidelines, tools, standards, procedures, and documents.

- *Across organization boundaries:* Communities of practice are not bound by company affiliation. With the emphasis on the extended enterprise, they often become useful precisely by crossing organization boundaries. For instance, in fast-moving industries such as computer hard drives, engineers who work for suppliers and buyers often form a community of practice to keep up with constant changes in technology, even though it is not part of their job description.[3]

Spontaneous or intentional. Many communities of practice start without any intervention or development effort from the organization. Members spontaneously come together because they need each other as peers and learning partners. In other cases, organizations have intentionally developed specific communities to steward a needed capability. Whether a community is spontaneous or intentional does not dictate its level of formality. Some highly active and mature communities remain very informal while others are highly structured, calling meetings, setting agendas, defining specific roles, and creating community artifacts such as Web sites or knowledge bases.

Unrecognized to institutionalized. Communities of practice have a variety of relationships to organizations, ranging from completely unrecognized to largely institutionalized.[4] Consider the group of nurses on a ward who met regularly for lunch and discussed patient cases. Over time, they created a history of cases they all knew about and could use to examine new problems. Yet they were not explicitly aware that these lunches had become one of their main sources of new knowledge. And of course, the hospital administration had no awareness of the value of these informal lunch discussions. At the other end of the spectrum, some communities have been found so valuable that they have been incorporated into the official structure of the organization. Such institutionalization—when well managed—can confer legitimacy and resources to a community of practice without violating its internal drive. Between invisibility and institutionalization there is a whole range of possible relationships, as described in table 2-1. The point is not that one kind of relationship is necessarily better than the others, but that different issues arise as the relationship changes.

A Structural Model: Domain, Community, and Practice

D ESPITE THE VARIETY of forms that communities of practice take, they all share a basic structure. A community of practice is a unique combination of three fundamental elements: a *domain* of knowledge, which defines a set of issues; a *community* of people who care about this domain; and the shared *practice* that they are developing to be effective in their domain.

- The *domain* creates common ground and a sense of common identity. A well-defined domain legitimizes the community by affirming its purpose and value to members and other stakeholders.

TABLE 2-1 RELATIONSHIPS OF COMMUNITIES TO OFFICIAL ORGANIZATIONS		
RELATIONSHIP	DEFINITION	TYPICAL CHALLENGES
Unrecognized	Invisible to the organization and sometimes even to members themselves	Difficult to see value and be aware of limitations, may not involve everyone who should participate
Bootlegged	Only visible informally to a circle of people "in the know"	Getting resources, having an impact, keeping hidden, gaining legitimacy
Legitimized	Officially sanctioned as a valuable entity	Broader visibility, rapid growth, new demands and expectations
Supported	Provided with direct resources from the organization	Scrutiny; accountability for use of resources, effort, and time; short-term pressures
Institutionalized	Given an official status and function in the organization	Fixed definition, overmanagement, living beyond its usefulness

The domain inspires members to contribute and participate, guides their learning, and gives meaning to their actions. Knowing the boundaries and the leading edge of the domain enables members to decide exactly what is worth sharing, how to present their ideas, and which activities to pursue. It also allows them to recognize the potential in tentative or half-baked ideas. To you, an apple falling from a tree is just natural, but to a physicist who is trying to understand the dynamics of gravity, the very sight can reconstruct the whole universe.

- The *community* creates the social fabric of learning. A strong community fosters interactions and relationships based on mutual respect and trust. It encourages a willingness to share ideas, expose one's ignorance, ask difficult questions, and listen carefully. Have you ever experienced this mixture of intimacy and openness to inquiry? Community is an important element because learning is a matter of belonging as well as an intellectual process, involving the heart as well as the head.[5]

- The *practice* is a set of frameworks, ideas, tools, information, styles, language, stories, and documents that community members share. Whereas the domain denotes the topic the community focuses on, the practice is the specific knowledge the community develops, shares, and maintains. When a community has been established for some time, members expect each other to have mastered the basic knowledge of the community, just as biochemists expect members of their discipline to understand basic chemistry. This body of shared knowledge and resources enables the community to proceed efficiently in dealing with its domain.[6]

When they function well together, these three elements make a community of practice an ideal *knowledge structure*—a social structure that can assume responsibility for developing and sharing knowledge. Let us explore in more detail how each element contributes to a community's ability to steward knowledge.

Domain

Arlene is a consultant. Today she takes the time to document a client problem and its solution, because she can see that it has broad implications. It is a great case for the new e-business practice she belongs to, and she knows that her colleagues will appreciate the issues it raises. The solution her team came up with is innovative and will change the way the firm approaches this type of engagement; it may even suggest a new line of business.

It is her understanding of her community's domain that enables her to recognize that this particular problem will be interesting to others. It is her commitment to a shared learning agenda that motivates her to contribute her insights to the practice of her community. Her appreciation for the cutting edge of the domain demonstrates her leadership role in the community. She understands what matters to this community and is able to contribute something that everyone will find relevant. She knows what to communicate and how to present information in useful ways—an outsider would not appreciate why sharing a certain detail, such as the size of a meeting room or the personality of an executive, is important to the story.

Without commitment to a domain, a community is just a group of friends. A shared domain creates a sense of accountability to a body of knowledge and therefore to the development of a practice. Communities may be more or less explicit about everything that their domain includes, but whether explicit or implicit, the members' shared understanding of their domain—its purpose, its resolved issues, its open questions—allows them to decide what matters. The domain guides the questions they ask and the way they organize their knowledge. It helps them sort out what to share and how to distinguish between a trivial idea and one with real promise.

The domain of a community of practice can range from very mundane know-how, like eating healthy food, to highly specialized professional expertise, like designing aircraft wings. It is a lot easier to define a domain when there is already an established discourse, as is the case with a professional discipline, but what brings members together is not always based on recognized topics. Members of a community may indeed share a profession or a discipline (cardiologists, history teachers, petrophysicists), have the same job or role (insurance claims processors, safety managers), or deal with the same clients. But they may also face similar problems that are not officially recognized as domains (online facilitation, document management, aggressive customers, low-status job).

For instance, members of a group of medical insurance claims processors each have to process a certain number of claims per day. That is the official version of their task, if you view them as a workgroup. But if you view them as a community of practice, their domain goes beyond this simple goal. They care about the competence needed to meet production quotas, but they are equally concerned about preserving a sense of identity, despite the status of the job. In practice, their actual domain is as much about how they survive their work environment as it is about production goals. As a community, they hold each other accountable to the latter commitment—preserving their identity—even more stringently than to the company's demands. For them it is okay to miss your daily quota—it happens to everyone at times—but it is not okay to show too much interest in the job. This would violate the distance that, as a community, they are working to maintain from the company. What guides the actual learning of the community is an insider's view of the domain. This view may or may not be easily articulated by members, and it may not always align with the organization, but it nevertheless shapes the knowledge, values, and behaviors to which they hold each other accountable.[7]

Whatever creates that common ground, the domain of a community is its *raison d'être*. It is what brings people together and guides their learning. It defines the identity of the community, its place in the world, and the value of its achievements to members and to others. In this regard, the identity of the community depends in good part on the importance of its domain in the world, which in turn makes the domain important to members. For a group of engineers with whom we worked to form a community of practice, what turned out to be exciting and rewarding to them was not merely sharing knowledge, but also discovering that the company actually considered their voice to have professional authority.

A domain is not a fixed set of problems. It evolves along with the world and the community. A community of Web designers will shift its focus as languages like HTML or Java become popular or certain applets come into demand. In any domain, hot topics periodically arise and generate fresh energy. In science, most notably, each discipline has one or two burning questions that researchers pursue at any given time. As these problems are solved and new ones appear, as new technologies pose new challenges, as the next generation of members brings fresh perspectives, the community's sense of what it is about evolves and grows. And yet, through these changes, the community maintains a sense of identity rooted in a shared understanding of its domain.

Mapping domains and defining their content and scope is an art.[8] A good domain is not merely a passing issue, like the choice of a new supplier, which can be addressed by a temporary task force. It concerns complex and long-standing issues that require sustained learning. One consulting firm uses the heuristic that a domain should have a "half-life" of at least eighteen months.

A domain is not an abstract area of interest, but consists of key issues or problems that members commonly experience. An insurance organization had started a community around "technical skills" because it was a term and an issue that many people recognized as important. But in practice, this topic turned out to be too general to pique anyone's professional interest. They had to restructure the group into more specialized communities addressing specific techniques, skills, and responsibilities, such as claims processing or training.

The most successful communities of practice thrive where the goals and needs of an organization intersect with the passions and aspirations of participants.[9] If the domain of a community fails to inspire its members, the community will flounder. Moreover, if the topic lacks strategic relevance to the organization, the community will be marginalized and have limited influence. This intersection of personal meaning and strategic relevance is a potent source of energy and value. Domains that provide such a bridge are likely to inspire the kind of thought leadership and spirit of inquiry that are the hallmarks of vibrant communities of practice.

A well-developed domain becomes a statement of what knowledge the community will steward. It is a commitment to take responsibility for an area of expertise and to provide the organization with the best knowledge and skills that can be found. In turn, when an organization acknowledges a domain it legitimizes the community's role in stewarding its expertise and capabilities. A firm with such communities would not dream of making important decisions relevant to their domain—a large purchase of equipment, an acquisition, a new business line, an executive hire—without consulting members. Indeed, a well-honed domain can boost a community's visibility and influence within the organization.

Community

Quantitative biologists from two sites at Eli Lilly and Company, one at the corporate headquarters in Indiana and the other at an affiliate site in North Carolina, recognized the challenges that go along with collaborating effectively on projects. The affiliate site was an acquired company, and the two sites had cultural differences, which led to differences in methodology, terminology, and mission. The geographical distance also made working and personal relationships difficult. Both sites had an incomplete understanding of project histories and an inability to easily identify and contact experts. As a result, there was significant duplication of effort, redundancy of competing technologies, and ineffective transfer of project work from one site to the other. A small group of scientists from both sites considered creating a community of practice to solve these problems.

At first, the community concept was met with some skepticism, since most of the scientists did not understand the scientific benefit that a community would bring. It was at a launch meeting of the core group that the skeptics' points of view began to change. Working toward a common vision for community is what allowed them to build trust and relationships. At the behest of the facilitators, the members started to talk about the value of community, beginning with their experiences outside of work. What kept them in a community? What made them leave? They also agreed on what their practice was—quantitative biology—which allowed them to see it as a connecting thread among them.

Now the groups meet face-to-face quarterly, alternating sites for each meeting. Between meetings, they have bimonthly teleconferences. They also publish their travel schedules so members from different sites can meet if they happen to be in the same place. Their roster is growing fairly rapidly. The community has designed a charter and the members have made a commitment to avoid finger pointing. They have also decided to break down the traditional hierarchy among scientists and to involve everyone from senior research scientists to lab technicians, though at first the lab technicians were a bit reluctant to express their opinions in front of the senior scientists. At a recent meeting they even organized a contest to adopt a mascot—the "Q-Bee"—for quantitative biology.

The effect of all this community work is showing up in the group members' job performance. They have created a joint strategy for developing new technologies that reduce replication and pool resources. In addition, they have found that by combining orders for chemicals from the two sites, they could save money through bulk discounts. The sites have begun sharing compounds for testing, which for one group had not happened in the past. Their success is a combination of two key factors. First, they have removed barriers to relationships by addressing head-on initial trust issues, problems in the work environment, and challenges from skeptics. But this focus on relationships, which has become extremely important to the group, has always been in the service—not at the expense—of their focus on science, which is equally important to them both organizationally and personally. Their community helps them to better deliver the value of their scientific discipline and experience more fully their cultural identities as scientists. As one member said: "Relationships are what science is all about."

The community element is critical to an effective knowledge structure. A community of practice is not just a Web site, a database, or a collection of best practices. It is a group of people who interact, learn together, build relationships, and in the process develop a sense of belonging and mutual commitment.[10] Having others who share your overall view of the domain and yet bring their individual perspectives on any given problem creates a social learning system that goes beyond the sum of its parts. Members use each other as sounding boards, build on each other's ideas, and provide a filtering mechanism to deal with "knowledge overload."[11] Interpersonal relationships are also critical. Knowing each other makes it easier to ask for help: You know who is likely to have an answer and you can feel confident that your request is welcome. Experts can also assume that community members who ask for help are competent enough not to waste their time.

To build a community of practice, members must interact regularly on issues important to their domain. Having the same title, for instance, is not enough. You can all be safety managers in different business units, but unless you interact, you do not form a community of practice. Moreover, these interactions must have some continuity. A good conversation on an airplane ride or a workshop at a conference does not constitute a community of practice. Interacting regularly, members develop a shared understanding of their domain and an approach to their practice. In the process, they build valuable relationships based on respect and trust. Over time, they build a sense of common history and identity.[12]

The concept of community often connotes commonality, but it would be wrong to assume that the hallmark of an ideal community of practice is homogeneity. Although long-term interaction does create a common history and communal identity, it also encourages differentiation among members. They take on various roles, officially and unofficially. They create their own specialties or styles. They gain a reputation. They achieve a status and generate their own personal sphere of influence. In other words, each member develops a unique individual identity in relation to the community. Their interactions over time are a source of both commonality and diversity. Homogeneity of background, skills, or point of view may make it easier to start a community of practice, but it is neither a required condition nor is it a necessary result. In fact, it is not even an indicator that a community will be more tightly bonded or more effective. With enough common ground for ongoing mutual engagement, a good dose of diversity makes for richer learning, more interesting relationships, and increased creativity.[13]

We are often asked if there is an ideal size for a community of practice. As mentioned earlier, we have seen them in such a wide variety of sizes that it is difficult to give absolute numbers. On the one hand, you need a critical mass of people to sustain regular interaction and offer multiple perspectives. On the other hand, if the community becomes too large, it can inhibit direct interaction. Communities change in structure and characteristics as they grow. Communities with fewer than fifteen members are very intimate. Between fifteen and fifty participants, relationships become more fluid and differentiated. Between fifty and 150, communities tend to divide into subgroups around topics or geographic location, and beyond 150 members, the subgroups usually develop strong local identities.[14] As will be discussed further in chapter 6, these nested subcommunities within a single large community allow members to be very engaged locally while retaining a sense of belonging to the larger community.

Another question that people often ask is whether membership in a community of practice has to be voluntary. A community of practice is not like a team that management can assemble unilaterally; its success depends too much on personal passion for coercion to be effective. Membership may be self-selected or assigned, but the actual level of engagement is a personal matter. In this sense, participation is voluntary. Participation can certainly be encouraged, of course, but the kind of personal investment that makes for a vibrant community is not something that can be invented or forced. Sometimes it takes a bit of prodding for people to discover the value of learning together. Nothing says communities of practice must be purely spontaneous. In the end, however, the success of the community will depend on the energy that the community itself generates, not on an external mandate.

All communities of practice depend on internal leadership, but healthy communities do not depend entirely on the leadership of one person. Leadership is distributed and is a characteristic of the whole community. Recognized experts certainly help to legitimize the community's role and voice, but they are not necessarily the ones who bring the community together or take the initiative to explore new territory. Rather than think in terms of specific leaders and followers, it is more useful to think of such roles in terms of an ecology of leadership. Leadership in a community of practice can be very diverse, including community organizers, experts and "thought leaders," pioneers, administrators, and boundary spanners.[15] Roles may be formal or informal. They may be concentrated in a small subgroup or widely distributed. But in all cases, those who undertake leadership roles must have internal legitimacy in the community. External leadership roles are also important, especially as communities mature, because communities depend on external sponsors for access to influence and resources and for building credibility with teams and business units.

Anthropologists who study communities have noted the importance of reciprocity in community participation. Members of a healthy community of practice have a sense that making the community more valuable is to the benefit of everyone. They know that their own contribution will come back to them. This is not a direct exchange mechanism of a market type where commodities are traded. Rather it is a pool of goodwill—of "social capital," to use the technical term—that allows people to contribute to the community while trusting that at some point, in some form, they too will benefit.[16] This kind of reciprocity is neither selflessness nor simple tit for tat, but a deeper understanding of mutual value that extends over time.[17]

Learning requires an atmosphere of openness. Each community develops a unique atmosphere—intense or laid back, formal or informal, hierarchical or democratic. Whatever norms members establish, the key is to build a foundation for collective inquiry. An effective community of practice offers a place of exploration where it is safe to speak the truth and ask hard questions.[18] Trust is key to this process. Meetings are intense, rich in content, engaging members in good discussions. Effective communities are not necessarily without conflict. In fact, the stronger a community, the better it is able to handle dissension and make it productive. In good communities strong bonds withstand disagreement, and members can even use conflict as a way to deepen their relationships and their learning.

Practice

Tom is an electronics engineer specializing in a commonly used but delicate type of circuit called phase-lock loops. This is the kind of circuit that (among other things) will tune your radio to the frequency you select. Today, Tom has a vexing problem with a promising design and he decides to bring it to the community meeting to get help. He goes to the white board and draws a quick diagram using weird symbols. In a matter of minutes, all his colleagues at the meeting are ready to discuss his new idea. They can see it is a promising idea and they understand where his problem lies. They all get to work, ready to think, invent, and find solutions together. Eric, a newcomer to the community, is in awe.

For him, this is an ideal context to learn the craft. Through its practice—its concepts, symbols, and analytic methods—the community operates as a living curriculum.

One of the tasks of a shared practice is to establish a baseline of common knowledge that can be assumed on the part of each full member. This does not mean that all members are cognitive clones. People specialize and develop areas of individual expertise. They may belong to slightly different schools of thought. But they share a basic body of knowledge that creates a common foundation, allowing members to work together effectively.

A community's practice explores both the existing body of knowledge and the latest advances in the field. As a product of the past, it embodies the history of the community and the knowledge it has developed over time. You can't be a real electronics engineer unless you are familiar with the repertoire of your community: the hieroglyphic symbols Tom was using, Ohm's law, last year's disaster that resulted in a recall of a whole batch of chips, the design guidelines on the Web site, or the stock of stories about relationships with people at the plant that may help you address tricky manufacturing problems. At the same time, the practice is oriented to the future: It provides resources that enable members to handle new situations and create new knowledge. Music is a good example of a craft where a base of masterful techniques makes for artful improvisation. A shared practice supports innovation because it provides a language for communicating new ideas quickly and for focusing conversations.[19]

The term *practice* is used here in the sense it has in an expression like "reasonable medical practice" used to justify a doctor's action in a malpractice lawsuit. It denotes a set of socially defined ways of doing things in a specific domain: a set of common approaches and shared standards that create a basis for action, communication, problem solving, performance, and accountability. These communal resources include a variety of knowledge types: cases and stories, theories, rules, frameworks, models, principles, tools, experts, articles, lessons learned, best practices, and heuristics. They include both the tacit and the explicit aspects of the community's knowledge. They range from concrete objects, such as a specialized tool or a manual, to less tangible displays of competence, such as an ability to interpret a slight change in the sound of a machine as indicating a specific problem. The practice includes the books, articles, knowledge bases, Web sites, and other repositories that members share. It also embodies a certain way of behaving, a perspective on problems and ideas, a thinking style, and even in many cases an ethical stance. In this sense, a practice is a sort of mini-culture that binds the community together.[20]

An effective practice evolves with the community as a collective product. It is integrated into people's work. It organizes knowledge in a way that is especially useful to practitioners because it reflects their perspective. Each community has a specific way of making its practice visible through the ways that it develops and shares knowledge. Some use stories. Traditional midwives in the Yucatan discuss how to proceed with a birth by sharing stories relevant to each decision.[21] Similarly, Xerox repair technicians tell war stories to communicate their insights and to help solve difficult encounters with recalcitrant machines.[22] Some document formulas and procedures in articles, as do scientists and researchers. The EBoK at DaimlerChrysler is a mixture of procedures, best practices, and lessons learned that reflect the way an automotive engineer thinks about design. In each case, the mode of communicating and capturing knowledge matches the demands of actual use.

A community must have a shared understanding of what aspects of its domain are codifiable and which are not, and what to do in each case. Successful practice development depends on a balance between joint activities, in which members explore ideas together, and the production of "things" like documents or tools.[23] It involves an ongoing interplay of codification and interactions, of the explicit and the tacit. Documentation is not a goal in itself, but an integral part of the life of the community. At DaimlerChrysler, communities of practice spend a good part of their meetings discussing the chapters of the EBoK that their members are writing and debating what should go in them. Engineers report that participating in these discussions is just as important to them as having the final documents. Some say they don't really need to read the documents after they have participated in the discussions.

The twin goals of interacting with peers and creating knowledge products complement each other. On the one hand, the goal of documenting and codifying focuses community activities, and on the other hand, these activities give life and legitimacy to the documentation.

Successful practice building goes hand-in-hand with community building. The process must give practitioners a chance to gain a reputation as contributors to the community's practice. At Xerox, all tips in the repair technician database prominently carry the name of the contributor, and at DaimlerChrysler EBoK chapters are always signed. In addition, there must be a process by which the community validates and endorses new submissions as accepted communal knowledge. At Xerox, all new tips are explicitly endorsed by reputable experts. Debates about practice frameworks and methods allow the community to own its standards. Agreeing on standards and best practices inevitably involves disagreements and conflicts. When this process takes place in the context of an ongoing community, however, each specific debate is part of a longer debate to which members have committed. This ongoing commitment puts the process of dealing with disagreement in perspective. As one DaimlerChrysler engineer reports, you know that issues can be revisited and that new issues will come up: You lose this one, you'll win another one.

Implications of the Model

DEVELOPING A MODEL of communities of practice in terms of these three constituent elements is not merely a theoretical exercise; it is useful in many concrete ways. For starters, the model provides a common language that facilitates discussion, collective action, and efforts to gain legitimacy, sponsorship, and funding in an organization. Defining domain, community, and practice also clarifies the definition of communities of practice as a social structure distinct from other types. In addition, these elements provide a means to understand the different ways in which participation is meaningful to members—some may be more interested in the community than in the practice aspect, for instance. Finally, the three elements guide community development efforts by indicating the various areas on which one needs to focus in order to foster a well-rounded community.

How Communities of Practice Differ from Other Structures

This model reinforces the significance of the term *community of practice*. Not every community is a community of practice. Although a neighborhood is commonly called a community, it is rarely a community of practice as we define it.[24] Similarly, not everything we call practice—such as practicing the piano—gives rise to a community. Together the terms *community* and *practice* refer to a very specific type of social structure with a very specific purpose. Providing some contrasts with other, more familiar structures will help elucidate what is distinctive about communities of practice as knowledge structures. (See table 2-2.)

Communities versus Business or Functional Units

At the core of a business or functional unit is the responsibility for managing a business goal, such as serving a specific market segment, manufacturing a product, or fulfilling an administrative function. This responsibility includes allocating resources, managing business processes, and assigning formal roles, reporting relationships, and accountability for business outcomes. By contrast, the primary purpose of communities of practice—to develop knowledge—does not make them a very good vehicle for, say, delivering a product to the market. Communities of practice are more loosely connected, informal, and self-managed than business units, even when they are highly institutionalized. They are based on collegiality, not on reporting relationships, and membership depends on participation rather than institutional affiliation. Production targets, allocation of resources, and reporting relationships distract a community of practice from its purpose of stewarding knowledge and fostering learning.

This focus on knowledge does not mean that members of communities of practice do not care about these other objectives, just that as

TABLE 2-2 **DISTINCTIONS BETWEEN COMMUNITIES OF PRACTICE AND OTHER STRUCTURES**

	WHAT'S THE PURPOSE?	WHO BELONGS?	HOW CLEAR ARE THE BOUNDARIES?	WHAT HOLDS THEM TOGETHER?	HOW LONG DO THEY LAST?
Communities of Practice	To create, expand, and exchange knowledge, and to develop individual capabilities	Self-selection based on expertise or passion for a topic	Fuzzy	Passion, commitment, and identification with the group and its expertise	Evolve and end organically (last as long as there is relevance to the topic and value and interest in learning together)
Formal Departments	To deliver a product or service	Everyone who reports to the group's manager	Clear	Job requirements and common goals	Intended to be permanent (but last until the next reorganization)
Operational Teams	To take care of an ongoing operation or process	Membership assigned by management	Clear	Shared responsibility for the operation	Intended to be ongoing (but last as long as the operation is needed)
Project Teams	To accomplish a specified task	People who have a direct role in accomplishing the task	Clear	The project's goals and milestones	Predetermined ending (when the project has been completed)
Communities of Interest	To be informed	Whoever is interested	Fuzzy	Access to information and sense of likemindedness	Evolve and end organically
Informal Networks	To receive and pass on information, to know who is who	Friends and business acquaintances, friends of friends	Undefined	Mutual need and relationships	Never really start or end (exist as long as people keep in touch or remember each other)

community members they focus primarily on knowledge and learning. Nor does this focus on knowledge mean that there are no differences in power among community members. An expert will certainly have more power than a novice, but this power derives from the ability to contribute to the knowledge of the community, not from formal authority to control resources, give orders, or grant promotions.

Communities versus Project or Operational Teams

The essence of a team is a set of interdependent tasks that contribute to a predefined, shared objective. The team makes a commitment to this goal and ensures that individual commitments are kept. The team leader keeps the team focused on its deliverable and coordinates individual contributions to the overall objectives. By contrast, the essence of a community of practice is the members' personal investment in its domain. A domain is different from a task; it is not so much a specific achievement as a territory, an area of shared interest that the community explores. Members are connected by interdependent knowledge, not by interdependent subtasks. A community coordinator does not "lead" the community in the traditional sense, but brings people together and enables the community to find its direction. A community may undertake specific tasks and projects in the course of developing its practice. It may charter a team to establish a standard or to document a procedure. But the community is not defined by any of these tasks. Rather, it is defined by its fundamental commitment to exploring its domain and to developing and sharing the relevant knowledge.

Communities versus Informal Networks, "Communities of Interest," and Professional Associations

All organizations have informal networks of people who communicate, share information, and build relationships and reputations.[25] A community of practice is different from such a network in the sense that it is "about" something. It is not just a set of relationships. Its domain gives it an identity, and the commitment to care for this domain gives it a cohesiveness and intentionality that goes beyond the interpersonal nature of informal networks.

A shared interest alone, however, does not necessarily yield a community of practice. You can be interested in French cinema and enjoy reading postings on a newsgroup, but the members of this newsgroup are not developing a practice. Caring for a domain goes beyond mere interest. It entails developing a shared practice, which directly affects the behaviors and abilities of members. But again, having a shared practice by itself does not constitute a community of practice. Many professional associations, for instance, act more as lobbying or advocacy entities than communities of practice, though they may include specialized subgroups that create practice-development relationships among members.

Obviously, all these distinctions exist in varying degrees; they are not black and white. The extent to which any group is or is not a community of practice is not something that can be determined in the abstract by its name or by characteristics of members. You have to look at how the group functions and how it combines all three elements of domain, community, and practice.

Forms of Participation

Domain, community, and practice are not merely useful terms for defining communities of practice. They represent different aspects of participation that motivate people to join a community. In fact, to some extent they characterize basic types of members in a community of practice. Some people participate because they care about the domain and want to see it developed. Others are drawn by the value of having a community; they are looking mainly to interact with peers, people who share something important. For those who have devoted most of their lives to learning one profession, connecting with others who share that passion is rewarding in itself. Communities are also a place where people can make a contribution and know it will genuinely be appreciated. Other members simply want to learn about the practice: what standards have been established, what tools work well, what lessons have been learned by master practitioners. The community is an opportunity to learn new techniques and approaches in their personal desire to perfect their craft.

Although the impetus to join may be an overriding interest, one driving factor naturally leads to others. People who join a community because they are interested in the domain often stay because they become emotionally connected to the community. Still, it is useful to perceive these distinctions because a varied mix of people who care about each element in differing degrees will yield a balanced community.

These elements also show what a complex thing knowledge is for human beings. Knowledge involves the head, the heart, and the hand; inquiry, interactions, and craft. Like a community, it involves identity, relationships, and competence; meaningfulness, belonging, and action. A community of practice matches that complexity.[26]

A Practical Model as a Guide to Development

FINALLY, AND MOST IMPORTANT, the three elements provide a practical model to guide community development. A good model is useful for developing communities of practice because it helps ensure that you address all the relevant issues and maintain a proper balance among the elements.

- *Domain.* The work of negotiating a shared domain is critical to community development. A community must ask itself: What topics and issues do we really care about? How is this domain connected to the organization's strategy? What is in it for us? What are the open questions and the leading edge of our domain? Are we ready to take some leadership in promoting and developing our domain? What kind of influence do we want to have? Addressing these types of questions will help a community develop a shared understanding of its domain, find its legitimacy in the organization, and engage the passion of its members.

- *Community.* The community element needs attention, organization, and nurturing: What roles are people going to play? How often will the community meet, and how will members connect on an ongoing basis? What kinds of activities will generate energy and develop trust? How can the community balance the needs of various segments of members? How will members deal with conflict? How will newcomers be introduced into the community? Addressing these types of questions will enable the community to find its specific ways to operate, to build relationships, and to grow.

- *Practice.* Any community with sustained interactions in a domain will develop some kind of practice over time. Nevertheless, a community can become proactive in taking charge of the development of its practice. What knowledge to share, develop, document? What kinds of learning activities to organize? How should the knowledge repository be organized to reflect the practice of members and be easily accessible? When should processes be standardized and when are differences appropriate? What development project should the community undertake? Where are sources of knowledge and benchmarks outside the community? These are the kinds of questions that will help a community intentionally become an effective knowledge resource to its members and to other constituencies that may benefit from its expertise.

It is important to develop all three elements in parallel. Focusing too much on one while neglecting the others can be counterproductive. For instance, trying to design a knowledge base without a clear domain or a coherent community can easily produce a useless tool, as demonstrated by the numerous databases, built without involving a well-defined community, that are now collecting digital dust. Conversely, a community that does not focus on building a shared practice will remain a diffuse friendship group that may be socially satisfying, but ineffective.

Developing domain, community, and practice together is a balancing act; each element requires a distinct kind of developmental attention and work. At the same time, the three elements interact, and it is their interplay that makes for a healthy community. All three elements of a community of practice are dynamic. The domain evolves as the focus shifts from one hot topic to another. Members join the community and others move on. New practices arise and old ones are discarded.

We have found that if all three elements are in flux at the same time, the community is at risk. People may become unsure of the community's purpose, leadership, or value. It is difficult to proceed. But stability in one element can help facilitate a transition in another. For instance, if the domain is clear and the practice is well established, then people can come and go without harming the community. Similarly, if members have a strong commitment to each other, the community can survive a deep transformation of its practice by an innovation and members can push the edge of the domain with confidence that they are not at risk. The art of community development is to use the synergy between domain, community, and practice to help a community evolve and fulfill its potential.

Conclusion

WE HAVE ARGUED in this chapter that community members and sponsors alike benefit by understanding the three basic elements of a community of practice. Indeed, the process of writing this book has been an effort to "walk our talk" and, as mentioned in the preface, to help catalyze a latent community of practice around communities of practice. We have defined the domain of issues that we consider relevant to communities of practice—including those related to business strategy, innovation, organizational learning, organization design, leadership, and knowledge management. We have introduced the key elements of our practice—definitions, models, methods, and stories. We owe this knowledge to colleagues—clients, scholars, mentors, and friends—particularly those that we acknowledge and cite throughout this book. The influence of this work as a community-building artifact will depend ultimately on the continuing relevance of its domain in the world and on the diverse, distributed, and growing community of practitioners who make use of it.

Seven Principles for Cultivating Communities of Practice

I N SILICON VALLEY, A COMMUNITY OF CIRCUIT
designers meets for a lively debate about the merits of two different designs developed by one of the participants. Huddling together over
the circuit diagrams, they analyze possible faults, discuss issues of efficiency, propose alternatives, tease out each other's assumptions, and make
the case for their view. In Boston, a group of social workers who staff a help
line meet to discuss knotty client problems, express sympathy as they discuss difficulties, probe to understand each other's feelings, and gently offer
suggestions. Their meetings are often deeply challenging and sometimes
highly emotional.

The fact-driven, sometimes argumentative, meetings of the Silicon Valley circuit designers are extremely different from the compassionate meetings of the social workers in Boston. But despite their differences, the circuit designers' and social workers' communities are both vibrant and full of
life. Their energy is palpable to both the regular participants and visitors.

Because communities of practice are voluntary, what makes them success-
ful over time is their ability to generate enough excitement, relevance, and
value to attract and engage members. Although many factors, such as man-
agement support or an urgent problem, can inspire a community, nothing
can substitute for this sense of aliveness.

H OW DO YOU design for aliveness? Certainly you cannot contrive
or dictate it. You cannot design it in the traditional sense of spec-
ifying a structure or process and then implementing it. Still, aliveness
does not always happen automatically. Many natural communities
never grow beyond a network of friends because they fail to attract
enough participants. Many intentional communities fall apart soon
after their initial launch because they don't have enough energy to sustain themselves. Communities, unlike teams and other structures,
need to invite the interaction that makes them alive. For example, a
park is more appealing to use if its location provides a short-cut
between destinations. It invites people to sit for lunch or chat if it has
benches set slightly off the main path, visible, but just out of earshot,
next to something interesting like a flower bed or a patch of sunlight.[1]
The structure of organizational relationships and events also *invite* a
kind of interaction. Meetings that contain some open time during a
break or lunch, with enough space for people to mingle or confer privately, invite one-on-one discussion and relationship building. Just as a
good park has varied spaces for neighborhood baseball games, quiet
chats, or solitary contemplation, a well-designed community of practice
allows for participating in group discussion, having one-on-one conversations, reading about new ideas, or watching experts duel over cutting-
edge issues. Even though communities are voluntary and organic, good
community design can invite, even evoke, aliveness.

Designing to evoke aliveness is different from most organizational
design, which traditionally focuses on creating structures, systems, and
roles that achieve relatively fixed organizational goals and fit well with
other structural elements of the organization. Even when organizations
are designed to be flexible and responsive to their environment, organic

growth and aliveness are typically not primary design goals.[2] For communities of practice, however, they are paramount, even though communities also need to contribute to organizational goals. Designing for aliveness requires a different set of design principles.[3] (Vibrant neighborhoods also embody design principles, as Boston's Prince Street demonstrates—see box 3-1.) The goal of community design is to bring out the community's own internal direction, character, and energy. The principles we developed to do this focus on the dilemmas at the heart of designing communities of practice. What is the role of design for a "human institution" that is, by definition, natural, spontaneous, and self-directed? How do you guide such an institution to realize itself, to become "alive"? From our experience we have derived seven principles:

1. Design for evolution.

2. Open a dialogue between inside and outside perspectives.

3. Invite different levels of participation.

4. Develop both public and private community spaces.

5. Focus on value.

6. Combine familiarity and excitement.

7. Create a rhythm for the community.

These design principles are not recipes, but rather embody our understanding of how elements of design work together. They reveal the thinking behind a design. Making design principles explicit makes it possible to be more flexible and improvisational.

1. Design for Evolution

BECAUSE COMMUNITIES OF practice are organic, designing them is more a matter of shepherding their evolution than creating them from scratch. Design elements should be catalysts for a community's natural evolution. As they develop, communities usually build on preexisting personal networks. For example, when Schlumberger

BOX 3-1 ARCHITECTURAL ALIVENESS

PRINCE STREET in Boston's North End is a typical old-city neighborhood, full of life and visually welcoming. Low red brick buildings line the narrow street, with apartments on the upper stories and restaurants, spas, bakeries, butcher shops, and gift stores below. Many stores have little alcoves at the door, just large enough for a few people, or a few chairs, to gather. Big plate glass windows let you see the activity inside, and some merchants have placed their wares on the street, extending the buying range of the store and blurring the distinction between inside and outside. Side streets punctuate Prince Street. They gently curve out of sight, the same low red brick buildings on either side. Occasionally you can see a small park down a side street, the inviting paths that crisscross it clearly laid down by footsteps long before they were paved.

Prince Street was not architecturally designed; it emerged as people settled Boston. However, it still embodies a number of principles for creating architectural aliveness.[4]

1. **Integrate different uses.** Prince Street integrates residential and commercial use, which invites people of different ages, occupations, and with different purposes to mingle on the street.

2. **Use repeating patterns that are similar, but not exactly the same.** The buildings are similar, red brick with black shutters on the windows above. However, the windows vary in height and size from building to building.

3. **Create transitions at entrances.** Rather than just a door in the middle of the building, many storefronts have small alcoves at the doorway. These invite people to pause, to mingle and talk, as they transition from the street to the building.

These architectural principles echo ones that are also relevant to communities, where a mix of familiar and exciting activities that span both public and private spaces are key characteristics of "aliveness."

launched a series of communities of practice in its research division, most people were already part of networks connected through the company's extensive bulletin board system.

The dynamic nature of communities is key to their evolution. As the community grows, new members bring new interests and may pull the focus of the community in different directions. Changes in the organization influence the relative importance of the community and place new demands on it. For example, an IT community that was only marginally important to an organization suddenly became critical as the company discovered the potential of a few e-business pilots. Changes in the core science or technology of a community constantly reshape it, often bringing in professionals from neighboring disciplines or introducing technological advances that change their way of working. Because communities are built on existing networks and evolve beyond any particular design, the purpose of a design is not to impose a structure but to help the community develop.

Community design is much more like life-long learning than traditional organization design. "Alive" communities reflect on and redesign elements of themselves throughout their existence. Community design often involves fewer elements at the beginning than does a traditional organization design. In one case, the coordinator and core members had many ideas of what the community could become. Rather than introduce those ideas to the community as a whole, they started with a very simple structure of regular weekly meetings. They did not capture meeting notes, put up a Web site, or speculate with the group on "where this is going." Their first goal was to draw potential members to the community. Once people were engaged in the topic and had begun to build relationships, the core members began introducing other elements of community structure—such as a Web site, links to other communities, projects to define key practices—one at a time.[5]

The key to designing for evolution is to combine design elements in a way that catalyzes community development. Physical structures—such as roads and parks—can precipitate the development of a town. Similarly, social and organizational structures, such as a community coordinator or problem-solving meetings, can precipitate the evolution of a community. Which community design elements are most appropriate depends on the community's stage of development, its environment, member cohesiveness, and the kinds of knowledge it shares. But evolution is common to all communities, and the primary role of design is to catalyze that evolution.

2. Open a Dialogue Between Inside and Outside Perspectives

G OOD COMMUNITY DESIGN requires an insider's perspective to lead the discovery of what the community is about. When designing teams, we know a team's output requirements in advance and can design to achieve that output. But effective community design is built on the collective experience of community members. Only an insider can appreciate the issues at the heart of the domain, the knowledge that is important to share, the challenges their field faces, and the latent potential in emerging ideas and techniques. Only an insider can know who the real players are and their relationships. This requires more than community "input." It requires a deep understanding of community issues.[6]

Good community design requires an understanding of the community's potential to develop and steward knowledge, but it often takes an outside perspective to help members see the possibilities. Because intentional communities are new for most organizations, members often have a hard time imagining how a more developed community could improve upon their current personal networks or help them leverage dormant capabilities. Good community design brings information from outside the community into the dialogue about what the community could achieve. Sometimes this involves educating community members about the role of communities in other organizations. It might mean bringing an "outsider" into a dialogue with the community leader and core members as they design the community. As a result of this dialogue, the people who understand the issues inside the community and have legitimacy within it are also able to see new possibilities and can effectively act as agents of change.[7]

The well-connected leader of a new community on emerging technology was concerned about how to develop the community when many of the "prima donnas" of the industry were outside his company. When he saw how a similar community in another organization was structured to involve outside experts in multiple ways, he started rethinking the potential structure of his own community. He realized that the key issues in his community were less about technology and more about the business issues involved in developing the technology. This understanding of the business perspective of the other community gave him a sharper sense of the strategic potential of his own.

3. Invite Different Levels of Participation

GOOD COMMUNITY ARCHITECTURE invites many different levels of participation. Consider the variety of activities we might find in a city neighborhood on any given day: solitary shoppers, people walking briskly to work, friends out for a casual stroll, couples chatting at an outdoor café, a crowd watching a street performer. Others are on the periphery, watching the action from the windows above the street. A community of practice is very similar. As we saw in chapter 2, people participate in communities for different reasons—some because the community directly provides value, some for the personal connection, and others for the opportunity to improve their skills. We used to think that we should encourage all community members to participate equally. But because people have different levels of interest in the community, this expectation is unrealistic.

Alive communities, whether planned or spontaneous, have a "coordinator" who organizes events and connects community members (see chapter 4 for more on the role of the community coordinator). But others in the community also take on leadership roles. We commonly see three main levels of community participation, as illustrated in figure 3-1. The first is a small *core* group of people who actively participate in discussions, even debates, in the public community forum. They often take on community projects, identify topics for the community to address, and move the community along its learning agenda. This group is the heart of the community. As the community matures, this core group takes on much of the community's leadership, its members becoming auxiliaries to the community coordinator. But this group is usually rather small, only 10 to 15 percent of the whole community. At the next level outside this core is the *active* group. These members attend meetings regularly and participate occasionally in the community forums, but without the regularity or intensity of the core group. The active group is also quite small, another 15 to 20 percent of the community.

A large portion of community members are *peripheral* and rarely participate. Instead, they keep to the sidelines, watching the interaction of the core and active members. Some remain peripheral because they feel that their observations are not appropriate for the whole or carry no authority. Others do not have the time to contribute more actively. In a traditional meeting or team we would discourage such half-hearted involvement, but these peripheral activities are an essential dimension of communities of practice. Indeed, the people on the sidelines often are not as passive as they seem. Like people sitting at a café watching the activity on the street, they gain their own insights from the discussions and put them to good use. They may have private conversations about the issues being discussed in the public forum. In their own way, they are learning a lot. In one community, a peripheral member attended nearly all meetings for two years, but almost never contributed. Then he was transferred to another division and, to everyone's surprise, started a similar community there.

Finally, outside these three main levels are people surrounding the community who are not members but who have an interest in the community, including customers, suppliers, and "intellectual neighbors."

Community members move through these levels.[8] Core members often join the sideline as the topic of the community shifts. Active

FIGURE 3-1   DEGREES OF COMMUNITY PARTICIPATION

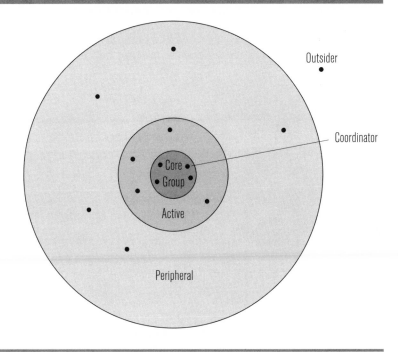

members may be deeply engaged for a month or two, then disengage. Peripheral members drift into the center as their interests are stirred. Because the boundaries of a community are fluid, even those outside the community can become quite involved for a time, as the focus of the community shifts to their areas of interest and expertise. The key to good community participation and a healthy degree of movement between levels is to design community activities that allow participants at all levels to feel like full members. Rather than force participation, successful communities "build benches" for those on the sidelines. They make opportunities for semiprivate interaction, whether through private discussion rooms on the community's Web site, at a community event, or in a one-on-one conversation. This keeps the peripheral members connected. At the same time, communities create opportunities for active members to take limited leadership roles, such as leading a development project that requires a minimal time commitment. To draw members into more active participation, successful communities build a fire in the center of the community that will draw people to its heat.

4. Develop Both Public and Private Community Spaces

L IKE A LOCAL NEIGHBORHOOD, dynamic communities are rich with connections that happen both in the public places of the community—meetings, Web site—and the private space—the one-on-one networking of community members. Most communities have public events where community members gather—either face-to-face or electronically—to exchange tips, solve problems, or explore new ideas, tools, and techniques. These events are public in that they are open to all community members, though they are often closed to people outside the community. Sometimes they include formal presentations, but most often they are informal discussions of current problems and issues as described in the introductory vignette in chapter 2. Public community events serve a ritualistic as well as a substantive purpose. Through such events, people can tangibly experience being part of the community and see who else participates. They can appreciate the level of sophistication the community brings to a technical discussion, how it rallies around key principles, and the influence it has in the organization.

As we've emphasized before, communities are much more than their calendar of events. The heart of a community is the web of relationships among community members, and much of the day-to-day occurs in one-on-one exchanges. Thus, a common mistake in community design is to focus too much on public events. A community coordinator needs to "work" the private space between meetings, dropping in on community members to discuss their current technical problems and linking them with helpful resources, inside or outside the community. These informal, "back channel" discussions actually help orchestrate the public space and are key to successful meetings. They ensure that the spontaneous topics raised at the meetings are valuable to the whole and that the people attending will have something useful to add. The one-on-one networking creates a conduit for sharing information with a more limited number of people, using the coordinator's discretion as a gate. Every phone call, e-mail exchange, or problem-solving conversation strengthens the relationships within the community.[9]

The public and private dimensions of a community are interrelated. When the individual relationships among community members are strong, the events are much richer. Because participants know each other well, they often come to community events with multiple agendas: completing a small group task, thanking someone for an idea, finding someone to help with a problem. In fact, good community events usually allow time for people to network informally. Well-orchestrated, lively public events foster one-on-one connections. As one coordinator said, "I like to see who walks out of the room together, who hangs around and talks. The more new connections I see, the better the meeting was." The key to designing community spaces is to orchestrate activities in both public and private spaces that use the strength of individual relationships to enrich events and use events to strengthen individual relationships.[10]

5. Focus on Value

COMMUNITIES THRIVE BECAUSE they deliver value to the organization, to the teams on which community members serve, and to the community members themselves. As we argued in chapter 1, value is key to community life, because participation in most communities is voluntary. But the full value of a community is often not apparent when it is first formed. Moreover, the source of value often changes over the life of the community. Frequently, early value mostly comes from focusing on the current problems and needs of community members. As the community grows, developing a systematic body of knowledge that can be easily accessed becomes more important.

Rather than attempting to determine their expected value in advance, communities need to create events, activities, and relationships that help their potential value emerge and enable them to discover new ways to harvest it. A group of systems engineers thought that sharing project proposals would be useful. Once they began, however, they discovered that the proposals themselves were not that helpful. What they needed was the engineers' logic for matching *that* software with *that* hardware and *that* service plan. This logic, of course, was not explicit in the proposal. These engineers needed to meet, discuss their proposals, and unveil the logic that held their systems together.

Many of the most valuable community activities are the small, everyday interactions—informal discussions to solve a problem, or one-on-one exchanges of information about a tool, supplier, approach, or database. The real value of these exchanges may not be evident immediately. When someone shares an insight, they often don't know how useful it was until the recipient reports how the idea was applied. The impact of applying an idea can take months to be realized. Thus, tracing the impact of a shared idea takes time and attention.

In fact, a key element of designing for value is to encourage community members to be explicit about the value of the community throughout its lifetime. Initially, the purpose of such discussion is more to raise awareness than collect data, since the impact of the community typically takes some time to be felt. Later, assessments of value can become more rigorous, as we discuss further in chapter 8.

Several months after it started one community made discussing value part of its monthly teleconferences. Most community members were not able to identify any particular value when these discussions began, even though they all felt participation was useful. Soon, however, one community member was able to quantify the value his team gained by applying a new technique he learned from another member. Another said the real value of the community was more personal and less quantifiable; he knew who to contact when he had a problem. Once these examples surfaced, other community members were better able to identify the specific value they derived from participation. Although people often complain about the difficulty of assessing community value, such early discussions greatly help community members as well as potential members and other stakeholders understand the real impact of the community.

6. Combine Familiarity and Excitement

S UCCESSFUL COMMUNITIES offer the familiar comforts of a hometown, but they also have enough interesting and varied events to keep new ideas and new people cycling into the community. As communities mature, they often settle into a pattern of regular meetings, teleconferences, projects, Web site use, and other ongoing activities. The familiarity of these events creates a comfort level that invites candid discussions. Like a neighborhood bar or café, a community becomes a "place" where people have the freedom to ask for candid advice, share their opinions, and try their half-baked ideas without repercussion. They are places people can drop by to hear about the latest tool, exchange technical gossip, or just chat about technical issues without fear of committing to action plans.

Communities of practice are what Ray Oldenberg calls "neutral places," separate from the everyday work pressures of people's jobs.[11] Unlike team members, community members can offer advice on a project with no risk of getting entangled in it; they can listen to advice with no obligation to take it. These are reasons why a group of scientists in a pharmaceutical company, driven by urgency to develop new products, see their community as a place to think, reflect, and consider ideas too "soft" for the development teams.

Like a well-planned, challenging conference, vibrant communities also supply divergent thinking and activity. For example, a community of immunologists invites a controversial speaker to their annual conference, a Nobel Prize winner whose ideas are respected by the community but controversial enough to challenge their normal way of thinking. P&G invites its communities to its science fair, where the latest ideas and inventions are displayed and discussed. Conferences, fairs, and workshops such as these bring the community together in a special way and thus facilitate a different kind of spontaneous contact between people. They can provide novelty and excitement that complements the familiarity of everyday activities.

Lively communities combine both familiar and exciting events so community members can develop the relationships they need to be well connected as well as generate the excitement they need to be fully engaged. Routine activities provide the stability for relationship-building connections; exciting events provide a sense of common adventure.

7. Create a Rhythm for the Community

OUR EVERYDAY LIVES have a rhythm: waking up and preparing for work, commuting, checking e-mail, attending meetings, commuting home, engaging with kids' activities, enjoying quiet time. Although there are different rhythms for different people, most of our lives do have a rhythm, which contributes to its sense of familiarity. Towns also have a rhythm. Take the college town of Boulder, Colorado. Throughout the year it has a series of monthly festivals: a river festival, a road race, an arts festival, a Fourth of July celebration, a World Affairs Conference, and a few festivals whose occasion hardly anyone remembers. Like most towns, it also sponsors numerous projects—an arts fund drive, clothing for the homeless. These events and community projects give residents an opportunity to assemble, converse, share opinions, spout off (Boulder's fairs even have an official soapbox), and have fun together in a way that punctuates the life of the town. They give the town a beat.

Vibrant communities of practice also have a rhythm. At the heart of a community is a web of enduring relationships among members, but the tempo of their interactions is greatly influenced by the rhythm of community events. Regular meetings, teleconferences, Web site activity, and informal lunches ebb and flow along with the heartbeat of the community. When that beat is strong and rhythmic, the community has a sense of movement and liveliness. If the beat is too fast, the community feels breathless; people stop participating because they are overwhelmed.

When the beat is too slow, the community feels sluggish. A community of library scientists had an annual meeting and a Web site with a threaded discussion. Not surprisingly, six months after the conference there was very little activity on the Web. An engineering community, on the other hand, held a biweekly teleconference as well as several focused, face-to-face meetings during the year. In this community there is typically a flurry of activity on the Web site just before and after the teleconferences and meetings. The events give the community a beat around which other activities find their rhythm.[12]

Sometimes key projects and special events create milestones for the community, breaking up the regular rhythm. Members of a community on team development at the Veterans Benefits Administration traveled to regional offices around the country. They gave workshops and coached local team members and managers. These office visits made the community's contribution to the organization visible and marked a major step in the community's development.

The rhythm of the community is the strongest indicator of its aliveness. There are many rhythms in a community—the syncopation of familiar and exciting events, the frequency of private interactions, the ebb and flow of people from the sidelines into active participation, and the pace of the community's overall evolution. A combination of whole-community and small-group gatherings creates a balance between the thrill of exposure to many different ideas and the comfort of more intimate relationships. A mix of idea-sharing forums and tool-building projects fosters both casual connections and directed community action. There is no right beat for all communities, and the beat is likely to change as the community evolves. But finding the right rhythm at each stage is key to a community's development.

Conclusion

ALTHOUGH COMMUNITIES of practice develop naturally, an appropriate amount of design can be a powerful engine for their evolution, helping members identify the knowledge, events, roles, and activities that will catalyze the community's growth. The organic nature of communities of practice challenges us to design these elements with a light hand, with an appreciation that the idea is to create liveliness, not manufacture a predetermined outcome.

Because communities of practice are living things, they require an approach to organization design that more fully acknowledges the importance of passion, relationships, and voluntary activities in organizations. Rather than focusing on comprehensiveness and fit, community design concentrates on energizing participation. Rather than designing finished structures, it uses design as a catalyst for community growth and development. This approach intermingles design and implementation, making design a recurring aspect of the life of the community, not a precursor to its existence—a part of the community itself, not an outside-in activity. The challenge of designing natural structures like communities of practice is creating an approach to design that redefines design itself.

The Early Stages of
Development

Planning and Launching
Communities of Practice

IT IS 1994. AFTER TEN YEARS OF ADVANCED TECHNICAL *development Auger, the Deepwater Tension Leg Platform developed by Shell Oil's U.S. division, begins operation in the Gulf of Mexico. Anchored to the ocean floor by high-tension wires, it floats on the surface, gently rocking with the waves, as it pumps 90,000 barrels of oil and 300 million cubic feet of gas a day.[1]*

When Shell first started deepwater exploration in the Gulf, the division was organized by function. Now that Auger was operational, the company needed to improve efficiency and replicate the design. Shell redesigned its deepwater operation so that the core organizational units were cross-disciplinary project teams, called asset teams, responsible for exploring or developing a geographic region of the Gulf. Each asset team operated as a separate profit and loss center, with full responsibility for both sound scientific analysis and financial return. Asset team members were housed together and reported to the same general manager. Having adjacent offices helped the scientists and engineers to understand the full spectrum of issues in exploring and developing the site. This integrated work space facilitated much tighter integration between disciplines. Sharing goals helped scientists and engineers better understand the financial as well as the scientific implications of the tools and approaches they used.

Yet, the very thing that made these teams work well—common goals, shared focus, physical proximity, working rapport—led to the isolation of the professional staff. In the new organization, people literally had to track down colleagues on other teams, often several floors away, or make an appointment for an informal discussion. As a result, staff members spent far too much time looking for information from other teams or past projects. The new organization had eliminated the old functional silos, but the project teams had become a new kind of silo that isolated people from other members of their discipline.

To address this problem, Shell created "networks" of people who shared a common discipline or interest. Since the networks were formed around technical topics, their members knew what information was useful, what they should document, what help other network members really needed. The networks linked professionals across the project teams. One of these networks brought together geologists, reservoir engineers, petrophysicists, and other geoscientists interested in turbidite structures, a geological formation fairly common in the Gulf. They called themselves the "Turbodudes."

The Turbodudes started with a small group of about fifteen geoscientists meeting weekly to discuss key issues in developing turbidite reservoirs. The group consisted of leading experts in the field. Like most early communities of practice at Shell, they talked about technical problems they were having in their work and thought through alternative approaches. They had a lot of energy for these discussions. As one geologist said, "With so many meetings that aren't immediately relevant to your work, it's nice to go to one where we talk about rocks."

Several years later, the Turbodudes are still going strong. Their discussions continue to be very informal. Typically, a member poses a question or problem and the group makes observations and suggestions. The community coordinator lightly facilitates the discussion by helping people explicate the logic or assumptions behind their observations. If a speaker seems defensive and closed to the ideas of others, the coordinator reminds him (as the name reflects, most Turbodudes are men) that the purpose of the meeting is to raise many different ideas. When the group seems to be "grilling" a speaker, asking many detailed questions but offering few alternatives, he reminds them that they owe the speaker some ideas of their own. He then suggests they shift focus and discuss other ways the speaker could approach the problem. These community discussions seem very spontaneous, but this spontaneity is more intentional than it appears.[2]

Between meetings the coordinator "walks the halls." He drops in on community members, follows up on action items, asks people about hot issues to discuss at the next meeting, and informally lets others know about upcoming agenda items on which he would particularly like their input. These informal, one-on-one discussions ensure that the "spontaneous" topics raised at the next meeting are truly valuable to the community and that those attending will have something useful to add. In fact, the Turbodudes' coordinator tracked the number of people attending the meetings and found that the strongest predictor of high attendance was how much time he had spent the previous week walking the halls. Still, he was not able to get all the people he wanted to join the meetings. One turbidite expert was reluctant to attend the Turbodudes meetings regularly because he "didn't have time." The coordinator then offered tailored invitations, encouraging him to come when the topic was particularly important to him.

Turbodude members also connect through small projects. The Turbodudes frequently identify technical problems that are too big to solve completely by the end of a meeting. The coordinator works through some of these on his own with the input of a few community members. Small teams of community members handle other issues.

As the Turbodude community developed, the number of potential projects increased. They identified many more issues that could be resolved or turned into guidelines than they had time for. As the Turbodude coordinator said, "At the weekly Turbodudes meeting, I feel like I am in the middle of a rushing stream, with so many ideas and potential improvements to our work rushing by."

As a result of the Turbodude meetings, one-on-one connections, and projects, Turbodude members have developed a real understanding of each other's work, needs, and perspectives. When they walk into a Turbodude meeting, they do so with many relationships already forged. Like people walking in their neighborhood, they come to the meeting with multiple purposes, and those purposes intermingle on "the street" of community meetings. Of course, the Turbodudes did not begin with the relaxed intimacy their meetings have come to possess. The character of the community evolved as the community matured. The planners of the Turbodudes could not dictate this character. Instead they had to find the topics, the people, and the forums that would help the community develop.

The Stages of Community Development

L IKE OTHER LIVING THINGS, communities are not born in their final state, but go through a natural cycle of birth, growth, and death. Many go through such radical transformations that the reasons they stay together have little relation to the reasons they started in the first place. Although communities of practice continually evolve, we have observed five stages of community development: potential, coalescing, maturing, stewardship, and transformation. (See figure 4-1.) They typically start as loose networks that hold the potential of becoming more connected and thus a more important part of the organization. As members build connections, they coalesce into a community. Once formed, the community often grows in both membership and the depth of knowledge members share. When mature, communities go through cycles of high and low activity, just like other living things. During this stage, communities often take active stewardship of the knowledge and practices they share and consciously develop them.

As communities evolve through these stages, the activities needed to develop them also change. This chapter and the next trace the issues communities face during these stages and the activities that can help them develop.[3]

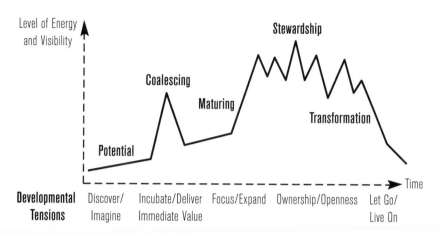

FIGURE 4-1 STAGES OF COMMUNITY DEVELOPMENT

The jagged line represents the level of energy and visibility that the community typically generates over time.

A community's development, like an individual's, is rarely smooth. It frequently involves painful discoveries, difficult transitions, and learning through hard-won experience. One community stalled when its passionate leader changed roles. Community members were so dependent on him they found it hard to take on the tasks he had so invisibly assumed. A community of production engineers was reluctant to welcome new members. They didn't want to let go of the intimacy they had developed, even though they knew they had to expand to survive. Each stage of community development, like each stage of human development, confronts the community with a central challenge. We will describe each challenge as a tension between two opposing tendencies that the community must address before it can move to the next stage. Of course, each community experiences these tensions differently. Some view them as major problems and conflicts, with community members aligned on opposite sides. Others consider them an opportunity to grow and solidify the community.[4]

Although a developmental model provides some direction, it cannot be taken too literally. These stages and their sequence are merely typical, and there can be wide variations in the ways communities experience them. Just as many of us still experience adolescence at fifty or some children grow up very quickly when faced with extreme circumstances, communities vary widely in their developmental sequence. Some communities go through one stage rapidly; others spend much time in the same stage. Some seem to skip a stage and may later go back to deal with earlier issues; others appear to struggle with unresolved tensions from several stages at once. Some do not make it all the way through. Sometimes communities reach their full potential at stage 2 or 3. For example, one community of production engineers felt that the most valuable thing they could do was help each other solve everyday production problems. They realized that they could also rationalize production schedules, develop collective procedures, and more fully steward their knowledge. But they chose to continue focusing on sharing tips. There is nothing wrong with this decision. It may have been the very best thing for them to do. Still, having a sense of stages and associated issues helps you foresee problems you are likely to face, understand the changing needs of the community, and take appropriate action. It helps you be patient when a community needs to deal with its development in its own time and prod appropriately when it is time to move on.

In this chapter, we discuss stages 1 and 2, which cover the process of launching a community of practice. We will discuss stages 3, 4, and 5 in the next chapter, where we address the challenge of sustaining a community through its growth and maturity, and possible midlife crises, until its end or transformation.

Stage 1: Potential

Community development begins with an extant social network. Any important topic in an organization usually attracts an informal group of interested people who begin networking. Whether they are simply a loose network or have already begun to see themselves as community of practice, these are the people who are likely to form the core group of the community and take the lead in pulling it together. Like an embryo, a potential community already comprises some basic elements of a developed community and has the full potential of becoming one. At some point, the idea of forming a community is introduced into this loose network, and this prospect starts to redirect people's attention. They start to see their own issues and interests as communal fodder and their relationships in the new light of a potential community. As the sense of a shared domain develops, the need for more systematic interactions emerges and generates interest. Some people usually step up to take responsibility for getting the community started.

Typically the key issue at the beginning of a community is to find enough common ground among members for them to feel connected and see the value of sharing insights, stories, and techniques. At this early stage, what energizes the potential community is the discovery that other people face similar problems, share a passion for the same topics, have data, tools, and approaches they can contribute, and have valuable insights they can learn from each other. The more passionate people feel about those concerns, the more drive the community is likely to have. But passion alone is not enough to make a community. A community is driven by the value members get from it, so people need to see how their passion will translate into something useful.

- As the community begins, the key *domain* issue it faces is defining the scope of the domain in a way that elicits the heartfelt interests of members and aligns with important issues for the organization as a whole.

- The key *community* issue is finding people who already network on the topic and helping them to imagine how increased networking and knowledge sharing could be valuable.

- The key *practice* issue is identifying common knowledge needs.

These three dimensions are related. As you establish the scope of the domain, the dimensions of the community become clearer. As you build the community, people identify common knowledge needs.

Discover and Imagine

Starting a community of practice involves balancing discovery and imagination—discovering what you can build on and imagining where this potential can lead. This is a delicate balance. If you ignore the networks that currently share knowledge about the topic, you will fail to enlist the participation of the most likely early contributors. But if you focus only on current networks, you will not cross enough personal boundaries to bring new ideas into the community.

To build the community, the leaders and organizers need to discover who talks with whom about the topic, what issues they discuss, the strength of their relationships, and the obstacles that impede knowledge sharing and collaboration. Building on these networks and appreciating the common ground people already have is key to success in the early phases of community development. People actively networking on the topic often already know what knowledge is important to share and what problems are involved in connecting with each other. These same people are likely to be core members of the emerging community. By conducting either a formal or informal social network analysis, the organizers can identify who is involved in this current network and where the ties between people are strong.[5] If the community does not build on current networks, it risks losing credibility with, or even alienating, these important potential members.

At the same time, community members need to imagine how a community can be more than just a personal network. Well-connected practitioners often believe that they already know the people who matter and sometimes have a hard time imagining the value a more extended network could add—especially if it includes people less knowledgeable than themselves. Imagining a wider, more fully developed community often involves seeing new possibilities. For example, a group of software configuration management (CM) experts had trouble imagining what a community could do until they learned that part of their company was about to adopt a new CM software. Realizing that focusing on that software would involve people outside their current network, they began to see how the community could become an extremely valuable resource.

Sometimes imagining the community is difficult because it is so different from the team environment people are used to. Even in the early phases of a team's launch, it is possible to define its outputs and performance goals and assign member roles. Because communities *evolve* toward their potential, rather than define it up front, developing them involves imagining possibilities their members have not yet considered. Unless community leaders and members have had the experience of how a community can provide value, this can be difficult to imagine. In fact, many of us have limited or even negative experience with the more commonplace geographic notion of community (see box 4-1), which may further limit our imagination.

Planning Communities: A Typical Work Plan

It is tempting to develop a detailed plan of the structure, roles, membership requirements, documentation system, and so forth for a community, as we would for a team. But as we said in chapter 3, planning a community is more a matter of finding the triggers to catalyze evolution than creating a full design. The overall goal in the planning stage is to promote community development around each of the three key elements—domain, community, and practice—by defining the community's focus, identifying and building relationships between members, and identifying topics and projects that would be exciting for community members.

Determine the Primary Intent of the Community. Communities of practice can start with different intents. For instance, an exploratory study by the American Productivity and Quality Center (APQC)[6] found four different strategic intents for forming communities for professionals on different teams or locations: (1) to help each other solve everyday work problems in their discipline, (2) to develop and disseminate a set of best practices, (3) to develop and steward the tools, insights, and approaches needed by members in field assignments, and (4) to develop highly innovative solutions and ideas. (See box 4-2.) Although most communities serve more than one purpose, communities tend to focus on one and adapt the structure, roles, and activities most suited to that intent. Then they fit other activities into those structures.

BOX 4-1 FOOD FOR THOUGHT . . . LIFE WITHOUT COMMUNITY

I T MAY BE more difficult for us to design communities of practice today than it would have been fifty years ago. Many of us have had little or no first-hand experience of what it is like to live in a traditional community. Few Americans, for instance, shop for dinner by walking to the corner store, where they run into neighbors and exchange the local gossip. It has become a nostalgic wish to have morning coffee at the neighborhood diner, a place to offer opinions and spout off as well as exchange news. Few can visit a local tavern "where everyone knows your name." The television show *Cheers* is as close as many Americans get. Mostly this is because the local grocery, diner, and tavern have gone out of business, replaced by supermarkets, fast-food drive-through windows, and chain restaurants. As the population has become more mobile, it has moved from neighborhoods to "neighborhoodless" suburbs. The public places that anchored local communities are, on the whole, absent in the suburbs.[7]

Communities of practice are, of course, different from neighborhood communities. But like neighborhoods, they are a place where people live, think, and converse in the presence of others, in a "public" place. What we have lost in the transition to a suburban society is the knowledge and experience of conversing and thinking in public with others we know.

It is ironic that as we move further away from the traditional neighborhood experience in our own lives, communities of practice are becoming a more important part of organizational life. Perhaps some of the appeal of communities of practice is that they are an avenue through which we can recover some of our lost sense of community.[8]

Different intents require different community structures and activities. "Helping" communities, for instance, require forums for informally sharing ideas. "Knowledge stewarding" requires some structure and roles for verifying the knowledge the community manages. Identifying the strategic intent helps define the scope of the community and the kind of knowledge it will share. When communities begin, trying to play all these roles can overwhelm members. Clarifying the primary intent of the community can make its development more natural and easier for members to imagine. As the community matures, it can expand its focus to include other areas.

Define the Domain and Identify Engaging Issues. As communities evolve, they frequently change the scope of their domain, either by changing their boundaries or by completely redefining them. Thus the first objective is to define the domain in a way that will engage potential members, rather than determine its final shape. Frequently, senior managers and support team members identify the overall domains around which the company will form communities. But within that general definition the community leader and core members need to identify the topical and social boundaries of the domain, whether it will focus deeply on a narrow topic or on a broad range of issues; whether it will address a small group of people or a larger, more diverse membership. We have found three criteria help define the scope of the domain.

1. Focus on dimensions of the domain that are particularly important to the business. Managers are more likely to give support when the community focuses on such issues. This is especially true at the beginning of a community-building effort, when the legitimacy of the community is at stake. For example, Shell's first communities were formed around technical disciplines. Because Shell is a very technical company, these were seen by both practitioners and organizational leaders as important.

2. Focus on aspects of the domain community members will be passionate about. This assures that the community will be attractive enough to members to grow and develop.

3. Define the scope wide enough to bring in new people and new ideas, but narrow enough that most members will be interested in the topics discussed. When some community members have more knowledge and experience than others in certain areas, it is more likely that knowledge sharing will be valuable from the start. This is especially useful when expertise is located in isolated pockets of the organization. Community members can

BOX 4-2 **STRATEGIC INTENT**

E XAMPLES OF STRATEGIC intents for communities of practice include:

1. **Helping communities.** Most communities have some mechanisms for community members to help each other solve everyday problems and share ideas. Communities that focus on helping typically create forums for people to connect across teams, geography, or business units and decide for themselves what knowledge to share, how to assess its value, and how to disseminate good ideas to the rest of the community. For example, Schlumberger's technical communities, composed of scientists and engineers, post requests for help or ideas on a customized, threaded discussion; typically several people respond. The intent of helping communities is to make peer-to-peer connections among colleagues.

2. **Best-practice communities.** These focus on developing, validating, and disseminating specific practices. Whereas helping communities rely on members' knowledge of each other to verify new practices, best-practice communities have a specific process to verify the effectiveness and benefits of practices. Because best-practice communities have a structured vetting process, they typically rely on sharing documented practices. For example, Ford Motor Company's best-practice replication (BPR) process includes a structure for operators and engineers to describe a new practice and its value, several reviews in which the local best-practice manager and community administrator (subject matter experts) assess the practice's effectiveness and benefits, and a process for ensuring that the practice is distributed and seriously reviewed in each of Ford's 150 manufacturing plants worldwide.

3. **Knowledge-stewarding communities.** Like other communities, those that primarily steward knowledge host forums for members to connect, develop, and verify practices, but their main intent is to organize, upgrade, and distribute the knowledge their members use every day. Cap Gemini Ernst & Young estimates that they have 1.2 million documents in their general, unfiltered repositories; 875,000 documents in their discussion databases; and 50,000 documents in comprehensive

packs of materials on specific topics. The primary focus of their 150 communities is to find, organize, and distribute this information throughout the organization.

4. **Innovation communities.** All communities innovate by encouraging individuals to develop and contribute practices. But the specific intent of some communities is to foster unexpected ideas and innovations. They are similar to helping communities, but they intentionally cross boundaries to mix members who have different perspectives. DaimlerChrysler's Austauschgruppe community connects 240 world experts from many different parts of the company to assess new directions in research. The community is designed to encourage engineers to be innovative and provides a channel for their ideas to be realized in new or improved products.

These intents are, of course, likely to shift as needs change and the community matures.

---

of course develop new knowledge areas, but at this early stage of development, opening the channels of communication through knowledge-sharing activities has a better chance of quickly creating value for community members and the organization than forging into uncharted territory.

Build a Case for Action. Because communities typically depend on middle and senior managers for funding and encouragement to participate, it is important to offer them well-researched, convincing proposals to build a case for action. This case describes the potential value of the community to the organization and the rationale for supporting it. It also markets the value of participation to members. It highlights benefits such as those listed in chapter 1 in terms of specific problems: the time people lose looking for information or reinventing tools and approaches that already exist in other pockets of the organization, the speed with which competitors share technology, or opportunities missed by failing to share technology. Even if you have made a convincing argument for sharing knowledge and community building in general within the organization, it is often useful to build a case for specific communities as well. One organization made a commitment to using communities of practice as its primary vehicle for sharing knowledge across sites, funded a community support team, and started several communities. But even with this commitment, some managers were unwilling to actively support their staff's participation in communities unless they had a specific rationale for each community. This company found that it was necessary to build a case for action on two levels—one for the organization as a whole, and one for each specific community.

Describing the case for action for each specific community also gives the community a focus. Sometimes communities are formed to address a specific problem, such as transferring technology between sites or strengthening technical competence in an area. Occasionally, a company will see communities of practice as stewards of core competencies and will launch them with that intent. Building a case for action clarifies the importance of the domain to the organization and to community members.

Identify Potential Coordinators and Thought Leaders. Community coordinators and thought leaders are key to community success. While community coordinators sometimes emerge without intervention, frequently the management team or a community sponsor will request well-respected community members to assume this "official" coordinator function. Whenever possible, it is important to involve community coordinators in the very early stages of community development to recruit, interview, and persuade potential community members to join and to ask sponsors for support. This way, they begin right away to weave relationships among members and establish their community-development role.[9] (See A Critical Role: Community Coordinator.)

In most domains there are some individuals regarded as "thought leaders," people in the organization who are defining cutting-edge issues in the domain, or are well seasoned and well respected practitioners. Involving these thought leaders early on helps to legitimize the community and attract other key members who will want to know "Who else is coming?" When SAP America started its business-to-business community, it engaged a very well known and respected "business-to-business" consultant to participate. His reputation, both within and outside SAP, signaled to potential members that the community would focus on cutting-edge issues.

Interview Potential Members. Interviewing potential members is a very useful way to discover the issues they share and the opportunities to leverage knowledge. Interviews can also serve to introduce the notion of community. This is the first chance to discuss the community's potential value to individuals and to the organization. For this reason, interviews are conducted more as discussions than traditional question-and-answer interviews. These interviews not only identify the potential value of the community, they also begin to identify its potential scope, membership, and hot topics around which to link community members.

We have found it is very useful to conduct these interviews as a team that includes a support staff and the potential community coordinator. One can take notes while the other discusses. This gets the coordinator involved early in understanding community issues and building relationships. Because conducting the interviews involves one-on-one networking with community members, it foreshadows one of the primary roles of the coordinator and is often good training for that person.

Connect Community Members. Interviews are great opportunities to begin developing the private space of the community. Rather than treating them as purely data-collection activities, whenever someone mentions a problem that you know others share or might be able to solve, try to link them together. This makes it possible for potential members to experience the value of community even before the first meeting or visit to the Web site. Beginning by forging one-on-one connections fosters the relationships that will strengthen the community. The interviews for the Turbodudes revealed that many of the people interested in turbidites were not well connected. The interviews themselves, as much as the first meetings, served as the initial way to connect people for mutual benefit.

Create a Preliminary Design for the Community. Creating ideas and models of how the community might work is particularly useful. A preliminary design for the community might include a description of its scope, hot topics, structure, roles, knowledge-sharing processes, and names of key members. The straw model should be detailed enough to initiate community activity, but not so detailed that it leaves little room for improvisation and new ideas. The community will modify itself along multiple dimensions as it develops. In keeping with the principle of designing through dialogue, community leaders should be invited to help develop the straw design.

A Critical Role: Community Coordinator

A number of studies have found that the most important factor in a community's success is the vitality of its leadership.[10] The community coordinator is a community member who helps the community focus on its domain, maintain relationships, and develop its practice. The coordinator's time—typically 20 to 50 percent—is frequently funded through a dedicated budget created for this purpose. Community coordinators perform a number of key functions:

- Identify important issues in their domain.
- Plan and facilitate community events. This is the most visible aspect of the coordinator role.
- Informally link community members, crossing boundaries between organizational units and brokering knowledge assets.
- Foster the development of community members.
- Manage the boundary between the community and the formal organization, such as teams and other organizational units.
- Help build the practice—including the knowledge base, lessons learned, best practices, tools and methods, and learning events.
- Assess the health of the community and evaluate its contribution to members and the organization.

Effective community leaders typically are well respected, knowledgeable about the community's domain, well connected to other community members (they know who's who in the community), keen to help develop the community's practice, relatively good communicators,

---

**BOX 4-3 A SUCCESSFUL COMMUNITY COORDINATOR
AT DAIMLERCHRYSLER**

EMILE, A FULL-TIME community coordinator at DaimlerChrysler, was an engineering supervisor before Chrysler restructured into cross-functional car platforms. Emile began organizing monthly meetings of windshield wiper engineers, about thirty of them, from all five platform teams. He invited vendors to speak to the group about their products and future developments. He organized ongoing projects to pursue innovations and supervised community activities to develop standards for components, select vendors, and propose enhancements that would support product-design activities. For example, he has led an effort to propose and then design a new million-dollar simulation system to help test and develop windshield wipers under a variety of adverse conditions and car configurations—all of which affect wiper performance. Emile's community is one of the company's most successful, based on member attendance, innovations, skill development, and reputation with the platform teams. Much of this is due to Emile's leadership—planning meetings, recruiting outside experts, coordinating with platform leaders, keeping contributors to the EBoK on track. And, of course, networking. Although Emile is very good at organizing and facilitating meetings, he spends most of his time as a coordinator on the telephone with community members.

---

and personally interested in community leadership. Some of the best community coordinators are midcareer professionals who see networking with other community members as useful for their own career development, or as a way to leverage their capabilities more broadly.[11] (For an example, see box 4-3.)

Good community coordinators are knowledgeable and passionate about the community's topic. They are well respected by their peers as practitioners, but they are generally not leading experts in their field. Since a coordinator's primary role is to link people, not give answers, being a leading expert can be a handicap. Good coordinators also need good interpersonal skills for networking and the ability to recognize the development needs of individuals. They understand group dynamics well enough to see when the community is moving toward a factional split or becoming dominated by a subgroup with a limited perspective. Finally, they must have the strategic and political savvy to create a bridge between the community and the formal organization. Given how different this role is from team leader and other common leadership roles, community coordinators can easily fall into some common leadership traps. (See box 4-4 for a description.)

Stage 2: Coalescing

When a community is able to combine a good understanding of what already exists with a vision of where it can go, it is ready to move to the coalescing stage. During this second stage, the community is officially launched by hosting community events, though community building has already begun with networking in the planning stage. During this time, it is crucial to have activities that allow members to build relationships, trust, and an awareness of their common interests and needs.

The main issue in the second stage of community development is to generate enough energy for the community to coalesce. As we saw in the principles discussed in chapter 3, communities thrive when members find value in participating. But it often takes time for a community to develop to the point that people genuinely trust each other, share knowledge that is truly useful, and believe the community provides enough value that it has a good chance to survive.

- The key *domain* issue of the coalescing stage is to establish the value of sharing knowledge about that domain.

- The key *community* issue is to develop relationships and sufficient trust to discuss genuinely sticky practice problems. Trust is paramount in this coalescing process; without it, it is difficult for community members to discover what aspects of the domain are most important and identify the real value of the community.

BOX 4-4 COMMON COORDINATOR FAILURES

COORDINATORS ARE CRUCIAL to a community's success, and weak coordinators can significantly limit a community's effectiveness and long-term growth potential. We have seen four common reasons for coordinator failures.

1. **Time.** The most common cause of failure is that the coordinator simply does not make time to perform the role, even when they have been allocated time for this purpose. They too easily let other things take priority over community work.

2. **Public versus private space.** Sometimes coordinators focus their attention on the public space of the community—such as community meetings and Web discussions—and ignore the private space, where they should be connecting individuals or walking the halls between meetings to see what issues are current.

3. **Networking skills.** Some coordinators lack the ability to network with community members. One coordinator complained that the community was not working because community members were not calling him to ask for help or to submit information to the community's Web site. He just did not feel comfortable going to their offices to "technically socialize" about community issues.

4. **Technical knowledge.** When coordinators do not have the background to understand the technical issues in the community, it is difficult for them to take the initiative to move the community forward. As one coordinator said, "I feel like an outsider. How can I ask them to do things I don't have the knowledge to do?"

- The key *practice* issue is to discover specifically what knowledge should be shared and how.

Incubate and Deliver Immediate Value

The main challenge for most communities at this stage is to balance the need to let its members develop relationships and trust against the early need to demonstrate the value of the community. By focusing solely on relationship building, the community risks being dismissed by both the organization and its members before it ever provides value. By focusing on delivering immediate value, the community risks a superficial treatment of the practice. Communities often begin with a spike of interest and energy, particularly if the community has a highly visible launch event. However, after the first event, the reality of community work—networking, sharing ideas, maintaining the Web site—typically sets in, and people's energy for the community can fall off sharply. Other commitments pull people away from participating; leaders don't really know what to do to keep the energy alive; people expect—and don't always find—great immediate value. They often interpret this loss of interest as a lack of real value and become impatient with the community.

During this incubation, communities are particularly fragile. Building trust, exploring the domain, and discovering the kind of ideas, methods, and mutual support that are genuinely helpful take time. Most of all, community members need to develop the habit of consulting each other for help. As they do this, they typically deepen their relationships and discover not only their common needs, but also their collective ways of thinking, approaching a problem, and developing a solution. However, most people, and most of their managers, have a personal limit on the time they are willing to contribute before realizing value. Because community participation consumes time, most community members experience both internal and external pressure to discover and deliver value soon after the community starts.

Knowing what is most useful to share is often more subtle than it would seem. Sometimes community members can share some information that turns out to be extremely valuable during their first few encounters. But usually they need to first understand each other's work, dilemmas, and way of thinking or approaching a problem before they can provide really useful advice. Getting to this stage involves sharing, thinking about, and applying small hints and tips as they get to know and understand each other. After some time spent sharing these "light value" tips, community members come to understand each other's work well enough to see gaps in their approaches and opportunities to share more valuable insights. During this time they also learn to gauge each other's reactions to feedback, as well as the depth and style of each other's thinking. The trust community members need is not simply the result of a decision to trust each other personally. It emerges from understanding each other. As one oil reservoir engineer observed, "Sometimes you can share an insight that is so useful it saves a well from going down, but you don't save a well at the first meeting." At the heart of a community's incubation period is the development of this deep insight into each other's individual practice, each other's reactions and style of thinking, and a collective understanding of the practice as a whole.[12]

Community coordinators and support staff can be particularly helpful during this stage because most communities need a good deal of nurturing to address these challenges. Some of this nurturing occurs in the public space of the community, by facilitating meetings, managing the Web site, or organizing community documents. But most nurturing occurs in the private space of the community, talking with members one-on-one about their needs, connecting them with others, and finding people outside the core group who can provide needed insights, solutions, or ideas. Nurturing a community at this stage involves helping it to do what it will naturally do on its own once it gains momentum.

Nurturing Communities: A Typical Work Plan

A number of activities can help communities move through this incubation time and coalesce into a well-functioning community. These activities help members balance the need to build a solid foundation with the need to demonstrate value. Although communities vary in the order of these activities, the following is a typical sequence.

Build a Case for Membership. Sometimes the focus of the community or the reputation of its members is enough to galvanize interest. Some members of SAP America's business-to-business community participated simply because they wanted to hear its primary thought leader speak. But community coordinators and support staff typically need to personally recruit potential community members. This usually involves building a two-pronged case for membership: the benefits of contributing and the value of learning from others' experience. Some community leaders and core members argue that making contributions is the cost of getting insights from others. One community's best contributor said that when he started contributing more, the quality and quantity of responses to his requests rose. In some companies, contributing adds to an individual's visibility and reputation. At McKinsey, for example, contributing to a community is one way consultants gain enough visibility to become known to senior partners, thus increasing their chances of being chosen for important consulting projects. But contributing also has intrinsic value. For some contributors, the simple satisfaction of helping their peers and making their mark on the field is a significant benefit. Others say that contributing helps them focus and articulate their thoughts. Building a case for membership not only helps invite people into the community, it helps to bind the core group together and strengthens their relationships.

Launch the Community. There are several different strategies for launching a community and moving it through this early coalescing process. One is to start with a highly visible and dramatic kickoff. For example, Schlumberger initiated communities of practice by holding elections. Potential coordinators wrote position papers and gave campaign talks, mostly through the company's Web site, on why they would be good community leaders. A few candidates even debated their competing visions of the community. Once the elections were complete, the organization brought the leaders of the eighteen new communities together for a large kickoff meeting held at a local country club. In other cases, the entire community comes together for a launch event. This approach is most effective when members already have a sense of common identity and are longing to connect. Some of the communities in Shell's New Orleans operation were well-established disciplines that had been housed together before the company reorganized into teams. People missed the interaction and relished the opportunity to reconnect. While a dramatic kickoff does not mean a community will not need to incubate, it can provide momentum that helps sustain it through that period.

Other communities begin very quietly, with little or no fanfare. A community of machine operators and engineers started as a small group that simply met for lunch one Wednesday a month to discuss "screening" issues with engineers and operators. There was no official launch, no announcement—just the coordinator talking with potential members and sending out a notice. While company support staff had been involved in selecting the focus, leader, topics, and members, the community kept its initial work quiet and unobtrusive. The community used its invisibility to build enough trust for operators to become more comfortable discussing problems and ideas and even disagreeing publicly with the engineers. The quiet approach can give the community enough time to develop a rhythm and demonstrate its value before it becomes visible to the organization. This approach works best when the domain of the new community is not a well-established discipline but an emerging issue whose implications and relevance need to be explored.

Which approach will work best depends on the culture of the organization and the type of community. On the one hand, with a visible launch, particularly one with senior management endorsement, more people become aware of the community, its focus, and their own possible roles. Supervisors and managers are more likely to recognize the importance of the community and be more supportive. The community itself is likely to attract broader and more active participation at the outset. A quiet launch, on the other hand, gives the community additional time to bond, discover the true value of the knowledge they share, and develop their own rhythm of meetings and collaboration.

Initiate Community Events and Spaces. Regular events help to "anchor" communities. Immediately after the launch, most communities start to implement knowledge-sharing events, such as weekly meetings, teleconferences, or Web events. It is best to begin these right away in order to tap the energy generated during the launch. Scheduling a series of regular events helps to establish a sense of familiarity and create a rhythm that becomes part of the members' everyday life. As we saw in chapter 3, such events are the heartbeat of the community. They need to be frequent enough to become familiar and routine, while respecting the time availability of members. To create this sense of familiarity, some communities meet in the same space. One community built a library to house their data, which they also used as a meeting space.

Other communities create small rituals to establish a routine. A global competitive intelligence community begins its monthly phone meetings with a brief check-in, asking each member to describe in less than two minutes the biggest technical issue at their site. They end every meeting by asking members to rate the value of the current meeting and what they could do to improve the next.

Legitimize Community Coordinators. Most of the work of community coordination, such as networking, is invisible both to community members and to the organization. Unfortunately, many coordinators find they do not have the skills they need to develop a community—especially skills such as networking, listening, and managing conflicts and disagreements. Coordinators thus can find themselves in a bind, facing work that is both difficult and unrecognized. In technical areas, where specific technical contributions are highly valued, the social side of community coordination—networking within and outside the community, facilitating meetings, making telephone calls, and moderating Web sites—can seem unimportant. The organization is more likely to attract talented people to the role and leverage their time and effort when it legitimizes the role by recognizing and rewarding coordinators early in the community's life. For example, one company held a high-status annual meeting for community coordinators and contributors that demonstrated the value the organization placed on their contributions.

Build Connections Between Core Group Members. The incubation period is a critical time for building the core group. During this time community coordinators often feel a pull to involve peripheral members and to recruit new ones so the community feels like it has enough members to grow and thrive. But during the coalescing stage, building membership is actually much less important than developing the core group. It is through the collaboration of the core group that the community discovers its value; making connections between core group members is the most important networking the coordinator can do. When the core group is cohesive, the community can withstand the growth pressures typical of the next stage.

Find the Ideas, Insights, and Practices That Are Worth Sharing. The main activity for most communities during this period is sharing ideas, insights, and practices as they discover what knowledge is most important and valuable. Communities approach this in many ways. Some commission teams to develop technical procedures and standards. Some post material from their personal files in a common space. We found one of the most useful ways for a core group to explore this issue is for community members to begin helping each other solve everyday work problems that fall within their domain. This provides a good forum both for experiencing the value of sharing knowledge and for coalescing as a community. Focusing on current work projects also ensures that the community explores cutting-edge topics, which generates excitement. By being candid and helpful about real problems they face, community members build relationships of trust and reciprocity. Although the community is likely to have an idea of what knowledge and practices will be useful to share during the potential stage, it is typically during the coalescing stage that members discover the true value of their community, which can be quite different from what was originally anticipated.

Document Judiciously. When communities coalesce, members often discover that they have a great deal of overlapping and disorganized tools, databases, and background information. It is tempting to begin by "getting the house in order" and reorganizing all this material, but this generally does not energize the community. Focusing on current problems jump-starts the community with high-energy issues. Heavy documentation responsibilities, particularly at the beginning of a community's life, can easily kill it. They make participation a burden, another action item or chore to do. If documentation is an early goal, it is best to find a way for the community coordinator or core group to manage the effort themselves. IBM Corporation's Intellectual Capital group, for example, contracted with a core group of about eight to ten community members to organize the community's documents in its very early stages.

Identify Opportunities to Provide Value. Because generating value is critical to a community's viability, coordinators and organizers need to look for opportunities to provide value early in the community's life. Linking people who have problems with others who might have solutions, focusing meetings on topics relevant to members' everyday work, linking with outside experts, developing material that community members need—all of these can help generate value. When the community develops through the incubation period and community members determine what ideas and insights are really useful, the community usually begins to deliver some real value. During this time, community coordinators and organizers should be able to collect anecdotes that illustrate the value the community provides both to individuals and to the organization. Because community members typically do not develop the habit of tracing value until later in the community's life, it is important for the community coordinator and organizers to acknowledge and appreciate both obvious direct financial benefits and less obvious value, such as knowing who knows what, feeling more connected to the organization, or having more confidence in decisions. At this stage of development, the more intangible value of a community is often easier to identify. It frequently leads to a more tangible value as the community continues to develop.

Engage Managers. Management support is critical while communities are coalescing. At this stage, managers legitimize community participation, direct communities to issues of long-term importance to the business, and protect nascent communities from the need to show immediate value. Engaging managers and supervisors in understanding the role of the community is an important activity at this stage, though it of course continues (with a somewhat different focus) throughout the life of the community.

Conclusion

I N THIS CHAPTER we have identified the steps to plan, launch, and nurture a community through its early development. Our approach is quite different from traditional organization design and implementation. Rather than construct and then implement a design, community development involves helping the community through the tensions of each stage—first, by striking a balance between discovering the natural networks and imagining the value of enriching those relationships; and second, by nurturing strong, lasting relationships while at the same time quickly demonstrating the value of communities. Like human maturation, there are many variations in how communities deal with these tensions. By the end of the coalescing stage, the community has demonstrated that it is viable. It is up and running and has a good chance of survival.

As the community moves into the next stage of development, it faces the challenges of more mature communities—sharpening its focus as it grows and balancing a sense of ownership of the domain with openness to new ideas.

The Mature Stages
of Development

Growing and Sustaining
Communities of Practice

D URING ITS INCUBATION, THE TURBODUDE COM-
munity regularly attracted an average of fifteen members.
But after about six months, word spread that some of the company's leading geoscientists were engaging in cutting-edge discussions about turbidite
reservoirs. Attendance grew, averaging forty to fifty people per meeting,
topping off at 125 people.

The meetings evolved to reflect that growth. A small group of ten regular
members contributed most to the discussion. A much larger group of about
thirty attended regularly. Some of them spoke occasionally, but most rarely, if
ever, contributed. Although the people changed somewhat during the life of
the community, the percentage of participation remained fairly constant.

After several months of watching the onlookers, the community coordinator felt he should try to get more even participation and considered forcing

the issue. First, however, he interviewed some of the nonparticipants and discovered that many were new to the organization or the field and were using the community to learn, madly taking notes during the meetings. They asked not to participate more actively, because they felt their own contributions would dilute the quality of the discussion. So, to keep discussions focused on cutting-edge issues, the coordinator let the leading experts dominate. Still, the community continued to be a training ground for people new to turbidites. The Turbodudes coordinator estimated that about forty people had used the community as a vehicle for learning about turbidites. The Turbodudes continued to have informal "water-cooler" discussions, with little agenda and a lightly facilitated exchange about technical problems and analyses.

As the Turbodudes grew, they faced many of the growth problems of other communities. Several team leaders, knowing their reputation for probing and thoughtful analysis, decided to use the Turbodudes as an informal review board for projects. But without a real problem, these were more "rubber stamp" presentations than genuine discussions. As a result, the coordinator began screening discussion topics more carefully to keep the focus on truly cutting-edge issues. New members sometimes suggested that the community expand or change its focus to accommodate the issues they were interested in. For example, several reservoir engineers proposed including discussions of other kinds of reservoirs. After conferring privately, the core group decided that this would dilute the focus on turbidites and suggested that the reservoir engineers start another community focused on the reservoir issues they wanted to explore. The Turbodudes found they constantly had to balance their desire to meet the needs of newcomers and keep the core group engaged by maintaining focus on cutting-edge turbidite issues.

As the Turbodudes matured, they became clearer about the real value of their discussions. They discovered that one of their greatest contributions was to reduce uncertainty in deciding whether or not to develop a site. Exploration involves extrapolating from sketchy data and comparing the site to known geological structures, called analogues. Analogues are important because so little site data is available before drilling a well; they *help the geoscientist determine if the oil reserves are sufficient to warrant drilling. Reviewing the site with community members helped geoscientists consider different explanations of their data, sharpen their interpretations of the characteristics of the reservoir, and reduce their uncertainty about developing it. Turbodude discussions of analogues and alternative inter-pretations of data have avoided unnecessary drilling and testing at three sites per year—this represents a cost of $20 million to drill and another $20 million to test each well, a total savings of $120 million annually.*

The more recognition the community received, the higher the com-mitment of community members. By the end of the first year, the Turbo-dudes' core group realized that they were onto something. Several of them started devoting more time to the community. As the core members' commitment grew, they became more willing to take on additional issues related to stewarding their practice. They commissioned small task forces to develop these areas. For instance, in order to be more systematic about the way they analyze turbidites, they began distinguishing between dif-ferent types of turbidite structures. The distinction helps them under-stand how turbidite data should fit together and makes it easier to predict what the structure is likely to be. Another project involved helping geol-ogists assess the volume of oil and gas in prospects where there was little or poor data. In the past, geologists' estimates had varied widely. A task force from the Turbodudes researched the estimating methods commu-nity members used and developed a standard methodology that is now used throughout the organization. The standard helps ensure that varia-tions are really variations in the prospect, not just calibration differences among geologists.

Although most Turbodude discussions still focus on helping each other, these activities reflect a shift in the community from pure helping to organ-izing, systematizing, and creating standards of good practice for turbidite analysis. As the community adopted these new responsibilities, the role of the community coordinator changed somewhat. In addition to "walking the halls," which is still his main task, he coordinates these knowledge-stewarding activities. Rather than being made obsolete by the maturing of the commu-nity, his role remains important, but with a shift in focus.[1]

From Starting to Sustaining

W E MAY BE tempted to think that maturity is a time of stability, but communities, like people, change and grow during their maturity as much as they do during their formation. The ongoing life of an active community, like an active town, is rich and complex. It contains many relationships, many levels of connection, and many subgroups within it. New members bring new interest; high contributors get pulled away by other assignments; market and organizational needs change; the community's relationship to the organization shifts. These changes pull the community's focus in new directions. Sometimes these changes drive the community to new levels of activity; sometimes they drain its energy. Thus, mature communities go through cycles of high and low energy as they respond, adjust, and reorganize. As communities progress from getting started to becoming a viable part of the organization, the core challenges they face also shift. Instead of overcoming inertia, they must now figure out how to keep their informal peer focus as they become more recognized and integrated with more formal organizational structures.

Because communities grow and change throughout their lives, they continue to need support. If the passion of the core members is strong enough, communities can, of course, sustain themselves with that energy. But like adults, they greatly benefit from reflection and active development efforts as they take on more mature responsibilities. Chapter 4 focused on how to get communities up and running, beyond a launch event, to the point that they are truly viable. This chapter deals with how to help communities grow, change their relationship to their domain, and truly integrate with the organization as a whole. These stages of development we call maturing, stewardship, and transformation.

Of course, some of the activities that were useful in starting a community continue to be important for growth. Mature communities continue to benefit from regular measures of their value and health. Coordinators still need to connect people one-on-one in the private space of the community. They still require help and coaching to deal with the changing demands of their role. And company managers still need to be engaged as the community develops, shifts, and redefines its role in the organization.

Stage 3: Maturing

During the maturation stage, the main issue a community faces shifts from establishing value to clarifying the community's focus, role, and boundaries. Once a community has demonstrated its viability and its value, it might grow rapidly, as the Turbodudes did. When word spreads that the community is effectively sharing knowledge, it can move from relative isolation to an onslaught of newcomers and onlookers. One community met informally in a small conference room for three months. Then, seemingly from nowhere, there was a line at the door for seats. But it is not just physical growth that challenges a community during this time. Shifting from sharing tips to developing a comprehensive body of knowledge expands the demands on community members, both in time and in the scope of their interests. Projects to develop new areas of knowledge draw heavily on core group members, increasing the time they must devote to community matters.

- The key *domain* issue as a community grows is defining its role in the organization and its relationship to other domains.

- The key *community* issue at this stage is managing the boundary of the community, which is no longer just a network of professional friends. In defining new and wider boundaries, the community must ensure that it is not distracted from its core purpose.

- The key *practice* issue at this point shifts from simply sharing ideas and insights to organizing the community's knowledge and taking stewardship seriously. As the community develops a stronger sense of itself, the core members frequently begin to see gaps in the community's knowledge, identify its cutting edge, and feel a need to be more systematic in their definition of the community's core practice.

During this stage, communities often find that their domain, membership, and practice are all expanding simultaneously.

Focus and Expand

Communities often experience a strong tension at this stage between welcoming new members and focusing on their own interest in cutting-edge topics and expert interactions. Maturing communities often develop a sort of "craft intimacy." Community members get to know each other's style and approach to technical problems. In conversation and joint projects, they discover their strengths and weaknesses and come to appreciate others' contributions, energy, interest, perspectives, and individual styles. They learn who in the community says little but has great insight as well as whose ideas need to be verified. They know whom to contact for what kind of help. They learn who does meticulous analysis and who thinks in broader, more intuitive ways. They can predict which topics are likely to produce a dead-end discussion or a rousing debate, which will invite quiet members to join, and which will stir community members' interest or ire. This intimacy makes community discussions considerably richer. They are not just exchanges of information, but a dance of styles and perspectives.

Growth can multiply relationships and make the community more exciting, but success in number of members can be a mixed blessing. When a community grows rapidly, it often shifts tone. New members disrupt the pattern of interaction the core community has developed. They ask different questions, have different needs, and have not established the relationships and trust that the core group enjoys. Growth often seems to occur just as the community's core members have developed relationships strong enough to discuss really important topics. For core members, growth is more than a disruption. It threatens the intimacy and sense of identity that make the community attractive.

After four months of meeting regularly, one small community of six senior engineers began to grow rapidly. People from neighboring disciplines heard about their weekly discussions. The six senior engineers reluctantly welcomed these newcomers, but within a month found that the informal discussion had shifted from cutting-edge issues to more basic topics in the field. The community no longer met their needs. One week, much to everyone's surprise, the six senior engineers were all missing. The coordinator found them down the hall, meeting in a separate conference room. They had gone underground. To bring them back, he acknowledged that the newcomers had shifted the focus and inquired what they would need to return to the fold. Everyone agreed that community meetings would remain focused on cutting-edge ideas. They also decided to organize a mentoring program for newcomers. This way basic questions could be addressed outside community meetings.

A community resolves the tension between focus and growth when it learns how to preserve relationships, excitement, and trust as it expands membership, and when it can maintain helping interactions while systematizing its practices. Resolving this tension typically drives the community to a deeper sense of identity and greater confidence in the value of its domain.

Maturing: A Typical Work Plan

Maturation is a very active stage for community coordinators and support staff. The tensions community members feel can be quite strong. Communities often break apart or reorganize during this phase, so the community generally needs considerable support.

Identify Gaps in Knowledge and Develop a Learning Agenda. During this stage, communities continue to refine their domain. However, their emphasis changes from defining to developing. The domain itself, rather than individual needs, becomes the primary driver of activities. As a community matures, it often finds areas where it collectively needs to develop more knowledge. Identifying knowledge gaps can be a very healthy process. It can induce a more honest discussion of a community's needs and build identity as members develop new areas. Some communities track ongoing development areas and progressively focus community meetings, Web sites, or task teams on these topics. In this way, the community's learning agenda continually evolves. McKinsey communities scan industry leaders and canvass members of client service teams to discover what knowledge will be most useful to develop. Some communities systematically develop their learning agenda by mapping out what they already know, what they need to know, and the projects and resources they will need to fill the gaps. The focus of the community shifts from simply sharing tips and advice toward the broader goal of stewarding knowledge.

One of the ways many communities take charge of their domain and pursue an explicit learning agenda is to commission project teams to explore a new topic area, create guidelines, or identify different approaches to a practice. These teams usually report the results of their work to the community as a whole. These projects can become developmental milestones. A manufacturing community commissioned a team of operators and engineers to analyze a machine that was not operating well. When the team jointly decided to get rid of the machine, it marked an important moment in the community's life. From the operators' point of view, it was the point when the engineers actually listened to them.

Define the Community's Role in the Organization. During this maturing stage, a community often assumes a more important role in the organization. For example, the well-established Turbodudes came to be known as stewards of turbidite knowledge. When someone had a problem with a turbidite reservoir, team leaders expected their geoscientists to bring the problem to the Turbodudes. Sometimes, however, managers and other outsiders expect a community to take on more responsibilities than it thinks appropriate. The community needs to be clear about the responsibilities it can assume. The division manager asked one community to become responsible for technical quality, formally reviewing each other's work. This made sense, because the community had the technical expertise to conduct the reviews. However, the community was concerned that this would turn them into the "methods police" and undermine their ability to share ideas informally. The community turned down the request. Because this community was explicitly concerned with the relevance of its work to the organization— beginning every meeting with an update from the leadership team representatives on current issues—it was able to preserve its legitimacy with senior management. Because maturing communities begin to act more collectively, rather than as a group of individuals that help each other, they often gain more influence in the organization, as did the chemical engineers described in box 5-1.

**BOX 5-1 TAKING ON IMPORTANT ISSUES:
A SOURCE OF LEGITIMACY**

ONE CHEMICAL ENGINEERING community is a small group of seventeen members, peripheral to the core business of the organization. As the coordinator of that community remarked, "When we do our job well, nothing happens." That is, there are no chemically related problems in the core production processes. Community members meet monthly for a day-long collaborative session. Three-quarters of the chemical engineering staff regularly attend these meetings, which focus largely on sharing ideas, tips, and advice. But a few years ago, the community began to take on some issues that were important problems for the organization. One was the procurement of chemicals, formerly done by each of the organizational units independently. The community developed a process for supplier management and competitive bidding. They reduced the number of chemical suppliers to a few highly qualified companies and negotiated a collective purchasing arrangement. As a result of their new process, they lowered the cost of the organization's chemical supplies to one-third that of other operators in the region. By taking on an important issue and contributing substantial value to the organization, the chemical engineering community has gained considerable legitimacy—both as a group and as a profession—within the organization.

Redefine Community Boundaries. A maturing community becomes more intentional about involving everyone with an appropriate relationship to the domain—for instance, by linking across departments and geographical areas or by connecting practitioners in related disciplines. This kind of growth often entails some restructuring. Sometimes communities subdivide into topical or geographic sub-communities so people can stay connected to the whole community while maintaining a stronger tie to a smaller group. Because they rearrange relationships, these reorganizations can be difficult; following natural lines of connection can make the rearrangement much less cumbersome.

Routinize Entry Requirements and Processes. When new members join a well-established community, the process can be daunting for newcomers and time-consuming for current members. More important, it can break up existing well-established relationships. A well-defined entry process can alleviate these problems. After struggling to update new members, share knowledge, *and* make decisions during its quarterly meetings, DaimlerChrysler's knowledge-management community established expectations for new members. They agreed that new members should be sponsored by a current member and sit down with that member before attending their first meeting to get the background on the community's purpose, history, scope of activities, and norms of interaction.

Measure the Value of the Community. As more newcomers join a community, it becomes even more important for the community to measure its value. Uninvolved stakeholders generally need more traditional and clear demonstrations of value. By the time the community is in the maturing stage, there are usually sufficient examples of value to make a convincing case for its existence and potential members' involvement.

Maintain a Cutting-Edge Focus. As we saw in the core group of engineers that went underground, a growing community's focus can easily shift from cutting-edge to more basic issues. Coordinators need to keep well connected with core members to ensure that their needs continue to be met. Frequently what draws newcomers at this stage is the stature and activity of the core members. If they withdraw their time and attention, they reduce the appeal of the community overall.

Build and Organize a Knowledge Repository. As the community exchanges information, it often creates a body of knowledge through meeting notes or threaded discussions. This information can easily become a junkyard of disorganized insights, particularly if they are organized according to only one taxonomy, such as the dates of the meetings. Usually topics overlap, sometimes skipping a few meetings in between; likewise with threaded discussions. They quickly grow into lengthy streams, interspersed with hidden gems. Organizing the repository appropriately is a crucial objective. Johnson & Johnson, for instance, commits substantial resources to ensuring that the organization of a community's knowledge-sharing space reflects how members seek and share knowledge. The Knowledge Networking team has developed a systematic methodology for analyzing the main work activities of community members in order to identify relevant knowledge requirements—both tacit and explicit. This analysis produces a customized language for describing their knowledge-seeking and -sharing behaviors, which provides the core structure for organizing the space. Basing the design on a taxonomy so closely tailored to the practice makes both contributions and access to the community's knowledge more efficient and more engaging for members.

A Useful Role: Community Librarian

A community's ability to grow from a network of friends into a legitimate, influential player in the organization also depends on its ability to develop and provide access to knowledge, tools, and guidelines about its domain. When communities begin to form, they often discover that they have a plethora of materials that have never been systematically collected and organized.

If a community's practice is dynamic, members soon realize they need to continuously gather, assess, and organize materials to keep the practice repository up-to-date and accessible to practitioners. Coordinators frequently take on this task, but when the community has a large body of information, the task can be overwhelming, and it becomes necessary to hire a librarian to fill this role. Community librarians play more than a backroom, information-organizing role. They are often active community members. Sometimes the librarians are right-hand resources for community members. A librarian might handle any of the following activities:

- Scanning for relevant articles, books, cases, and other resources
- Reviewing and selecting material; writing summaries, reviews, or annotations
- Organizing materials into the community's taxonomy
- Providing on-call research services for practitioners about what resources may be most helpful
- Taking and editing notes at community meetings
- Connecting community members with others experts in the field

Librarians need some basic understanding of library science applications and technical knowledge of the domain they are supporting. They also typically need Web skills, familiarity with online and physical resources relevant to the domain, and interpersonal skills to consult with practitioners and help connect people with shared or complementary interests. Some communities use the librarian role to introduce people new to the domain. It is another way they can become familiar with the practice and its membership.

Stage 4: Stewardship

The main issue for a mature community is how to sustain its momentum through the natural shifts in its practice, members, technology, and relationship to the organization. Declining energy can, sometimes, become a vicious cycle. When other projects pulled away the main contributors to an IT community, none of the less active members took up the slack; for six months, the community went dormant. When one of the leading contributors returned, he had a hard time renewing member activity, and the community never fully recovered. As in any mature life, maintaining freshness and liveliness takes energy and attention.

- The key *domain* issue in this stage of community development is to maintain the relevance of the domain and to find a voice in the organization.

- The key *community* issue is to keep the tone and intellectual focus of the community lively and engaging.

- The key *practice* issue for communities in the stewardship stage is to keep the community on the cutting edge.

Ownership and Openness

Established communities regularly experience a tension between developing their own tools, methods, and approaches and being open to new ideas and members. For a community at the stewardship stage, this tension is not merely about growing up, but continuing to grow when it has already established a solid foundation of expertise and relationships.

As they build a common body of knowledge, communities often develop a strong sense of ownership of their domain. They take pride in the ideas they have developed, the guidelines they have written, the direction in which they have pushed their domain, and the efficacy of their collective voice. A community of physicists, feeling that they had some important insights to offer on the technical direction of the company, collectively wrote a white paper and submitted it to the executive management team. They all felt not just a desire to be influential, but an *obligation* to influence the company's strategy.

To maintain the relevance of their domain, communities need an influx of new ideas, approaches, and relationships. For example, a group of system engineers that had developed a cutting-edge technology felt that it was still the world leader years later, even when other groups outside the company had far surpassed it. A community needs to balance its sense of ownership with receptivity to new people and ideas. Openness is more than simply accepting new people and ideas when they pound hard enough on the boundaries of the community. It involves actively soliciting new ideas, new members, and new leadership to bring fresh vitality into the community. As the Turbodudes reexamine their core model of turbidite reservoirs, they are challenging their assumptions and drawing in new perspectives. However they finally develop their model, the discussion itself brings a healthy search for new thinking into the community. To remain vibrant, communities need to shift topics along with the market, invite new members, forge new alliances, and constantly redefine their boundaries.[2]

Sustaining Momentum: A Typical Work Plan

Actively stewarding a body of knowledge involves maintaining a balance between the tensions of ownership and openness. It is key for the community coordinator and core group members to identify opportunities to take on new challenges, expand the community's focus, and incorporate new perspectives. Coordinators need to be aware of the waxing and waning of community energy and take action to help the community meet the changing demands of its environment in a way that preserves or even develops its own sense of self. Following are activities that can help coordinators in this challenge. The order of these activities depends on the issues in the community.

Institutionalizing the Voice of the Community. When communities reach their maturity, they often feel a need to become a recognized part of the organization and to have a voice in the organization's strategy and direction. As keepers of the organization's core competencies, communities can be critical to the organization's long-term success. Once they have attained a capacity for reliable stewardship, they are often seen as such. Many organizations integrate these communities into their ongoing budgeting and planning activities, allocating resources such as staff time to community activities. When communities see themselves as a core part of the organization, they often need a structure, such as a senior management liaison or a process for influencing the organization. The community of physicists mentioned previously not only wrote a white paper, but wanted a method through which they could exert influence on the technical strategy of the company. Giving communities this kind of voice and influence can greatly strengthen them.

Rejuvenate the Community. Because communities naturally go through cycles of high and low energy, most regularly need to rejuvenate their ideas, members, and practices. Introducing new topics, controversial speakers, or joint meetings with other communities or with teams that draw on the community's knowledge all help to spur interest during the low periods. Sessions with vendors and suppliers can make the community aware of new technology or new practices. One community coordinator has a list of potential supplier presentations about exciting new technology developments. Whenever he sees the energy in the community begin to wane, he brings in one of these suppliers. Sometimes the developments they describe are so dramatic they generate interest among people beyond the community as well, so the meetings serve a dual purpose. For global community members, who have few opportunities to meet in person, just organizing a face-to-face meeting, even a regional one, can rejuvenate energy. When a community's energy begins to wane, it often loses its sense of rhythm. Sometimes the rhythm itself becomes too predictable. Changing the community's rhythm can also rejuvenate the community.

Hold a Renewal Workshop. Whatever method for rejuvenation, communities, like people, commonly experience a "midlife" crisis—even several of them. They face difficult questions about their direction. They need to decide whether to become a full part of the organization or remain somewhat underground, whether to remain informal or become more systematic in their approach to their domain, whether to keep their current boundaries or shift to include a dramatically new group of people. Sometimes they must decide whether to continue at all. A renewal workshop is like a launch meeting, but it is used to reaffirm the commitment to the community and to set new directions.

Actively Recruit New People to the Core Group. As a community develops, core members often absorb some of the leadership roles. However, core group members also experience turnover. Because people who contribute extensively to a community are very knowledgeable, they generally have many other demands on their time. As the community's topics shift, core members may lose interest in the community's current focus; others simply burn out. Finding new core members is an important task for coordinators of communities at this stage. Besides watching for people who are obvious potential core group members, such as thought leaders and expert practitioners, coordinators look for people who are midcareer, or involved in emerging topic areas, who would appreciate an opportunity to take a more active role in the development of their discipline.

Develop New Leadership. Community leaders also may be called to other projects, burn out, or simply run out of new ways to engage the community. Sometimes people who are good at galvanizing energy during the community's early phases are less effective at sustaining it. And someone who is capable of leading the community when it focuses on one part of the domain may not be as adept when the focus changes. Coordinators should regularly look for successors. When a community's energy wanes significantly, replacing the leadership can give it a new lease on life. Rather than develop new leaders, some communities regularly rotate leadership to distribute the "burden" of coordination among core members. Rotating leadership also builds stronger ties among core members. It tends to move the community more toward collective leadership. Schlumberger has developed an interesting variation on community leadership. Schlumberger communities elect leaders for a one-year term of office. Annual elections both invigorate the community and renew leadership. Some elections are hotly contested; others are all but shoo-ins. But the election process, with candidates proposing platforms for community development, brings the community's attention to how it could evolve.

Mentor New Members. As communities mature, they often realize the importance of systematically mentoring new members. One community found that new members were constantly turning to a few senior members for mentoring and development, which was creating an unacceptable burden on their time. To spread this more equitably among senior community members, the community took responsibility for mentoring, identified topic areas in which other community members could serve as mentors, and assigned newer members. By assuming mentorship as a community, they were able to regulate the burden among members. Some communities find that establishing a mentorship program helps them keep the focus of community events on cutting-edge issues by providing an outlet for newcomers' questions. At McKinsey, community leaders help junior members identify development directions and steer them to projects that support that development.

Seek Relationships and Benchmarks Outside the Organization. As communities move more to the cutting edge of their practice, they often find that they share interests with people and groups outside the organization. Input from outside the organization is one of the most effective ways to refresh a community's focus. This could involve benchmarking a current practice or using ideas from other companies, associations, and universities to build new knowledge and approaches. Active, mature communities often form ongoing relationships with other companies to compare and refine their practices or develop new ones. These associations are powerful development mechanisms because different organizations bring different perspectives, and often new ideas, to the practice. Benchmarking other world-class practices helps keep an established community from getting complacent about its own tools and approaches.

Stage 5: Transformation

The tension between a community's sense of ownership and its openness to new ideas and people is never fully resolved. It continues throughout the stewardship stage of the community. When the community widens its boundaries, it risks diluting its focus. New members feel less ownership of the community's topic, practices, and processes. When a community closes its boundaries, it risks suffocating itself. Most communities waver somewhere in the middle, with vacillating levels of activity. But sometimes a dramatic event, a sudden influx of new members, or a fall in the level of energy calls for a radical transformation—perhaps a return to an earlier incubation or growth stage, or even the community's ending.

The radical transformation or death of a community is just as natural as its birth, growth, and life. Even the healthiest communities come to a natural end.[3] Changing markets, organizational structures, and technology can render the community's domain irrelevant. The issues that spawned the community may get resolved. The community's practices can become so rote and commonplace that they no longer require a distinct community. Or, members may develop such different interests over time that there is no longer enough commonality to hold the community together. Whatever the cause, we have seen communities transform themselves in many ways.

- Many communities simply fade away, losing members and energy until no one shows up to community events or posts to its common Web space. A community of project engineers, after resolving some pressing problems in the company's approach to project engineering, slowly lost momentum.

- Communities also die by turning into a social club. A once-powerful community of IT managers became isolated from emerging ideas and influence in the organization. The core group had developed strong personal connections and continued to meet, but their focus slowly shifted from IT issues to organizational ones, and then to their personal lives. Although they felt well connected to each other, they lost their sense of stewarding a practice.

- Sometimes communities split into distinct communities or merge with others. One global community discovered that its topic overlapped considerably with another smaller community. Rather than continue side-by-side, these two communities merged.

- Some communities require so many resources that they become institutionalized. They are transformed into centers of excellence with a small staff that maintains a particular competence and links to the rest of the organization through community members. Or they become actual departments in the organization, taking on all the structures and functions of formal units, including reporting relationships, resource allocation responsibilities, recruiting, hiring, and individual performance reviews. Of course, even as a functional department they can be a vehicle for informal peer-to-peer knowledge sharing, but the institutional structure does constitute a radical transformation of the community itself and of its relationship to the organization.

To close a community with a sense of resolution, like closing any relationship, requires both letting go and finding a way to live on—in memory or in the form of a legacy. Closing a community has an emotional component. Officially closing a community gives its members an opportunity to decide what parts of the community to let go of and how to let other parts live on. Most of us feel regret at endings—opportunities we could have taken, contributions we should have made, relationships we wanted to develop more deeply. Conversations about ending can be difficult for communities, just as they are for families, teams, and partnerships, even when the ending is appropriate. So the natural tendency is to avoid the conversation altogether and either let the community drift apart or, like the IT managers, maintain the social relationships even though the community has lost its practice-based value. There is nothing wrong with this sort of "soft ending" for a community;

there is no *need* to address its closing. A soft ending simply means that the community closed without taking the opportunity to honor members' contributions and pass on the community's legacy.

Communities also die before their time. Senior managers fail to acknowledge their importance, factions within the community make participating more trouble than it is worth, or coordinators and key members attend to other priorities. But the ever-present possibility of death also enlivens a community of practice, just as the ever-present awareness of our own mortality can enrich our personal lives. It can help communities remember to focus on those issues genuinely relevant to members. It can remind community coordinators and core members that they are responsible for keeping the community alive. Indeed, deciding whether the community is truly dying or is simply in need of rejuvenation is always a judgment call. And it can help all community members remember that the community only lives on because they give it life through their participation. This fragility can help them appreciate their present experience of the community—its liveliness, engagement, and sense of camaraderie—just as the awareness of death helps us as individuals appreciate the preciousness of the present moment.

Conclusion

PROGRESSING THROUGH these stages, communities typically undergo several changes in their focus, relationships, and practice. They commonly shift from sharing ideas and tips to stewarding their practice—building, refining, and expanding the domain and its relationship to other domains. They move from a loose network of personal relationships to a group with a common sense of identity, combining intimate knowledge of each other's approach with a sense of collective responsibility for the domain. Their focus shifts from solving common problems within their practice to systematically exploring its subtleties.

Like individuals, communities go through periods of both relative stability and great discovery. Sometimes these periods of transition are exciting: building new relationships, seeing new opportunities to apply the practice, feeling on the cutting edge of new ideas. But just as often, they feel like things are falling apart, old relationships are losing their value, or ideas and approaches are growing tired or less relevant. Just as we experience the turmoil of human development, so do communities of practice. Leaders feel burnt out or underappreciated. Core members become frustrated trying without success to generate energy. Developmental challenges remain unresolved, or are resolved in inappropriate ways that stall the community's growth or ossify its practice. Some communities lose their way and become dysfunctional, a topic we address in chapter 7.

If the bonds of trust and respect and the sense of common direction are strong, these struggles can become temporary expressions of the community's aliveness. For communities, as for individuals, development is not just random change. Like life, it has a direction. For individuals, maturity often means having a richer, deeper experience of life. For communities, stewardship means developing deeper knowledge of their domain. Through a mastery of its domain, a community is able to increase the organization's ability to deal with problems, improvise solutions, and imagine new directions. No matter how narrow the domain, there are always new dimensions to discover. The exploration of a craft can continue as long as the domain is viable. As long as people think about the application of practice, they will come up with changes and improvements.

The Challenge of
Distributed Communities

W HEN A GEOLOGIST IN SHELL'S EXPLORATION
and Production International Ventures (SEPIV) group
learned how the Turbodudes informally share cutting-edge ideas and
insights, he realized that there would be tremendous value in establishing
the same kind of group globally. Of course, there would be daunting obsta-
cles—how to maintain informality and build trust across time zones and
distance; how to share ideas across different organizational units; and how
to honor different national and organizational cultures. He knew this
would not succeed if it was seen as a "U.S. initiative." But SEPIV manage-
ment also thought the idea was worth pursuing and formed a small cross-
functional team to identify, design, and implement a few pilots. Their goal
was to create a structure through which people could share knowledge
about oil exploration and development in deep ocean water (over 500
meters). To do this they planned to build a set of global, technically focused
peer communities. They planned to build these communities with people
from each of the operating Shell companies as well as representatives from
Shell's labs. In the end, they would span eighteen time zones and twenty

independent Shell companies. The team's vision was for these communities to bring the world's leading expertise, no matter where it was located, to bear on problems and issues, no matter where they occurred.

The team interviewed more than fifty people from the Shell companies to identify technical focus areas, barriers to global networking, and the level of energy people had for networking. They found that most people were excited about the idea, but concerned that global sharing would be inhibited by barriers such as not knowing who else was interested, reluctance to contact people in other units without a preexisting relationship, or business constraints on sharing information across boundaries.

From these interviews, the support team identified three important technical areas in which they would create pilot communities; one focused on geology, one on reservoir engineering, and one on well engineering. These areas included people from both the scientific and engineering disciplines.

Because the communities spanned many different companies, it was important to get the support of business unit managers. While most supported the general idea of communities, several were concerned about the amount of time their staff might spend with people from other business units. In addition, there were conflicting priorities among business units. Some, for example, invested heavily in cutting-edge technology; others were too small to do so. To build support, the community-development team created a video about the role and potential value of communities to the organization, gave talks at senior management meetings, and traveled the world, meeting with business unit leaders and potential community members. Most of this involved one-on-one discussions, which altogether took the support team six months to complete. Although they did not get the active support of all the business unit managers, they did convince a critical mass of business units to participate.

The structure of the global communities reflected their diversity. Given the disparity between business units in national and organizational cultures, and the variation in how community members in the local business units were organized, the design team created a structure for the communities that allowed local variation while linking to the larger structure. Each community was composed of a set of local "cells." This made it possible for each business unit, or regional groups of business units, to organize their community in whatever way they saw fit. Some held weekly meetings, like the Turbodudes. Others networked with each other informally. By having local community events and relationships, this structure also made the community visible. People could participate in community activities and experience being part of a local community while maintaining a global connection.

Local communities were knit together with a network of coordinators. Each local community designated a coordinator who not only facilitated local knowledge sharing but also connected people to the other cells around the globe. The local coordinators formed a network that shared ideas and offered advice; they held regular teleconferences and occasional face-to-face meetings. They got to know each other as well as the issues in each other's region.

This structure created a group of people—the network of local community coordinators—who ultimately felt collectively responsible for keeping the global community alive. But as in any community, it took some time to discover the value the community could provide. In one community, a local coordinator soon realized that the coordinators' network could be a valuable source of help with his local problems. He began regularly asking if other coordinators had ever used a certain supplier, tried a new pipe-fastening mechanism, or used a new tool. After several months, the other coordinators in the network learned from his example. Once the local coordinators realized the power of the community, they started to put more energy into building the global community as well as their respective cells.

Of the three pilot communities, two were quite successful. One of them remained rather small. The other grew rapidly, merged with another community, and eventually involved over 1,500 members. It became a model for other global Shell communities. The third never quite clicked, and after a year its members joined other global communities.[1]

Key Issues in Distributed Communities

F OR THE PURPOSE of this chapter, we will call "distributed" any community of practice that cannot rely on face-to-face meetings and interactions as its primary vehicle for connecting members.[2]

Typically, distributed communities cross multiple types of boundaries. Geographically distributed communities link people across time zones, countries, and organizational units. Like local communities, they share ideas and insights, help each other, document procedures, and influence operating teams and business units. They also knit organizations together. As we mentioned in chapter 2, in an era of globalization and worldwide communication networks, distributed communities are increasingly the norm.

Of course, all communities are distributed to some degree. They typically attract members from different parts of the organization, different floors, even different locations. But linking large numbers of people across vast distances, major organizational boundaries, and different cultures presents a new set of issues. When these four factors—distance, size, organizational affiliation, and cultural differences—are compounded, they make building and sustaining communities significantly more difficult.

Distance: Connections and Visibility

Different time zones and geographic separation obviously make it more difficult for community members to connect. They have to resort to technologies that are not real substitutes for face-to-face interactions. But the distance is not just physical; the community itself tends to feel more remote. Distance simply makes it more difficult to remember that the community exists. Of course, the "presence" of the community is always an issue. Because even local communities typically cross boundaries, there is usually some physical distance between community members. But members located in the same building or town often see each other by chance—in the hall, in the elevator, at meetings, or in the lunchroom. They can meet relatively easily to share ideas or collaborate. Most important, local communities typically have regular face-to-face meetings where they see other community members. Thus local community members can easily connect with each other, even when they are only marginally engaged in the community.

Distributed communities are generally less "present" to their members. On a teleconference call or on a Web site, community members are not visible unless they make a contribution, post a question, or ask for help. Members cannot see how many other people are reading—and benefiting from—a threaded discussion. Unlike in-person meetings, teleconferences and Web sites don't offer easy opportunities for informal networking. Because of these barriers, it takes more intentional effort for members to consult the community for help, spontaneously share ideas, or network with other members.

Size: Knowing People

Community size and geographical distance are not necessarily related. You can have very small global communities and large local communities. But because distributed communities usually draw from a wider base of membership, they can be very large, frequently hundreds of members and sometimes over a thousand. It is not possible to know that many people personally, even in a face-to-face meeting, let alone with the mediation of technology. We argued in chapter 2 that size has implications for the way communities structure themselves. When compounded with distance, size becomes an even more significant factor.

Affiliation: Priorities and Intellectual Property

Distributed communities typically cross more organizational boundaries than do local groups. Distributed communities can cross divisions of the same company, different business units within the same company, or entirely different businesses. Even though the companies in Shell's global communities are part of the same overall organization, each has its own goals and priorities, which sometimes conflict. For example, some Shell companies had partnerships with other oil companies that were direct competitors of Shell in other parts of the globe. Large, global communities often have more trouble than local ones in getting senior managers with conflicting priorities to genuinely buy into the idea of sharing knowledge with other companies or business units. This is complicated by the need to develop criteria for dealing with intellectual property. Such issues can be particularly big stumbling blocks for communities that span several different organizations, where intellectual property is a source of competitive advantage. Should all ideas and material developed in the community belong to all members? Does a convening group hold greater property rights? Are individual companies free to do whatever they will with ideas and material they develop with the community's input? Resolving these questions can greatly increase the time required for planning the community's launch. For example, in a cross-company community in which we participate, members spent time working out their own solution to the intellectual property issue. Rather than creating a complex ownership system, however, they simply agreed to share only knowledge that they thought could be disseminated within the other member companies without adverse effect to their own companies.

Culture: Communication and Values

Distributed communities are also likely to cross cultures. National cultures are the most obvious type, but organizational and professional cultures can also present problems in diversified companies or when there has been a lot of merger and acquisition activity. People from different cultural backgrounds can have very different ways of relating to one another and to the community, and this is likely to affect the development of global communities. People's willingness to ask questions that reveal their "ignorance," disagree with others in public, contradict known experts, discuss their problems, follow others in the thread of conversation—all these behaviors vary greatly across cultures. For example, who has the status or authority to speak to or for the community? How much deference should be shown to senior or elder practitioners? What is the appropriate level of formality or style of interaction between members?

Cultural differences can easily lead to communication difficulties and to misinterpretation. In one instance of a merger of an American and a European company, people realized that they had different interpretations of how to come to a meeting. The Europeans always came very well prepared, with an agenda and documents compiled in advance. They thought the Americans had not done their homework, either because they were lazy or because they did not care. The Americans, on the other hand, were used to building the agenda together at the meeting, and interpreted the well-meaning preparedness of the Europeans as an attempt to take over. Successful distributed communities have to learn to address cultural differences without either minimizing them or stereotyping people.

Language differences also introduce a very basic barrier to communication. They can intensify cultural boundaries, even when all parties agree to speak a common language. Non-native speakers may not understand the nuances and connotations behind certain terms or may hesitate to speak if they are uncertain of their ability to express themselves effectively. This can be further complicated when participants are speaking over the phone. Because computer-mediated conversations take place in writing, non-native speakers sometimes feel more comfortable contributing since they have time to check their text before posting.

Access to technology can be a barrier to communication. Communities are based on the connections of members. If simply connecting is difficult, people are less likely to make the effort, at least not regularly. It took a global community member in Nigeria twenty minutes to connect to the community Web site because his bandwidth was so narrow. Even though he did not need to be at his computer the whole time, he found the experience of connecting tedious and did so much less frequently than other community members. Compare this experience to that of a local community: One simply walks down the hall to find someone to talk to. Special effort to connect members raises the costs—in terms of time and effort—of participation, increases the inertia the community needs to overcome, and makes it even more important that the community deliver tangible value for its members.

Domain, Community, and Practice
in Global Communities

DIFFERENCES IN TIME ZONES, affiliation, and culture combined with large size and a heavy reliance on technology make distributed communities different from local ones in several important ways. They need to devote much more time to reconciling multiple agendas in order to define the domain and to building personal relationships and trust between members. They need to work harder to create a sense of intimacy among members without simply requiring that they all follow the same standard.

Defining the Domain: Reconciling Multiple Agendas

Distributed communities usually have a greater diversity of viewpoints, needs, interests, priorities, and expectations than local groups. At the same time, distance provides fewer opportunities to negotiate those issues. In one global community, for instance, headquarters and field people had very different understandings of what their community should be about. People in the field wanted to focus on specific action-oriented projects, whereas people at headquarters wanted to create a manual for general distribution. When a community is pulled in many different directions, it becomes more difficult to define the focus and scope of the domain. On one hand, each group brings in varied needs that may diverge and potentially dilute the community. On the other hand, the number and scope of topics in which they are all willing to invest are more limited.

Various business units may place different value on technical excellence or on stewardship of knowledge domains and may neglect these in favor of more immediate and concrete concerns, such as project deadlines, time, and cost objectives. As a result of these conflicting priorities, it is more difficult for organizational units to see the value of a community and agree to support it. Business unit managers are often willing to support distributed communities in theory, but reluctant to commit time and resources for local leaders to devote to global community development.

Distributed communities usually have to spend more time up front creating agreement, reconciling the priorities and needs of local groups, and dealing explicitly with competing pressures. Because participating in a global community is less easily folded into everyday work and may require travel, the need to convince managers of the value of stewarding the domain at a global level is greater.

Building the Community: Trust and Personal Relationships

Because members of large distributed communities have less contact, it is more difficult to build trust and personal relationships. As we have seen, a large part of the trust-building process takes place in the private space of the community by increasing the connections between individual members. In local communities, there are many opportunities for spontaneous networking and making new contacts. People can easily ask for help privately during a meeting break or test an idea with a colleague before sharing it with the whole community. Because there are fewer opportunities for spontaneous one-on-one networking in distributed communities, members tend to have fewer private conversations. Ideas or requests for help posted on the community Web site or in the collaborative software generally go to the whole community, not just to trusted members. As a member of a global community who was having trouble asking for help said, "It is sort of difficult to let your hair down in front of hundreds of people you don't know."

Different affiliations also make it more difficult for business unit managers and community members to trust others. Several of Shell's communities had to wrestle with the problem of what information the community would share with other units that had partnerships with competitors. Should they let partner company representatives (who worked side-by-side with the Shell staff) participate in the community? Should they trust the Shell employees to know what to share with partners and what not? Should they share only information that was not proprietary? Answering these questions in a way that allowed community members to freely trust others was key to making the communities effective.

Finally, cultural differences often make trust and deep personal relationships more difficult. For many people, connecting with others from their own cultural background is more comfortable. During the evening cocktail hour at the launch of one global community, people gathered according to their cultural backgrounds. These little knots of cultural identity increased members' sense of connection with people from different parts of their own country, but they diminished their sense of belonging to the whole.

Distributed communities have to work hard to create a base of trust between disparate members. They need to be more intentional about connecting people, finding opportunities for members to interact beyond their local circles, and building interpersonal relationships. They also need to address issues of norms and openness more explicitly; they cannot assume that norms are already shared or that there is enough interaction and common ground for norms to emerge.

Developing the Practice: Craft Intimacy

As we saw in chapter 5, successful communities develop a strong sense of craft intimacy—close interactions around shared problems and a sense of commonality. Obviously, such intimacy is more difficult to achieve in large distributed communities.

Different affiliations also make it more difficult to achieve craft intimacy. One small business unit in a widely distributed community could not afford the level of analysis their colleagues from larger and more technically sophisticated units recommended. As this community developed, the members from the smaller branches felt trumped by their peers with more organizational resources, who kept recommending courses of action the smaller units could not afford. Even though the resource-rich community members were very knowledgeable and approachable, the smaller business unit members had difficulty engaging with them.

The commonality required for craft intimacy can be more difficult to develop across cultures. When planning the development of Shell's global communities, the team found many Europeans skeptical of a U.S.-initiated community. They were concerned, perhaps rightly, that the Americans would try to impose a U.S. model of interaction on them. In one global community, two very different interpretations of the role of community leader surfaced, even though everyone was using the same role description. One group saw the role as a traditional group leader—directing the community, developing junior members, identifying key issues. These members felt that they should connect to the rest of the community through the coordinator, in deference to his leadership role.

Their counterparts from a different culture saw the community leader as an equal, a networker among peers, and wanted to connect directly with community members in other locations. Their respective perceptions of the role of the leader were consistent with their own cultural norms about deference to authority, but made the development of craft intimacy between sites difficult.

Common practices are not necessarily "standard" practices. Because distributed communities cross cultural and organizational boundaries, the application of an approach or tool in one location may not be the same as it is in another. A sense of intimacy does not mean that all local communities use the same practices. It does mean that they do understand and learn from each other's practice. Distributed communities give members a forum in which to "talk shop," solve problems together, and in the process find ways to learn from each other's perspectives and local conditions.

None of the factors and challenges discussed here prevent distributed communities from agreeing on a domain, developing strong personal bonds between members, or building a robust practice. They simply mean that creating distributed communities involves special effort. But if a community can overcome these obstacles, the rewards are also greater. As the local coordinator for one global community commented, "Feeling that you have a peer at the other end of the road dealing with the same kind of problems gives you some comfort that you are not just fighting windmills on your own."

Designing Distributed Communities

THE DESIGN PRINCIPLES and processes we use for local communities also work for distributed ones. However, designing and nurturing distributed communities so they can overcome the barriers of time, size, affiliation, and culture requires additional effort in four key development activities:

1. Achieve stakeholder alignment

2. Create a structure that promotes both local variations and global connections

3. Build a rhythm strong enough to maintain community visibility

4. Develop the private space of the community more systematically

Achieve Stakeholder Alignment

Overcoming differences in geography, affiliation, and culture generally requires more time and effort to define the domain and develop commitment from business unit managers. Engaging all players is key to getting a good start for any community. Given the conflicting priorities and lack of connection and trust among stakeholders of distributed communities, this is crucial. In a telecommunications equipment company, where most of the communities were centered in a single location, planning was complete in about six weeks. By contrast, as we saw, developing alignment for Shell's global communities took six months. Overcoming conflicting priorities and developing a common understanding of the potential value of the community typically takes such extensive preparation. Here are a couple of tips to keep in mind.

> *Going from 0 to 30 is the hardest part.* Because Shell's global communities involved so many stakeholders, the preparation had to be very extensive. But once Shell had eliminated several barriers that later would have interfered with the communities' effectiveness, other global communities had an easier time starting. More important, by increasing connections between business units and demonstrating the value of sharing knowledge, the communities themselves became an incentive to further minimize those obstacles.
>
> *Have a "hungry" business unit act as host.* It is useful to have a business unit act as a host for a global community. Hosting builds commitment and sets an example. A good candidate for this task is the business unit hungriest for knowledge in the domain. While planning their global communities, one organization found that the business unit with the most knowledge about the topic was reluctant to take overall responsibility for the community. They felt they were already inundated with requests for help, and sponsoring a

community seemed like an additional burden. However, the community support team realized that another business unit in the organization—one that was savvy enough to know who knew what in the field—desperately needed to expand their expertise. They made an ideal host. Because they had already planned an outlay of resources to develop their ability, they were willing to spend the resources (in terms of the coordinator's time) to facilitate the community overall. Most important, they had the passion to actively pursue new threads of knowledge, find the experts, and develop the relationships that hosting the community would entail. Like good midcareer professionals, they were poised to gain a lot from the task of developing the community.

Create a Structure That Promotes Both Local Variations and Global Connections

Large distributed communities often need a structure that is different from local or small ones. They need a design that allows for variations in culture, language, organization, and work without sacrificing the development of trust and connection between global community members. To design a structure that ensures local variation and global connectivity, you must avoid treating a global community as a massive monolith. It is built out of local subcommunities or "cells." One way to think about such a distributed community is as a kind of fractal structure.[3] The global community has many local incarnations. Community members belong to the global community by first belonging to a local one. You can't have a direct experience of community with a thousand people, but if you are affiliated with a smaller group, that subcommunity is your connection to other local communities as well as to the larger community. Obviously, this means how a community is divided and how those divisions are connected are crucial elements of the design.

There are different ways to divide a community into cells. At Shell, the cells are geographical localities connected to each other through a "hub-and-spoke" network of community coordinators. Each local community (or spoke) has a coordinator who maintains the local community and helps link people with problems to people with solutions in other parts of the world. Although most local communities are within a single business unit, several span business units within a particular region. The local community coordinators form a global network (the wheel's hub), which is held together by a global community coordinator.

Another way to divide large distributed communities is to create topic-focused cells. Community members typically participate in more than one area. If the topics remain integral to the overall domain, members can be exposed to the larger flow of ideas while maintaining their connection to a smaller group. One global community, for example, is divided into a dozen topic areas. But requests for help and special "hot topic" notices go to everyone. Community members can sign up to be notified through e-mail of new postings in their topic specialties, or to receive weekly digests. As a result, community members see an active, lively global exchange, even when their own topic area is relatively quiet, and feel connected to the community as a whole.

Combine Diversity and Connection

The structures just described work only for fairly large communities, because they need a minimum critical mass for each local site. Whatever the formula for subdividing cells, the purpose is to enable small group connection, local variation, and whole-community connection. Because the local coordinator is the primary link with the global community, this model allows the local communities substantial freedom while maintaining enough structure to support global community development. In some local communities, a senior functional leader is the local coordinator; in others, a midcareer professional. Some have regular community meetings, others do not. Some have formal processes for reviewing projects, others have informal ones. This flexibility makes it possible to accommodate variations in local culture and organizational structure. (See figure 6-1.)

Connect People

The role of the global and local coordinators is to create links between cells, or local groups, and thus tie them into a global community. When an individual has a question or problem, he or she posts it on

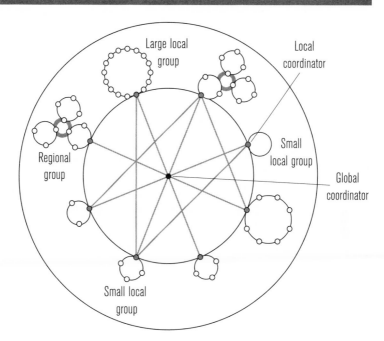

FIGURE 6-1   FRACTAL STRUCTURE FOR A GLOBAL COMMUNITY

Source: R. McDermott and J. Jackson, "Designing Global Communities."

the community Web site. The local coordinators and global facilitator shepherd the process of connecting, passing on the request to people in the network who are likely to have helpful information or insight and ensuring that the request is answered. Once they have found each other, members talk by phone, in person, via e-mail, or through the community bulletin board, exchanging the relevant information through whatever means is most appropriate. Given the tacit nature of much of the information, this flexibility allows people to use the most appropriate medium for what they want to share. When the community was first started and community members did not know each other, this personal touch was very important. As one person said, "I don't just want to send a blind e-mail to an expert across the globe. I need an introduction."

The community's ability to connect individuals worldwide relies on strong relationships at both global and local levels. Shell's three pilot global communities were launched in a two-day event that included all the local coordinators. Some communities continue this face-to-face contact by having coordinator meetings a few times a year. Coordinator meetings constitute the global level of the distributed structure and cell meetings the local level. This structure and the in-person meetings of coordinators provide enough intimacy at both local and global levels that community members can get to know each other.

Avoid Hierarchy

The subtle challenge for the coordinators is to work within a large structure while avoiding hierarchy. In this sense, their role is very different from that of a manager in a top-down organization. The purpose is to foster horizontal relationships, not to create a hierarchical channel of information through which members must navigate. Coordinators connect people; they do not convey information. They broker relationships, not knowledge. Once the relationships are established, people can make contact directly. Indeed, this is what happened in the global communities at Shell. As the communities grew, community members in different locations got to know each other and became more and more comfortable making direct contact. Through those direct relationships, the whole community became more tangible and more present to individual members.

Build a Rhythm Strong Enough to Maintain Community Visibility

Because their members don't bump into each other in the hallway, distributed communities are less visibly present than local communities and need, as much or more than local communities, a set of regular events to give the community a heartbeat. Many distributed communities use the Web as their primary form of connection. Differences in time zones often make live collaboration difficult, so asynchronous tools, such as threaded discussions, enable community members to participate in discussions in their own time. Days can easily pass between a request for help and responses. It can easily take weeks for a half-dozen exchanges concerning an ongoing topic discussion to take place. As a result, purely online connections can feel timeless and out of sync with the often urgent rhythm of everyday work. And when the community feels slow and out of sync, it can easily slip from people's consciousness. Regular events, such as teleconferences or meetings of local cells, regularly remind people of the community's presence. Special events, like global conferences, can give members a sense of connection in a way that threaded discussions cannot. As we mentioned in chapter 3, these events typically enliven the Web-based discussions with a flurry of postings before and after the event. Teleconferences and other events create deadlines for interaction. But more important, they increase the sense of social obligation community members feel to connect. Although distributed communities cannot have weekly face-to-face meetings like the Turbodudes do, they can use a wide variety of events to strengthen the community's presence. One global community has an annual two-day conference in three locations simultaneously. The first day ends for the European group with a videoconference with the U.S. group. The U.S. conference ends—late in the day—with a videoconference with the group in Sydney. The Sydney group ends its day in videoconference with the European group. Each group's discussion includes some common topics, which they summarize and pass on to the next group in the videoconference. While they would prefer a whole-community face-to-face event, this "circulating conference" gives them a feel of the community as a whole.

Arrange Teleconferences

One of the most common ways distributed communities create a rhythm is through regular teleconferences, as illustrated by the opening vignette of chapter 2. In that case, the community was small enough to include all members in the teleconference. Some larger communities have regular teleconferences for members interested in particular subtopics. In several of Shell's global communities, local coordinators participate in a biweekly teleconference, which sometimes focuses on how the cells are doing and other times on technical issues. Teleconferences are limited to relatively small groups unless they take the form of a lecture. But even when the whole community cannot participate,

teleconferences still allow members to interact directly, develop relationships, solve problems, and build a sense of craft intimacy. Several
additional factors can enhance teleconferences.

- *Conference software.* Some communities have found that
  augmenting these teleconferences with software such as Net
  Meeting or Same Time adds a stronger sense of presence to
  "virtual" meetings. Using this software, community members
  can see a slide show, white board, or text document as they
  talk. Some use the software for collaborative brainstorming,
  documenting their discussion as they go.

- *Video.* Video broadcast is useful for lectures. For interactive
  meetings, however, the three-second delay typical of the bandwidth available to most communities generally makes video
  links less effective as a discussion tool than the telephone.

- *Role of coordinator in teleconferences.* Coordinators also play an
  important role in managing teleconferences. They set up speakers,
  manage logistics, coordinate choice of topics, and facilitate the
  meeting. All the while they pay attention to virtual communication etiquette (such as muting background noise and drawing out
  participation where warranted), monitor links to online computer-
  based applications (such as Net Meeting), and arrange for notes
  or other follow-up points to be posted to a Web site or listserv.

Organize Face-to-Face Meetings

A recent study found that distributed communities usually have
face-to-face meetings one to three times a year.[4] These do not necessarily involve the whole community, especially if it is large. Ford's manufacturing best-practices community, for example, spans 150 manufacturing
plants around the world, with communities focused on different stages
of the manufacturing process. Within each plant, coordinators for each
community help develop, verify, share, and implement practices. The
company hosts annual face-to-face meetings for the plant coordinators
to discuss how their community is doing. Even though the meeting
doesn't include the whole community (which consists of thousands of

operators), it is an opportunity for community leaders to build connections with leaders from other plants. Several tips can increase the effectiveness of these meetings in weaving the community.

- *Rotate the location of face-to-face meetings.* One way to increase
  the connection of community members is to rotate meeting
  locations. This gives members an opportunity to see other sites,
  to get a feel for other members' particular issues and situations,
  and to develop stronger relationships.

- *Organize field trips.* Shell's geological community has a variation
  on this theme. They don't meet in a conference room; they find
  a geological structure relevant to the issues they are going to
  discuss and meet literally "on the rocks." These unique field
  trips to interesting geological sites increase the interest and
  personal draw of these events.

- *Form meeting design teams of members from different locations.*
  For each meeting, put together a team of members from various
  locations who will collaborate to prepare the meeting. These
  teams provide members other than coordinators an opportunity
  to get to know peers from other locations and take some
  responsibility for the development of the community.

Facilitate Threaded Discussions

Many communities use threaded discussions (or e-mail distribution lists) as one of their primary ways to connect members. These
enable community members to carry on a discussion on a topic of interest asynchronously. However, participants can see who else is there
only by their contributions; when a Web-based conversation goes
through natural cycles of low activity, it may look like the community is
dead. When members think the community is waning, it starts a vicious
cycle. Who wants to contribute if no one is listening? Just as visibility
spurs contribution, invisibility inhibits it. The community coordinator
can stimulate these discussions by occasionally stirring the pot with an
intriguing question or a provocative statement. Such interventions can
return the community to the awareness of members.

After a particularly long period of quiet, a distributed community member wrote a note asking, "Is anyone out there?" A few members responded and the coordinator, realizing that the community was on the verge of dissipating, introduced some new members and proposed the highly controversial metaphor of a toilet for understanding some of the community's core processes. This creative turn sparked enough response that members once again felt the community's lively presence, and several reengaged on more substantial topics. Even though the toilet metaphor was hardly serious, it sparked enough controversy for community members to begin actively connecting again.

Link Modes of Interaction

Increase the integration of different modes of communication by using the community's Web site (or threaded discussions) to prepare for meetings. The design-build community of a large engineering firm posts not only an agenda, but data and short analyses of issues on their Web site prior to meetings. Using a conference software, they review this material at their regular teleconference, including comments the community members posted in response to the material. After the meeting, they add information to the site about the meeting's conclusions and solicit feedback. Using electronic communication to feed teleconferences and face-to-face meetings makes the relationships between members a stronger and more visible dimension of the community.[5]

Make Judicious Use of Broadcast Technology

Many coordinators find it useful to broadcast information at regular intervals to keep the community in the consciousness of members.

- *Newsfeed.* Some communities link to member home pages so community news is visible when members log on each morning.

- *Subscriptions.* Many software packages allow members to be notified by e-mail when certain events take place on the community Web page, such as the publication of a paper. They can also receive a weekly digest of posts to the community's discussion board.

- *Newsletters.* Some communities publish newsletters that both inform members of community activity and, because of their regularity, are very good ways to maintain the community's visibility.

Like local communities, distributed communities use many forms of interaction and host both familiar and exciting events to create a rhythm of activities. But whereas local communities can rely on the momentum and natural networking opportunities that regular face-to-face events provide, distributed communities must be more intentional about creating a variety of reminders that reinforce the community's existence.

Develop the Private Space of the Community More Systematically

Differences in geography, affiliation, and culture increase the need for one-on-one networking in distributed communities. The personal networking that a coordinator does to launch a community is also necessary to start a distributed community. In fact, because it is generally more difficult to develop trust across distance and cultural boundaries, this networking is crucial. We found that focusing on core practices or methodologies is one of the easiest ways to build connections. Deeply engaging people in both practical and cutting-edge issues in their field can often create enough common ground for community members to overlook cultural differences.

Active networking by community coordinators also increases the exposure of community members to each other. Community leaders are sometimes tempted to strengthen the community by increasing the amount of material on their Web page, making it a full library. Although populating a database is useful, feeling related and responsible to other community members is a far stronger force for increasing participation and aliveness. As one global facilitator remarked, "My biggest learning is that it is all about the relationships. If you make the request based on 'I owe you a beer,' people will respond."

Coordinators bridge the boundaries between local communities.

By connecting people, they not only build an information network, they also create a web of trust. When a query on the Web site of one global community failed to generate a response, prodding by the global community coordinator resulted in a flurry of replies. The more time and energy coordinators spend networking, the more active their communities. Following are some specific ways coordinators may strengthen the personal network.

Personalize membership. It is useful to find ways to personalize participation, because it isn't easy for members to get to know one another from a distance, especially when the main topics of discussion are business-related. Many communities have pictures of all their members posted on the Web site, along with personal biographical details. A visual image makes it easier for community members to remember who's who. Some communities even have a small picture of the author with each posting on the discussion board.

Small group projects and meetings. Small group projects are important for creating personal relationships in all types of communities, but they take on a special value in distributed communities when they provide another way for small clusters of community members to connect with each other across sites.

Organized or impromptu site visits. Ford's best-practice communities regularly take small groups of community members to each other's plants to review the implementation of a manufacturing best practice. These small-group visits across sites create strong connections between the members involved. So do impromptu visits by a member who happens to be in town.

Be opportunistic about chances to interact. The community of quantitative biologists described in chapter 2 keeps a calendar so people know who is in town when they happen to be visiting. When the core members of a community of software developers were planning their events, they realized that the most important interaction for the community was for leading developers to discuss new developments in the platform. As they considered how to get this group of experts together, they realized that many of the same members would be attending a bimonthly business meeting completely unrelated to the community. The group added a day to that meeting for a community event. This saved travel time and cost while gaining a full day of direct interaction. Many discipline-based communities find that they have annual technical conferences to which community events can be added. Of course, they have to make sure they do not let the other conference activities shortchange their focus on the community, or vice versa.

Conclusion: Achieving True Globalization

TRUE GLOBALIZATION REQUIRES COMMUNITY. In the past, globalization often meant that a company had a very active international division to handle overseas sales, distribution, and management of overseas suppliers and manufacturing plants. But most company functions—such as research, marketing, core manufacturing, and administration—were located in the company's host nation. As companies moved to a more divisional or business unit structure, international business units became more influential, often operating as small, independent companies that developed their own marketing, technical service, and sometimes even their own research departments. The limitations of time, space, and integration of information often made it impossible to truly integrate the operations of these international business units. Some companies rotated staff to build greater connections between these divisions or trained managers centrally so they would know each other well enough to rely on each other throughout their careers.

Even though information technology has made deeper interdependence between operating units possible, it is communities of practice that create the relationships required for global integration. Strong human relationships are key to integration across geographically distributed business units as well as to effective partnerships.[6] By uniting people from different regions, countries, or divisions around topics they feel passionate about, communities increase the density of relationships between distributed business units. This occurs not only at the top of the organization but throughout the ranks, and on the level of everyday practice as well as business strategy. As communities enhance the sense of craft intimacy and trust between people in distributed divisions, they increase both the flow of information and the organization's capability to interpret and apply that information.

Unlike automated information systems, communities make it possible to share perspectives and frameworks. For example, the design-build community of a global engineering firm has developed a common approach to project proposals. Because the approach was developed by community members, they understand the inner logic of the approach and can easily adapt it to local circumstances. Thus, community members have both a common procedure and a shared understanding of the approach. In such a way, communities can create global practices without sacrificing a sensitivity to local circumstances. This provides an even deeper level of integration than universal standards.

Communities of practice create the common talent pool globalization requires. To be truly global—and competitive—companies need to be able to attract expertise, no matter where it is located in the world. By creating a set of relationships through which members know each other's expertise, communities of practice create a worldwide talent pool. A project manager in California responded to a request from a colleague in Brazil for input on a design-build proposal. After providing some information and feedback, the project manager told the Brazilian engineer that his workload was low, and he would be interested and available for the Brazil project if their bid was accepted.

Communities of practice create a point of stability in a world of temporary, distant relationships. Traditionally, people's sense of connection to an organization comes through their relationship with their manager and peers in their department or team. But in many companies, this level of connection is becoming weaker. As we saw in chapter 1, staff often work on interdisciplinary teams with a manager from a different discipline who cannot truly understand their technical contribution. They frequently work in departments or teams that change or reorganize as the market changes. When companies globalize, connections with other work team members may become even more temporary and tenuous. Community members who work on virtual teams often have relatively little contact with the whole team, working face-to-face only with the team members in their location. The team leader might be not only from a different discipline, but also from a different country or business unit. In some global companies, technical staff rotate among locations every few years. For people who change managers, team members, business units, and even countries every few years, communities can become a primary source of stability. By creating a group of peers who have long-standing relationships and who truly understand and appreciate each other's contributions, communities of practice can create a deep sense of organizational belonging independent of location and day-to-day job responsibilities. As one member of a strong global community commented, "I know I will be connected to the same group of [technical specialists] no matter where I am assigned, and this helps me feel more connected to the company as a whole."

In addition to strategic alignment among distributed business units and consistent information technology, true globalization requires a culture that encourages people to connect with staff in other business units and the capacity to adapt common, global frameworks to local needs. By uniting staff from distributed business units around key topics, forming stable, long-standing relationships on many levels of the organization, and creating forums that foster sharing and understanding, communities of practice provide the connective structure needed to build such an adaptive global organization. They are increasingly essential to knowledge-intensive organizations that seek to become truly global.[7]

CHAPTER seven

The Downside of
Communities of Practice

COMMUNITIES OF PRACTICE, LIKE ALL HUMAN institutions, also have a downside. They can hoard knowledge, limit innovation, and hold others hostage to their expertise. The medieval guilds, for instance, were often fortresses as much as they were stewards of knowledge. They focused as much on the interest of those who benefited from the status quo as on innovation in their practice. When some guilds started to make membership a right that was inherited from father to son, they became almost impossible for others to enter. Communities of practice can also reflect the narrow, unjust prejudices of their society. Most medieval guilds excluded women. Scientific communities in South Africa during the era of apartheid denied black South Africans access to opportunities to participate in research and knowledge-sharing activities. The Screen Actors Guild in the United States collaborated with rabid government officials in the 1950s to black-list actors for suspected political views. It is important not to romanticize communities of practice or expect them to solve all problems without creating any. They are not a silver bullet. In fact, because communities of practice have always existed in organizations, they are more than likely to be part of the problems they are expected to solve.[1]

In this chapter we examine the downside of communities, describe some common disorders, and propose some useful countermeasures. We address these issues at three levels. First, we explore how individual communities of practice can become an obstacle to learning. Then we look at problems associated not with single communities, but a constellation of them—a set of multiple communities related by organization affiliation, subject matter, or application. Finally, we consider how organizations can create barriers to the development of communities and fail to live up to the challenge they present.[2]

Given the positive connotations of the term community and the well-known tribulations of organizational life, it is tempting to idealize communities and demonize organizations. In discussing problems at these three levels—single communities, constellations of communities, and organizations—we do not divide the world into saints and devils. Rather, we emphasize the need to recognize the potential pitfalls at all three levels in order to avoid them wherever possible.

Single Communities: What Can Go Wrong

MOST COMMUNITY DISORDERS are of two general types. The first is obvious: a community may simply not be functioning well. The reasons are fairly straightforward. It may violate some of the basic principles introduced in chapter 3 or fail to achieve the balance of opposites related to the various developmental stages. For whatever reason, the domain may not arouse passion in members. Community members may fail to connect enough to develop trust. The practice may remain stagnant. Because of the reinforcing mechanisms that group processes can engender, a failed community is often worse than no community at all.

The other kind of disorder is more subtle; it reflects the human frailties of its members. The potential for this downside is inherent in all communities—they are, after all, composed of people—even when they are ostensibly functioning well. In fact, disorders often appear when some aspects of communities are functioning too well. In a tight community a lot of implicit assumptions can go unquestioned, and there may be few opportunities or little willingness inside the community to challenge them. The intimacy communities develop can create a barrier to newcomers, a blinder to new ideas, or a reluctance to critique each other. Like many human weaknesses, community disorders are frequently an extreme version of a community's strength. The very qualities that make a community an ideal structure for learning—a shared perspective on a domain, trust, a communal identity, long-standing relationships, an established practice—are the same qualities that can hold it hostage to its history and its achievements. The community can become an ideal structure for avoiding learning. When the qualities one seeks in a community are pushed out of balance, they turn into debilitating disorders that cause a community to stagnate or even die.

Learning to see community disorders is a useful lens for developing communities of practice and helping to ensure their continuing value. In this chapter we identify a few of the more common disorders that can affect communities of practice, either directly or through their environment. A useful way to approach this task is to associate disorders and corresponding remedies with the constituent element that they affect most directly: domain, community, or practice. Disorders can arise if some qualities essential to that element are either missing or pushed out of balance.

Domain: The Temptations of Ownership

Pride of ownership can induce a fall. Sometimes, the enthusiasm for the domain leads to excessive zealousness. Or the legitimacy of the community's hold on its domain is so widely recognized and well entrenched that arrogance sets in. It is not uncommon for engineers or technicians, for instance, to feel such exclusive ownership of their domain that they ignore the perspective of operators in analyzing a system. Being viewed as the expert in a domain also makes it easy to believe that what one knows is all there is to know. Arrogance can easily lead a community to claim exclusive ownership of that knowledge and hoard it from other communities or from the organization as a whole. When a community's hold on its domain becomes exclusive, outsiders are likely to feel hostage to the self-righteous expertise of specialists.

Imperialism

With the responsibility to develop a domain comes the ability to decide how to approach it, which issues matter, who can have a say, and what the organization should do about it. However, focusing on areas members are passionate about can lead a community to think that their domain is more important than others or that their perspective on the domain should prevail. For instance, if a new issue (such as e-business) arises, communities may start to vie for control over the initiative. In an IT firm, establishing standards for typical system configurations had become a hot topic. The firm had made substantial investment in the issue, and three practice centers had developed their own approach. But they were talking past each other, each claiming ownership of the issue. The reward for getting it right yourself and branding your ideas was perceived as more important than finding common ground and making progress together.[3]

In another organization, some communities have gained the reputation of acting as "the knowledge police." These communities feel such a strong sense of ownership of the domain that they believe anyone working in that domain should consult them, or even be forced to do so. A community that had developed an approach to entering new markets felt that any business unit entering new markets should use its framework, even if the unit was not convinced the framework applied to its situation. Imperialistic communities are not open to alternative views, outside experts, or new methodologies because of their passionate belief that their perspective is the right one. They need to be exposed to other perspectives in the context of real challenges that go beyond their domain and to problems that can be solved only by combining multiple approaches.

Other disorders derived from domain-related excesses and failures also reflect a human dimension: narcissism, marginality, and factionalism.

- *Narcissism.* A successful community takes pride in the integrity of its specialty. But taken to the extreme, this can result in members being overly concerned with themselves. One-upsmanship pushes them to technical prowess of questionable value. They pursue their own agenda with little regard for what teams or business units really need in terms of expertise or capability. Narcissistic communities often lack direct exposure to customers or the market.

- *Marginality.* Some communities are not taken seriously. They fail to assert the legitimacy of their domain or its importance to other constituencies. They remain marginal to the organization, either because they are not part of the organization's mainstream activity or because they are excluded from the decision-making power of the organization. Shared discontent, for example, can exert a strong emotional influence over members because it provides a sense of belonging for people who feel otherwise disenfranchised. But discontent has limited value as a domain in and of itself. The best of these communities serve as a gadfly, identifying gaps between the organization's aspirations and its reality. The worst become gripe communities, providing an outlet for members' dissatisfaction, but without any vehicle for initiating change. Marginality and discontent can create strong bonds between members, but the lack of effectiveness in making a difference is likely to become a drain on their energy and willingness to invest themselves. Bringing these communities into the fold of the organization and giving them visible responsibilities will make their cohesion constructive.

- *Factionalism.* To the extent that members have a strong commitment to their domain, their disagreements can turn into religious wars. Some communities are torn by internal strife over the definition or scope of the domain, with individuals or factions fighting for their own special interests, approach, or school of thought. Members can be consumed by these internal distinctions and spend more energy emphasizing differences with others than moving forward with practice development.

Treatments for Domain Disorders

Domain-related disorders often occur when the community or the organization fails to make a clear connection between the domain and the needs of the business, or when the needs of the business dominate to the point that the perspectives and interests of members are ignored. Because domain disorders reflect how the community defines itself in its environment, they often affect the relationship of the community to the organization and other constituencies. It is therefore by tending to these relationships that countermeasures can be developed. These might include establishing the legitimacy and strategic value of the domain, clarifying the link to business issues and finding ways for the community to add value, offering inspiring challenges, including the community in important decisions, holding it accountable for the reputation of the firm in the domain, or exposing it to other perspectives.[4]

Community: Too Much of a Good Thing

The term *community* has positive connotations for most people. It is a "warm" term that conjures images of harmony, sometimes with a dose of nostalgia. However, communities of practice are not havens of peace or unbounded goodwill. They reflect all the strengths, weaknesses, and complex interrelationships of their human members. They have their share of conflicts, jealousies, and intrigues. But even when there are tight bonds between members, the result is not always positive. Tight bonds can become exclusive and present an insurmountable barrier to entry. They can even embolden members to act in ways that would shock outsiders. This downside of community is what gives rise to the mobs that would burn a witch, lynch an African-American, or guillotine an aristocrat. Without vigilance, having a community may create a toxic coziness that closes people to exploration and external input.[5] In other words, too much community can become counterproductive.

Cliques

A community of practice can become a clique when relationships among members are so strong that they dominate all other concerns. Frequently, cliquish communities are dominated by a powerful core group that acts as an imperious gatekeeper. They become exclusive, either intentionally or as an unintended outcome of the tightness of their relationships.

An international community of consultants was formed to help each other with their consulting practice and to promote a particular methodology. They have been meeting annually for a number of years. They keep in touch between meetings through a listserv; some local cells even meet in person. Members in a solid inner circle have built such strong relationships that it is difficult for new members to enter. They are so well connected that their community is almost like a thicket. Though they do not intend to be exclusive, their efforts to recruit new members have been only marginally successful, and the core members feel satisfied to maintain their current relationships rather than expand membership. The community is not just a social network; members do talk shop when they meet. But their inability to recruit new members has made it unlikely that they would ever focus seriously on the second mission—to promote their methodology.

Cliquish communities also tend to stagnate. Pushed to an extreme, close friendship and the desire for a sociable atmosphere can prevent members from critiquing each other or from seeking to deepen their understanding of their domain. The community then becomes locked in a blind, defensive solidarity as members strive to protect each other from challenges. What cliquish communities need is new blood, people who are not overly caught up in the thicket of internal relationships and who can reopen the community's horizon.

Several other disorders are caused by excesses or failures in creating a sense of community.

- *Egalitarianism.* A community can constrain individual growth or creativity through the power of a group norm of equality. No one should stand out. It becomes difficult for any one member to take risks or engage in any activity that would distinguish him or her from the rest of the community. As in the Chinese Cultural Revolution of the 1960s, unity depends on uniform thinking, and any deviant idea or ambition becomes treason.

- *Dependence.* Too much dependence on the activity of a coordinator or on the charisma of a leader makes the community vulnerable to their departure. It is also tends to silence other voices and decrease the diversity of perspectives in the community. Thus, it becomes very important to spread leadership and share responsibilities.

- *Stratification.* Another reason for spreading leadership roles is the risk of stratification. An active core group is a key success factor, but too much distance between the core group, experts, and other participants creates distinct classes of members that prevent the community from developing a common identity.

- *Disconnectedness.* When a community is too large, diffuse, or dispersed to actively engage members, the sense of identification remains very superficial. Many people sign up, but they don't return or honor their commitments. Individual members don't connect in personal ways that show enthusiasm, enjoyment, and a willingness to give and reciprocate. Disconnected communities treat interactions as simply transactions. What these communities need are joint activities that build a meaningful sense of shared identity, one that binds members beyond specific exchanges.

- *Localism.* Sometimes a community lets geographical, departmental, or company boundaries define its own borders. It fails to transcend these boundaries to develop the range, intensity, and diversity of connections that would maximize the synergy between people and groups. Such communities need to be encouraged to move to the stewarding stage so they can view boundary expansion as part of caring for their domain.

Treatments for Community Disorders

Disorders related to the kind or the strength of relationships among community members affect a community's sense of belonging. As a result, such disorders often have a strong impact not only on how community members relate to one another, but also on how they relate to those outside the community. Countermeasures thus involve both internal and boundary work. Internally, trust comes from interactions that are mutually beneficial, such as engaging in shared problem solving. Involving new generations brings new blood to the community, but may require a framework such as apprenticeship or mentorship to connect newcomers with old-timers. Connections with other communities can be fostered by encouraging multimembership, supporting the efforts of knowledge brokers, or organizing boundary activities, such as joint sessions or projects.

Practice: The Liabilities of Competence

If all you have is a hammer, the whole world looks like a nail, as the saying goes. A shared practice is a liability as well as a resource. The cognitive and communicative efficiency it affords has a cost. When doctors talk about a patient, the specialized language and experience they share allow them to focus quickly on the core problem. All they have to do is to describe a few symptoms and they can start sketching some hypotheses. This very efficiency, however, can make it difficult for patients to understand what is happening. Not only does this efficiency create barriers to outsiders, it can also create boundaries for practitioners. The specialization of medical practice can transform the patient into a medical object and blind doctors to other aspects of a patient's illness. Indeed, the price of an efficient practice goes beyond communication with outsiders; it can prevent practitioners from seeing what does not fit in their paradigm. The practice of a community can hinder its own development.

Documentism

Successful communities capture and document insights, ideas, and procedures. They organize that information into a repository (usually in a database) so it is easily accessible to members. But carried to the extreme, this turns into a single-minded focus on documentation. Communities that fall into this pattern sometimes see amassing documents as a purpose in and of itself. They do not sufficiently screen and organize the documents to be genuinely useful.

A nationwide community of administrators had opened a Web site, which was to become one of the main vehicles for member connection. They let it be a repository for anything members wanted to post. Soon, however, it became merely a convenient place to put things. A lot of material was not directly related to the practice, and the design of the repository did not help clarify the content or its application to the practice. As a result, practitioners stopped using the Web site as a resource. It contained an impressive collection of stuff, but it was too disparate and disorganized. It ceased to be useful because it had accumulated material beyond anyone's ability to make sense of it.

Because documenting is important to developing a practice, this is an easy disorder to fall into, and many communities do. The papers, the memos, and the Web site come to define the community, displacing other aspects of community such as relationship building or collaborative problem solving. The result of documentism is typically an information junkyard, stockpiled with potentially useful but inaccessible information. It is a consequence of thinking that the documents are the main source of value of the community. To remedy it, communities need to think through their purpose, identify the documents that would genuinely be useful, and develop clear roles for managing them. Even though documentation is important for a community, most find that they need to integrate documentation with knowledge-sharing and problem-solving activities.[6]

Further disorders can result from a failure to develop and deepen the practice over time, including amnesia, dogmatism, and mediocrity.

- *Amnesia.* Amnesia is the opposite of documentism. Some communities do little more than discuss current member problems, without documenting the insights they develop. When similar issues arise, they rework ideas they have already discussed. The resulting sense of déjà vu can be deadly to a community since it makes participation feel unproductive. A community coordinator should ensure that insights and questions are recorded so that the community's activities are cumulative.

- *Dogmatism.* A strong sense of competence can lead to an unbending commitment to established canons and methods. Members refuse to accommodate any variation and sometimes even relish specialized knowledge and jargon that others cannot understand. Because dogmatism has to do with blind respect for authority, it usually takes some thought leaders to guide a community toward greater adaptability.

- *Mediocrity.* Building a practice means continually "sharpening the saw" by engaging in learning and innovation activities. However, it is sometimes easier to remain second-class and settle for less than cutting-edge. This is especially a risk when there is no one with enough knowledge to confront members with higher standards. In such cases, benchmarking activities can be really useful, as when the DaimlerChrysler Tech Clubs analyze competitors' cars to understand what other manufacturers are doing in their domain.

Treatments for Practice Disorders

Sharing the repertoire of a common practice is a very useful resource, both for leveraging past experience and for creating new knowledge. But a shared practice is also a blinder, and knowledge loses its value unless it is managed, updated, renewed, and extended. Disorders concerning how the community relates to the knowledge, tools, and methodology that make up its practice usually are internal. Frequently, practice-related problems end up crippling the community by causing members to lose interest. Countermeasures need to encourage members' involvement in the development of the practice: making enough time to participate actively; balancing joint activities with the production of artifacts; initiating exciting knowledge-development projects; benchmarking the practice of other communities, including competitors; challenging members to help teams with leading-edge issues; and valuing members' participation by allowing their contributions to build their reputation and affect their positions in the organization.

Living with the Downside

Many of these disorders are not fatal. Some, like mediocrity, can last for a while before being recognized as a problem, and some, like cliques, can persist for a very long time. Often disorders combine. In concert, imperialism in the domain, cliques in the community, and dogmatism in the practice will reinforce each other. Because many disorders are simply extensions of the qualities that make communities successful, they can affect any community, even seemingly effective ones. In fact, to some degree they are inevitable. You cannot benefit from the positive side of communities without confronting the negative aspects. Dealing with these problems does not mean denying, avoiding, or getting rid of them. Rather, living with the downside entails recognizing a problem, learning to manage it, and showing leadership when action is required. It is therefore important to spur communities constantly with new challenges, to hold them accountable (directly or indirectly) to outside issues, and to welcome the fresh ideas and agendas of new generations of members. The more quickly a community—or those leading and supporting it— can see a disorder emerging, the sooner they can act to correct it. Successful communities acknowledge their weaknesses and leverage this awareness to spur their growth and reaffirm their long-term vitality.

Constellations of Communities: What Can Go Wrong

COMMUNITIES OF PRACTICE do not exist in isolation. Their effectiveness is not a matter of their internal development alone, but also a matter of how well they connect with other communities and constituencies. We have looked at problems that can arise inside single communities, but some problems especially afflict the constellations of communities that form inside and across organizations.

As communities of practice focus on their domains and deepen their expertise, they inevitably create boundaries. This is a natural outcome of the focus, the intimacy, and the competence they share. All three elements of a community of practice can draw boundary lines. Different domains entail different interests, perspectives, perceptions of value, and sources of excitement. Membership in different communities makes trust more difficult. Different practices entail different vocabularies, styles, sets of experiences, and standards of performance. Boundaries of practice are often informal and even unspoken, but this does not make them less significant. Sit for lunch by a group of high-energy particle physicists and you know about boundary, not because they intend to exclude you, but because you cannot figure out why they are so excited. Shared practice by its very nature creates boundaries.

Boundaries of practice give rise to two challenges for managing knowledge in organizations: Because knowledge *sticks* to practice, it can be difficult to move inside an organization, but because it also *leaks* through practice channels, it is difficult to keep inside organizational boundaries.[7]

> *Stickiness.* Communities effectively steward knowledge in part by creating technical jargon, specialized methods, and customized environments. These make it easier for practitioners to learn and invent, but inevitably create boundaries for outsiders. Crossing boundaries of practice is rarely easy. Miscommunication and misunderstandings are commonplace along boundary lines—when there is communication at all. Because of different background assumptions, people from different communities often talk past each other even if they use similar terms. When researchers and marketing people, engineers and managers, or doctors and administrators talk to each other, the communication difficulties they encounter do not usually stem from interpersonal issues. Rather, they stem from the boundaries between their respective communities of practice, including language, purpose, perspectives, mistrust, professions, or position, and even different identities that entail different values and ways of being in the world.[8] Moving knowledge across boundaries is a notoriously difficult challenge.

Research on intra-firm knowledge sharing found that best practices (such as a new manufacturing method or an administrative
policy) typically took three years to transfer from source facilities
in one division to logical recipients in another. Key factors that
delayed or obstructed transfers were communication difficulties
and weak relationships between practitioners and business leaders
within the same organization.[9] Because people are often capable
of interpreting others' unfamiliar stories or experiences, there is an
implicit expectation that they should be able to transcend contexts
of practice, but it turns out that such differences in contexts are
very difficult to overcome. Knowledge "sticks" to practice in unexpected ways.[10]

Leakiness. Boundaries of practice do not follow institutional boundaries, nor are communities confined within the walls of organizations. Some communities exist even primarily across organizational
boundaries. In the wireless industry, for instance, the cutting-edge
knowledge is held by a few experts who move from company to
company. The same multimembership that connects teams and
communities inside an organization extends outside organizations as
well. The communicative efficiency that transports knowledge
smoothly within a practice can allow knowledge to flow easily past
organizational boundaries. For this reason, it is inherently easier for
your competitor's engineers than for your salespeople to gain deep
insights into your advanced product development. Actually, Shell's
move to organize communities of practice in one division was
prompted in part by a full-page ad in the *London Times.* In this ad
British Petroleum announced that it was beginning deep-sea exploration west of the Shetland Islands. Some people at Shell, however,
believed that BP had learned a key technology for deep-sea oil
exploration from its partnership with Shell in the Gulf of Mexico.
Firms in alliances often find they can gain knowledge faster from
the practitioners they know in other firms than from their coworkers
in other business units in the same firm. Knowledge can "leak"
easily outside the organization because shared practices that cross
organizational boundaries provide channels for sharing information
and ideas efficiently and insightfully.[11]

Managing Boundaries

Communities of practice make knowledge "sticky" and "leaky" at the same time. Knowledge has difficulty crossing boundaries of practice even within an organization, but it flows easily within a practice, no matter what other boundaries exist. You cannot avoid these risks, and therefore you have to live with them and manage them. The key remedy is to pay close attention to boundaries, both to avoid the problems they raise and to take advantage of the opportunities they present.

Boundaries usually have negative connotations. For many people, they connote limitations and exclusion. Properly understood, however, boundaries are sources of new opportunities as well as potential difficulties. Interacting across practices forces members to take a fresh look at their own assumptions. As a result, boundary crossing can be the source of a deep kind of learning. While the core of a practice is a locus of expertise, radically new insights and developments often arise at the boundaries between communities. A discipline such as psychoneuroimmunology still bears witness in its name to its origin at the boundary between practices. Something very creative can take place in the meeting of perspectives at these boundaries when participants make a genuine effort to listen to each other or to solve a common problem. So, boundaries are learning assets in their own right.[12]

There is increasing need to cross boundaries because today's complex problems frequently require solutions that are not confined to any one practice, or even to a single organization. An important developmental question for communities is with what other communities they should link, both inside and outside the organization. Most organizations are not designed to encourage boundary interactions. People are often rewarded for focusing on their own area. Managers view interactions with peers from other organizations with suspicion. Yet, for all the warnings of leakage, organizations usually benefit from informal—for the most part mutual—exchanges with practitioners from other firms.[13] Organizations have to develop procedures to avoid sharing that which should be private, yet disclose enough to enable communication and mutual learning.

Building robust constellations of communities within an organization allows practitioners to decide collectively, in their own community and with other colleagues, what to share and what to keep confidential.

For both the difficulties they create and the opportunities they present, it is important to pay as much attention to the boundaries of communities of practice as to their core, and to make sure that there is enough activity at these boundaries to prevent fragmentation and renew learning. Many forms of connection can enhance boundary activities: shared projects that are at the intersections of multiple domains, people who can act as "knowledge brokers" or translators because they have membership in multiple communities, boundary objects that can accommodate similar interpretations across practices (e.g., a well-written contract or design proposal).[14]

Crossing boundaries requires building trust not only inside communities but also through sustained boundary interactions. There is a definite tension between these two goals. Community development tends to turn a community within; boundary work turns it outward. Yet, communities of practice truly become knowledge assets when their core and boundaries evolve in complementary ways—creating deep expertise inside and constant renewal at the boundary. We would even argue that the learning potential of an organization lies in this balancing act between well-developed communities and active boundary management.

Organizations: What Can Go Wrong

COMMUNITIES OF PRACTICE usually develop in an organizational context, whether they are contained within an organization or cut across boundaries. We have seen how communities of practice can hinder organizational learning, when their disorders distract people from their most productive activities or their boundaries fragment the organization. Conversely, organizations can seriously hinder community development as well. They can be irrational, counterproductive, political, and rampant with suspicion and conflicts. Their design is often focused on accountability for short-term, local, or individual results and is not well-suited for communities. In one case, a community initiative among plant managers foundered in part because managers were measured and rewarded on their individual results; they had little incentive to share ideas and expertise with others who were competing for recognition and resources within the organization.

Just as it helps to anticipate disorders at the community level, it also helps to watch for organizational flaws that will affect the development of communities. There are two kinds of disorders at the organizational level. First are the perennial organizational dysfunctions that communities face. Second, some specific organizational problems—such as the risk of rigidity or increased structural complexity—are actually magnified by the focus on communities of practice.

Addressing Organizational Barriers

Communities of practice, like other organizational change initiatives, can encounter organizational barriers, which will affect their ability to steward knowledge. Sometimes these barriers can be so strong they become organization wide "learning disabilities."[15] Communities can even absorb these organizational problems and reflect them as community disorders. Typical examples of these perennial organizational problems include:

- *Irrational politics.* When ongoing internecine warfare hinders knowledge sharing between business units and teams, communities of practice tend to be right in the middle. Knowledge becomes a political football between warring factions with different strategic visions or between ambitious managers with clashing career aspirations. In one organization, communities of practice were considered with suspicion by business units that were fighting for more independence and viewed them as a scheme of centralization; in another the central office suspected communities were a strategy by line managers to subvert corporate standards. In very political organizations, communities will easily fall prey to factionalism through internal conflicts that reflect the tensions of the organization.

- *Short-term focus on tangible outcomes.* When an organization lacks a compelling vision of what communities can accomplish in relation to strategic priorities, communities are forced to focus on achievements that can easily be included in formal evaluations, such as technology or documentation, even if members do not believe that these are the most important priorities. A community disorder such as documentism or mediocrity then is a response to myopic pressures from the organization.

- *Anti-learning culture.* An organizational culture may discourage learning, reflection, and knowledge sharing—for instance, by putting value exclusively on individual tasks and performance. Often, policies and infrastructure also discourage participation. In such organizations, communities of practice are easily marginalized. Their very existence is constantly questioned, and their effectiveness is seriously limited.

Communities alone cannot develop countermeasures to most organizational disorders. They need engagement from senior managers and others outside the community to manage political issues, set priorities, and fine-tune organizational systems. Communities generally welcome this kind of attention when it is clearly offered in the spirit of magnifying the opportunities and influence of members, not merely appropriating their knowledge and expertise for exploitation by the firm.

Rigidity and Agility

One risk of organizing knowledge into communities is rigidity, a kind of global dysfunction that occurs as a result of disorders at the level of core practices in the organization. A practice is like a scientific theory. It is built over time and gains value and momentum as it solves problems. As social studies of science have demonstrated, theories are very resilient to disconfirming data. Their proponents can construct all sorts of ways to explain exceptions. In fact, it is one way their theories become stronger. But "patching" a theory creates new problems, and as a theory begins to generate more problems than it solves, it progressively becomes a liability.[16] Conversely, the more a theory has been successful, the more difficult it is to recognize its obsolescence.

Similarly, communities of practice can be impervious to signs of change. When a practice is successful and a community tightly knit, members understandably become reluctant to give it up. Communities can amplify inertia as members reinforce each other's perceptions and aspirations. The potential for inertia is not just individual but collective. Moreover, as an organization develops a successful strategy, the communities that provide critical capabilities gain status. This very status among communities creates inertia. It makes it more difficult to change, to consider other perspectives, and to listen to other communities. The resulting rigidity is always a danger lurking behind a capability.[17]

Communities of practice can also be a remedy for rigidity, because the same dynamics can work both ways. Certainly, overcoming rigidity can be more difficult when inertia is a characteristic of enduring social structures. It can be a challenge to change your perspective when you have a whole community to confirm the way you are looking at a problem. The converse is also true, however. Communities create a potential for organized change far beyond the individual capacity to change. It is easier to change radically if you have a community going through the process with you. When people share a passion for something and are invested in each other, they can form a collective identity around the need for change that will motivate and facilitate individual transformations. In this regard, a healthy community with a dynamic sense of inquiry can overcome inertia perhaps better than any other mechanism. Communities can dig you in deeper or pull you out. It depends on their competency and quality as well as their relationships with their environment.

Managing Complexity

Finally, because communities of practice introduce a new level of complexity, they can also test the limits of organizations. Of course, this complexity is a great resource. A constellation of communities in charge of focused knowledge domains increases an organization's capacity to respond to the demands of a complex world economy. It enables firms to track subtle changes and trends and to absorb information faster. Having the voice of practitioners at the table makes it easier to include multiple perspectives—customers, competitors, suppliers, and strategic partners. The complexity of multiple interrelated practices provides the "requisite" variety to remain adaptable and agile.[18]

Still, the new complexity presents a managerial challenge. There is something fundamentally unruly about a constellation of communities of practice. Communities are not just one more thing for managers to deal with, understand, and integrate with other concerns. They contribute to organizational complexity more than other approaches to knowledge because they create multiple centers of power based on knowledge. Less centrality of power entails more diversity and more stakeholders in forming the direction of the company—thus increased complexity in decision making. Business strategy has to become the consensus of a more disparate group of people. Such a knowledge organization is inherently more complex to manage than a traditional organization.

Executives have to understand that community initiatives invite this greater level of complexity. They must be careful about the management capability their organization actually has or can develop to handle complexity. They need to pace their progress so they don't run ahead of their capacity to integrate the voice of communities in the organization. But they should also understand that not all of this complexity must become part of the formal organization. One firm, for instance, tried to incorporate geography, community, and team multimembership into the formal system and ended up with such a complex design that it collapsed under its own weight; their restructuring project had to be abandoned. Companies have to resist two temptations: to shy away from this new complexity and revert to traditional control processes now applied to communities; or instead, to bring all this complexity into the formal system. Rather, they must allow the complexity of the informal to mesh with a manageable formal system.

Conclusion

THERE IS NO sure-fire protection from the disorders described in this chapter. In fact, the traditional means of preventing variability—highly bureaucratic structures and procedures—are likely to backfire with communities. There is something inherently uncontrollable about the informal, and therefore it presents an unavoidable risk of dysfunctional behaviors. To allow communities to flourish, it is more important to pay constant attention and fine-tune the process as it evolves. This will require leadership at multiple levels to address issues of community development, to foster the integration of an effective knowledge system, and to promote a compelling vision of the knowledge organization. It takes leadership inside communities to keep questioning the status quo, see what is possible in a domain, connect the people who care about it, and help develop an effective practice together. It takes leadership at the boundaries of communities so they remain open to the outside. Finally, it takes organizational leadership to provide an environment that is both supportive and challenging.

The value of the personal investment and sense of ownership that comes with forming a community around a significant domain will usually outweigh risks such as fragmentation, rigidity, or unruly complexity. The depth of knowledge that results compensates for the boundaries that inevitably arise. Communities can be instruments of agility in the face of change just as they can be sources of inertia. They present a complex management challenge, but the strategic capabilities they develop are worth the effort. Being aware of the risks they carry will increase the likelihood of a productive relationship among an organization, the communities that steward the knowledge it needs, and the members of these communities.

Measuring and Managing
Value Creation

McKinsey & Company has benefited from active and influential communities of practice for about as long as anyone—going back to the early 1980s, before the terms "knowledge economy" or "learning organization" became buzzwords. The firm began by launching several "practice centers" in areas where its leaders were convinced they were reinventing the wheel or missing opportunities to combine expertise across the growing number of globally dispersed offices. Since then, these "practices" (over thirty of them now) have been recognized by the firm's leaders, members, and clients as pillars of the firm's value proposition. Practices are self-governing groups of practitioners who dedicate part of their discretionary time to contribute to the stewardship of their shared area of expertise. They consist of a small core group of practice leaders, a broader band of active participants who engage in practice-related initiatives, and a wide network of consultants who have an interest in the area. The leaders of these practices are a group of senior consultants, not full-time coordinators, who agree to put their reputation on the line to push the practice forward.

McKinsey was quick to recognize the importance of giving internal practice leaders the leeway to determine their own learning agendas, fund their own projects, and organize conferences and other mechanisms for recruiting and developing members. In fact, except for a small number of full- or part-time practice staff, most of the time and energy that McKinsey consultants devote to practice activities is voluntary. This is noteworthy given that nearly all McKinsey's 6000-plus consultants are affiliated with at least one practice. Members (from senior directors to first-year associates) decide whether or not to participate in projects or attend conferences, weighed against other options to use precious discretionary time in activities related to practice development, professional growth, or client service.

McKinsey practice staff members integrate measures and management methods in their work. The Organization Practice, for example, is one of the most widespread in the firm, and its leadership group funds several practice staff members (often, former consultants who seek a less taxing work and travel schedule). These people systematically collect various kinds of data on practice activities while they answer requests from far-flung teams around the world. They record how often documents are requested from their Web site and which are "best-sellers." They also take note of the types of problems that client engagement teams are working on—restructuring a board of directors, for instance, or winning the "war for talent." They conduct interviews with members of consulting teams who have used practice resources to find out what the impact has been and to identify gaps or priorities. They are careful about tracking the time they spend helping engagement teams because they are funded largely through internal fund transfers from teams who pay for practice assistance. The practice's reputation is such that as a matter of course, teams call practice coordinators or tap into the Web site from all over the world to "get up to speed" on topics the practice is stewarding.

McKinsey's overall investment in its practices is huge—hundreds of millions of dollars per year. These investments include a corps of full-time coordinators, a world-class, Web-based knowledge repository and support staff, local and worldwide conferences, various practice-research efforts on emerging topics (for instance, Jon Katzenbach's best-selling books on teams), and, most significant, the opportunity costs of the professionals' time for participating. But the firm does not rely on practice statistics or funding transfers alone to account for its investments in these activities. Rather, over the last two decades, McKinsey has developed an approach to managing practice activities that works at multiple levels in concert.

Much of the "measurement and management" of practice activity is actually handled at the level of individual community members. This happens via the mental calculations of McKinsey's achievement-oriented consultants, who constantly ask themselves: "What can I do today that will contribute most to getting results or building capacity?" This performance ethic pervades the firm and provides a crucial foundation for the firm's practice-management efforts. Every consultant goes through an extremely rigorous biannual, 360-degree appraisal that determines bonuses and promotions. Members who lead specific practice-building initiatives include this work in their performance review. These initiatives are assessed in terms of the value that practice knowledge has contributed to client projects. Consultants' contributions to clients, the firm, and to colleagues are therefore highly visible, and this transparency provides a solid basis for measuring and managing the communities in which they participate.

At the level of the practice itself, practice leaders take the lead to review the strategy of the practice and what it has accomplished. Practice leaders and staff interview members of consulting teams to find out how the practice has created value for clients. They look for stories that tell how research has been applied to solve a client problem or how practice qualifications—such as research, client experience, and practitioner expertise—helped to persuade a client to engage the firm. They also review how well the practice is serving its members—in terms of their opportunities to develop expertise in areas of interest, build their professional network and reputation, and develop client relationships.

More recently, the firm has moved to develop organization-level measurement and management methods. McKinsey relied for many years on members and practice leaders to steward practice resources on their own, but as practices grew in value and strategic importance, it backed this up with methods that operated at a broader level. In the mid-1990s, the new managing director and the executive group responsible for overseeing McKinsey's practice activities decided that a more rigorous firmwide assessment approach was needed. There was much at stake. McKinsey's premium brand and distinctive ability to help clients increasingly depended on having deep expertise in specific topic areas. Meanwhile, the staff and travel costs devoted to practice development worldwide were significant and growing. Their sense was that not all practices were equally good stewards of their domains and that there was much to learn about the unique challenges of managing a practice successfully. They therefore launched an effort to help practice leaders evaluate their communities on a number of performance criteria, such as: Were they working with leading companies? Were they working on leading-edge topics? Were they attracting the participation of talented practitioners—and helping them to grow professionally? They launched a parallel effort to document practice-development expenses more carefully so these could be reviewed along with practice accomplishments.

The study found that practices fell into two self-reproducing patterns, as illustrated in figure 8-1. The more effective practices produced a high-energy cycle. They had high aspirations, which led to higher effectiveness, which led to higher recognition in the firm, which attracted people with high commitment. The less effective practices were caught in a low-energy cycle. The committee set about finding ways to enable more practices to achieve a high-energy cycle. The study included several recommendations to practices: ask leaders to make a substantial commitment of time and effort (usually a minimum of 20 percent of their time), set an agenda with high aspirations, start significant practice-development initiatives, and strengthen linkages with client service teams.

The firm manages its portfolio of practices largely by applying its standard appraisal process to practice leaders. This rigorous process provides the basis for in-depth discussions with the practice leader (or core group of leaders) responsible for each community. The oversight committee addresses deficiencies and recognizes achievements in discussions with practice leaders. If a leader is not able to develop the community as expected, they will

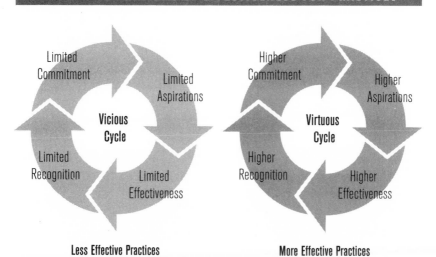

FIGURE 8-1   TWO PATTERNS OF EFFECTIVENESS FOR PRACTICES

Limited Commitment

Limited Aspirations

Vicious Cycle

Limited Recognition

Limited Effectiveness

Higher Commitment

Higher Aspirations

Virtuous Cycle

Higher Recognition

Higher Effectiveness

Less Effective Practices   **More Effective Practices**

Source: N. Foote, "Linking Communities of Practice and Performance" (paper presented at the Communities of Practice Conference, San Diego, CA, April 2000).

ask him or her to step down (after discussing this decision directly with the leader and making any appropriate attempts to support his or her efforts).

McKinsey's entire multilevel apparatus of measurement and management methods is based on a foundation of core operating values that have been held sacrosanct since the firm's founding—dedication to client service, professional development, and "building a great firm." These values serve as the basis for a practice-management approach that assumes that practice leaders will gladly scrutinize themselves and their practice on its ability to create value for clients, members, and the firm itself. If a community is not performing well, practice leaders in this culture expect to explain and address gaps—for example, why research expenditures have not garnered client interest, or why participation in practice conferences is falling off. Ultimately, McKinsey's success at measuring and managing communities of practice is due largely to its culture, where it is taken for granted that there is a strong causal link between knowledge and performance, and where leaders insist on managing this relationship at a world-class level.

The Knowledge System

ORGANIZATIONS THAT WANT communities to become a pervasive, integrated, and influential force for learning and innovation will need to measure and manage them.[1] Communities of practice create value by stewarding highly prized knowledge resources. It is in the best interests of both community members and managers to see that the value of this stewardship is fully realized and widely recognized.

Yet, many have argued that knowledge resources—like the communities that steward them—can't be measured and managed. And given what we know about the nature of knowledge—that it is tacit, dynamic, socially distributed, and realized through human acts—they're partly right.[2] As we've said before, you can't treat knowledge effectively as if it were a thing or a piece of property. But you can measure and manage the "knowledge system" through which it flows and creates value.

Every organization has a knowledge system, although it is generally not recognized or explicitly managed. A knowledge system includes two highly interdependent processes by which knowledge is produced and applied. The knowledge-development process takes inchoate knowledge assets—such as undeveloped ideas, latent skills, or isolated techniques—and converts these into visible, accessible knowledge resources. These resources are then applied in business processes to deliver products and services to customers. The application process, in turn, generates new problems, ideas, and innovative approaches that can be developed into knowledge resources.

"Managing knowledge" in this context means managing the knowledge-production and application processes throughout the knowledge system. This means coordinating the activities of a variety of players who help discover, diffuse, or apply knowledge—including teams, staff groups, research centers, communities, suppliers, customers, and other agents inside and outside the organization. Measurement activities support this management challenge by tracing and documenting the causal relationships between activities that produce and apply knowledge—for example, how a community translates a tentative idea into a new methodology that is used by teams to respond more quickly to customers. Without making these causal connections, you don't know whether community efforts have created value for teams. Communities of practice make it easier to measure and manage knowledge flows because practitioners track the entire process, from the learning and innovation activities where knowledge is generated to the business activities where knowledge is applied.

Measuring Value Creation

MANY FEAR THAT efforts to measure the value of knowledge will hurt more than help. Indeed, the risks of measures are well known—witness the distortions of behavior that result when teachers "teach to the test" or when a team focuses on an ill-conceived productivity target to the detriment of customer and profitability outcomes.

Nevertheless, we believe such measurement efforts are well worth the investment. Measures of value are instrumental for communities to gain visibility and influence, and to evaluate and guide their own development. Measures of communities' value legitimize their function in the organization, reinforce member participation, and provide a basis for prioritizing activities. Measures help communities translate the value of what they do for teams and business units into the *lingua franca* of the organization—bottom-line results. They support management processes—such as setting goals, reviewing accomplishments, and funding—that help to further integrate and institutionalize the role of communities in the organization. Finally, communities need measures to know how they are doing and to guide ongoing efforts to become more vibrant and effective.

How to Measure: Systematic Anecdotal Evidence

In recent years, a number of knowledge-measurement schemes have been proposed. Indicators such as patents, graduate degrees, training programs, and access to personal computers have all been used as elements of a measurement approach.[3] But to really understand the value of knowledge, you cannot merely count "things."[4] Static measures—such as participation rates, documents produced, or cycle times—only become useful in the context of stories that explain the causal links between them. Using our model, we would say that you have to go through the entire knowledge system, starting with the activities of communities of practice and following their effect through the application of knowledge resources in business processes, to create value for customers and other stakeholders. Our method relies on two complementary principles: demonstrate causality through stories and ensure systematicity through rigorous documentation.

Anecdotal Evidence: Telling the Story of Value

Stories are the best way to traverse the knowledge system in a way that explains the linkages between community activities, knowledge resources, and performance outcomes. Only a story can describe these complex causal relations while incorporating implicit contextual factors that may be crucial to appreciate but hard to codify or generalize.[5] Such stories depend on practitioners' involvement, because only practitioners can tell how the knowledge was put into action. The best way to assess the value of a community of practice, therefore, is by collecting stories.

In this context, the key elements of a good story describe how knowledge resources are produced and applied: What did the community do to convert a brainstorm or an isolated technique into a documented approach or proven standard? How were these resources applied through business processes to get results? The story thus consists of three main elements: (1) the initial knowledge-development activity to innovate, learn a skill, or solve a problem; (2) the knowledge resource generated by this activity—for example, a new insight, method, or relationship; and (3) how this resource was applied to create value. To make the story more complete as a measure of value, it helps to describe the initial problem and to explain what would have happened without the community.

At Granite Construction Incorporated, for example, a value-creation story begins by describing how a group of construction managers found that they were each working on their own form of project management manual. They started to hold weekly teleconferences to talk about common issues, pick the best from everyone's effort, and consolidate what they knew about project management. (See figure 8-2.) Their collective knowledge-development efforts produced new insights, improved project management guidelines, and developed stronger helping relationships among managers in various offices. These ideas, guidelines, and relationships were then applied by construction managers to improve project management, eliminate a lot of duplicate work, and even share workers and equipment. These outcomes helped them reduce costs and meet deadlines, but would never have happened without the formation of the community.

Good stories have a number of additional benefits, besides documenting how communities build, share, and apply knowledge assets. Stories provide recognition for their protagonists; they reinforce the importance of making one's practice visible in the organization; and they help build a culture that values innovation and knowledge sharing. Stories are a powerful component of any culture, and legitimizing the storytelling process encourages people to act out the stories they would like one day to tell.[6]

Systematicity

The solution to the conundrum of valuing communities of practice is to gather anecdotal evidence systematically. You can't just collect certain stories, perhaps the most compelling or available ones, because isolated events can be unrepresentative.[7] A systematic effort captures the diversity and range of community activities. Whenever possible, it also incorporates quantitative indicators from surveys and reports to flesh out the story and corroborate it with established measures.[8] This systematicity can go bottom-up, starting with the variety of activities that communities engage in. It can also be top-down, focusing on the range of possible values a community can be expected to deliver.

- *Bottom-up systematicity.* Bottom-up systematicity starts at the community level by identifying all activities. It attempts to

---

FIGURE 8-2   CAUSALITY THROUGH A VALUE-CREATION STORY

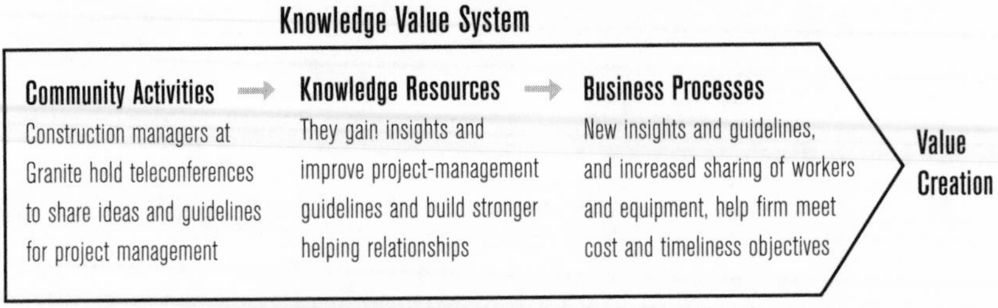

Knowledge Value System

Community Activities	→	Knowledge Resources	→	Business Processes	
Construction managers at Granite hold teleconferences to share ideas and guidelines for project management		They gain insights and improve project-management guidelines and build stronger helping relationships		New insights and guidelines, and increased sharing of workers and equipment, help firm meet cost and timeliness objectives	Value Creation

Template for building value-creation stories:
(a) What did the community do?
(b) What knowledge resources did they produce?
(c) How were those applied to get results?

---

discover the full value of community activities by following them rigorously through the knowledge system processes to understand their effect. The advantage of this method is that it may uncover value that was not predicted or even intended— for example, a partnership with another firm that increased access to new markets. The risk is that it will not address important business outcomes because extant communities have not decided to focus on them.

- *Top-down systematicity.* Top-down systematicity begins at the business-strategy or business-process level. It starts by identifying what knowledge the business needs in order to compete and then asks what communities are doing to help the firm build, share, and apply this knowledge. The risk of this method is that the measures will be used as drivers of community activities, even if members are not convinced of their intrinsic interest or value.

Bottom-up and top-down systematicity are not mutually exclusive approaches to measurement. Rather, they are two methods that complement each other to provide a comprehensive assessment of whether community activities are delivering sufficient value and whether the right value is being created.

A growing number of firms are using stories to document the value created by communities and to guide community-development efforts.

- At Shell, managers and community leaders use stories to justify investments in community initiatives. Community coordinators, sometimes accompanied by an external expert, conduct a series of interviews with a sample of community members to collect stories that document the causal links between community activities, knowledge resources, and value. These stories are then combined into an overall picture that provides a cost-benefit calculation of the value of communities to the business.

- An IT consulting firm organized an annual competition to identify the best stories. One year, by combining the stories they received, they were able to demonstrate savings of $5 million to $7 million and additional revenues of more than $13 million that could be attributed to participation in communities.

These firms and others have found that evidence of communities' value has to be anecdotal because stories are needed to explain causal relationships and to describe the contextual factors that must be taken into account. However, these stories must be collected systematically, because one story may not be representative of all activities or all possible outcomes. Hence the tongue-in-cheek but descriptive term "systematic anecdotal evidence."[9]

Steps in a Measurement Process

Measurement is costly. Therefore, it is worth considering carefully what the organization needs to learn from measures and where to focus scarce time and resources to collect and analyze them. The following considerations frame an approach for developing a measurement system that provides the information needed at an appropriate cost.

1. *For whom and for what purpose.* Measuring is always for some-
   body, and different people have different measurement requirements in terms of detail, completeness, frequency, and format.
   First, you need to identify the constituencies for measurements
   and then find out their requirements. Basic questions include:
   Who needs to know? What do they need to know? Why do they
   need to know it?

   Senior managers are most interested in the total return on
   investment for the company and the communities' contribution
   to strategic goals—for example, the ability of a construction
   firm to win highly profitable design-build contracts. Managers
   of projects, cross-functional teams, and business units want to
   know how communities have helped them achieve their goals in
   terms such as sales, customer satisfaction, cycle time, and cost.
   Community leaders want to know which community activities
   have been most valuable to members and stakeholders.

   It is impractical and too expensive to measure knowledge
   resources as comprehensively as companies account for physical or financial assets. One way to gauge the level of measurement needed is to identify how much value will justify community investments from the perspectives of key constituents.
   Senior managers, for example, may simply need to know that
   the annual time and travel expenses for running a community
   on deep-water drilling—about $500,000—are more than justi-
   fied by the benefits generated by the community—such as
   avoiding a dry well, which saves many millions of dollars. This
   does not mean that the community's value is limited to this
   quantifiable business outcome. In fact, its intangible contributions may be key to the company's ability to analyze deposits
   more accurately and therefore even more valuable in the long
   term. But these intangibles are trickier to measure (although
   surveys, social network analyses, and interviews all work well),
   and are often unnecessary to document. If the tangible benefits—such as new technologies or methods that save time and
   money—by themselves justify the community investment, then

all the intangibles of community participation—such as increased trust and expertise—can be viewed as bonus benefits that need not be measured in detail.

2. *What to collect and how.* The next step involves identifying the quantity and types of causal stories and related statistics that are needed to show how community activities, knowledge resources, and business value are related. It helps to have an interview protocol that specifies which questions to ask—and of whom—in order to document causal stories that link community activities to results. The protocol should also specify types of quantitative data to collect, such as participation rates, the number of responses in online discussion threads, how often documents are requested, as well as relevant business results. A community coordinator, for example, can use such data to see which discussion topics or speakers have been most useful for members, and which community activities have contributed the most to business performance. At Xerox, they collected statistics related to each of the elements of a good causal story and set goals related to community activities, knowledge assets, and performance outcomes. (See box 8-1.)

   As a supplement to an interview protocol, SafeCities, an intergovernmental community on public safety, developed a survey instrument that assessed strategic capabilities of members from eleven cities nationwide. The instrument behaviorally described the elements of expertise associated with the strategic capabilities (such as "building a local coalition" or "interrupting sources of illegal guns"), each of which was known to reduce gun violence—their bottom-line objective. This survey was distributed among members in various cities to assess the extent to which community participation had helped them learn to implement these strategies. Beyond its value as a measurement tool, the survey helped community members become more conscious of their learning objectives and specify more concretely who had what types of expertise to share. (Collecting such data—especially the causal stories and evidence of the

BOX 8-1 THREE LEVELS OF MEASUREMENT

THE COPIER REPAIR TECHNICIANS at Xerox use quantitative measures to account for the three main elements of a good "cause-and-effect" story, including community activities (sharing tips via the knowledge base), knowledge resources (the number of tips and the time to validation), and performance outcomes (reduced cost of repairs), as illustrated in the table. The measures of performance outcomes are derived by aggregating the value of hundreds of stories collected from practitioners. These measures help the community set goals as well as track progress.[10] (See table 8-1.)

TABLE 8-1 COMMUNITY GOALS AND MEASURES AT XEROX

	MEASURES	GOALS
Community Activities	Number of users connected	100 percent of population
	Percentage of users updating weekly	80 percent of population
Knowledge Assets	Number of solutions submitted by country	Tracking only, no target
	Number of days to validate solutions	80 percent validated in twenty-one days
Performance Outcomes	Number of customer problems resolved	300,000
	Percentage of reduction in service hours	5 percent
	Percentage of reduction in parts dollars	5 percent
	Total dollars saved in cost of service and support	$11.2 million

Source: T. M. Ruddy and R. Cheslow, "Eureka II" (presentation at the Communities of Practice Conference, San Diego, CA, April 2000). Copyright: Xerox Corporation.

value produced—often requires some digging on the part of the community's coordinator, as described in box 8-2.)

3. *How to raise awareness about measurement.* Useful knowledge measures are uniquely dependent on causal stories and hence

BOX 8-2 DIGGING FOR AWARENESS: INTERVIEWING TECHNIQUES

BECAUSE THE VALUE of community participation is often invisible, interviewing community members to collect stories takes some digging. You are not just asking people about what they already know, as in a survey. When first asked, community members often have trouble identifying the value they received from the community. The interviews themselves help raise their awareness. Interviews jog members' memories of problems they uncovered and resolved together, hot topics they discussed, or meetings and conferences they held. By asking who else they told about an idea or a tool, or where else it was applied, the interview helps them think about the social life of the idea or information beyond their own use of it. Community members often have trouble calculating the value of an idea or tool. Discussing what they would have done without it often helps them identify the incremental value.

To facilitate this discussion, the interviewer needs to know about the community's history, the ways people participate, and the issues they have raised. Community coordinators are ideally suited to conduct interviews because they have participated in many of the activities and know the players. However, the coordinator can also be too involved to see things clearly. It is often a good idea to combine a community coordinator and a specialist who is skilled in exploratory interviewing techniques and case-study research.

---

particularly dependent on practitioners who can tell them. Measuring the value of knowledge, therefore, is not only about collecting data, but also about creating a culture where practitioners understand the importance of contributing to the measurement process and take the time to do it. An overworked engineer or consultant has little patience for administrative overhead tasks, yet helping a coordinator document the value of the community is part of what it means to steward a practice; it is part of their commitment to the sustainability of the community. It helps, of course, if the measurement methods are simple and straightforward and if they recognize contributors.

4. *When and where to measure.* Once you know what to measure, you have to decide when and where to capture the evidence. Again, because measures consist largely of stories, this requires some careful thought. The data-collection process should define who collects the data, how frequently, what methods to use (such as interviews, surveys, and reports), and how to store and distribute it. Standardizing such a process reinforces the community's commitment to measurement and sets expectations for contributing to the effort—for example, by asking members to document value stories when they occur or to complete an annual survey. Coordinators often play a key role in shepherding the measurement process—helping members document stories, consolidating survey results, and so on.

5. *How to combine the data into an overall picture.* Ultimately, the causal stories and additional data should be aggregated to summarize the total value of community initiatives, given the investments made. For example, if the community invested in a knowledge repository to serve globally dispersed teams, then a collection of stories and data on use of the repository should be collected to describe and explain its overall impact. The stories and quantitative indicators both gain value when combined to paint an overall picture that links community activities to value created. (Shell communities and sponsors used a conservative method for calculating the value of community activities, as described in box 8-3.)

As the value of knowledge assets has become more salient in recent years, organizations have tried to measure knowledge in various ways, with limited success. They often miss the mark because they treat knowledge too much like a conventional asset with a specific and stable market value. Knowledge resources are protean by comparison, and highly dynamic. The best way to measure the value of knowledge is to see how it affects business processes—by solving a problem that saves costs, for example, or by producing information that closes a sale.

Because the value of knowledge is so dynamic and context-dependent, communities of practice—despite their perceived informality—are

BOX 8-3 CALCULATING ROI

SOMETIMES SENIOR MANAGERS and team leaders want a direct calculation of the return on investment in communities. It is a good idea to underestimate the value—intentionally and visibly—while overestimating the costs. When people approximate a numeric value, such as time saved, cost avoided, or additional revenue, we ask how much of that value they can attribute directly to their participation in the community. What are the chances that value would have been realized anyway? Then we ask how certain they are about that number. When reporting these results, we multiply the estimated value by the percentage attributable to the community and by the certainty expressed (also as a percentage).

numeric value * share of community * degree of certainty = reported savings

So, a $2 million savings, half of which the person estimates came from participating in the community, where they feel 80 percent confident in their estimate, would translate to:

$2M * 50% * 80% = $800,000

When calculating the costs of the community, we take all direct costs and add to them an estimate of average indirect costs. We are as generous in our cost estimates as we are conservative in our claims of value added.

Such conservative calculations will generally produce a very positive ROI for a healthy community. But being carefully and visibly conservative helps skeptics and finance people trust that you are not inflating the value of the community.

---

uniquely capable of providing a truly rigorous measure of it. Practitioners are in the best position to explain how knowledge is produced and applied to get results—because they are the ones doing it. They can tell you, for example, how a monthly teleconference of IT sales consultants led to the development of a pricing template, and how this has been applied to increase customer satisfaction and sales profitability. Ultimately, communities' collective measurement efforts in various domains enable the organization to assess the effectiveness of its entire knowledge system. Communities themselves benefit by telling their stories because these measures help to prioritize community activities, recognize members, and reinforce the community's legitimacy.

Managing the Knowledge System

THE KEY TO MANAGING a knowledge system is to link the processes that develop and apply knowledge to create value. Communities provide a unique point of leverage for managing the knowledge system, just as they do for measuring it. They are organized by knowledge domains, and they have direct responsibility for managing the knowledge resources associated with those domains. Communities thus provide a focal point for addressing basic questions associated with managing knowledge resources:

- How effectively has knowledge been developed and applied to support teams and business units?
- Are knowledge-development priorities aligned with the business strategy?
- Are teams and business units taking full advantage of knowledge resources, and have opportunities to capture and consolidate knowledge across units been fully realized?

These questions should, of course, also be asked by project and operational teams, staff groups, research centers, and other units throughout the organization. But communities can address these questions most effectively because they are organized around knowledge domains, not products or markets. Communities can identify specific opportunities, for example, in how teams apply particular methods based on their knowledge of methods used across teams. Communities can also provide a point of focus for accelerating the diffusion of best practices across business unit boundaries. If a particular business unit resists sharing its expertise with others, for example, the community can influence business unit practitioners and managers through direct appeals, or indirectly by asking senior managers to intervene.

When planning how to manage the value of knowledge resources, it is important to consider management as a set of functions managed by various players, not only managers. These functions include setting goals, managing performance, and funding. Community members act in partnership with formal team or business unit managers to manage the value of knowledge resources. Both parties negotiate to what extent these management tasks should be managed *inside* the community by its leaders and members or *outside* by business unit or corporate managers (or collaboratively, by both). The optimal balance of decision-making responsibility depends on the task itself—for example, setting goals or allocating funds. It is also influenced by the culture of the organization and of the community. For example, communities made up largely of autonomous professionals—such as scientists, software engineers, and management consultants—often insist on high levels of self-governance. Companies differ in their approaches, but community-based initiatives are not likely to thrive unless the balance of inside-outside decision making is determined through an open, good-faith negotiation between executive and community leaders. Of course, the balance of management responsibility may shift over time as the community matures, or if it loses competence and credibility.

There are several contingencies that influence how to apply the management approaches described here. Firms such as McKinsey that have established a rigorous and credible measurement system are more capable of managing community activities and outcomes. Communities that control more resources or are more formally established or strategic are managed more closely than ad hoc or informal communities. Finally, management approaches should be matched to the culture of the organization and to the developmental stages and requirements of specific communities.

Setting Goals

Goal setting, like performance management and funding, can focus on one or more elements of the knowledge system.

- *Community.* The organization invests in the community per se—defined by indicators such as the number of active members or types of activities that it coordinates—and the community takes responsibility for producing knowledge that creates value.

- *Knowledge resources.* The organization invests in community initiatives or projects to produce specific knowledge assets—such as a best-practice database—and organization leaders assume responsibility for making sure that these initiatives pay off.

- *Business value.* Communities are given value-creation goals (for example, to increase large-customer sales by 20 percent or to decrease packaging costs by $2 million); the community takes responsibility for producing useful resources and connecting with operating units to achieve results.

The first issue is to determine what goals to set and in what terms—community activities, knowledge resources, or business results, or some combination of these. Further issues include *how* goals should be set (for example, during annual reviews or as ad hoc, voluntary updates) and *who* will set the goals and with what input and negotiation. Community members are in the best position to know what capability targets are feasible with regard to skills, product and system innovations, and knowledge bases.

Community leaders partner with business unit leaders to determine which capability targets are priorities—both short- and long-term—for business unit performance. For example, at DaimlerChrysler, communities in the Chrysler Division set specific objectives each year to build up their knowledge base. In DaimlerChrysler's locomotive division, an aerodynamics community identified four key problems for the community to solve during its first year in operation. At McKinsey, practice leaders negotiate with client service teams (CSTs) to determine which types of knowledge and skills may be most useful to the CST's work with a major client. The practice leaders may not always agree with CST priorities, but they pay close attention to them because the CSTs ultimately determine which new concepts and methodologies will be applied in client work.

Managing Performance

Performance management issues include who takes responsibility for appraising the performance of the community and for addressing gaps or providing recognition for achievements. For example, at Daimler-Chrysler the "executive Tech Clubs" (consisting of platform engineering managers) are responsible for reviewing the results of engineering Tech Clubs—with special emphasis on knowledge assets such as the number of completed sections in the EBoK. These executives provide feedback and guidance to individual Tech Clubs based on their results. Of course, member input is crucial for determining what the community has done, could do, and would like to do in response to the assessment. Hence, it is particularly important that members understand executives' expectations and get sufficient support to meet them—or alternatively, renegotiate them.

The McKinsey story at the beginning of this chapter describes how the firm manages the performance of its communities at several levels simultaneously. It encourages active participation and high-quality contributions by individuals through its rigorous appraisal system. It reviews the success of specially funded projects through the oversight of community leaders. And it manages communities as a whole primarily through the appraisals of these leaders, who are responsible for setting the learning agenda and ensuring that communities create value for teams commensurate with the practice-development investments they have made.

At DaimlerChrysler, the Tech Clubs have matured to the point that engineers provide input on the appraisals of peers in the community, and this input influences their promotion in technical areas. Daimler-Chrysler and the World Bank have also adopted appraisal systems that explicitly recognize executives' support for building and sharing knowledge assets. These appraisal innovations were controversial at first, but they sent a message to members that senior leaders were serious about their commitment to building the knowledge organization.

Rewards depend to a great extent on the cultural norms in an organization or group. For example, at McKinsey's annual "Practice

Olympics," practice-development teams from various communities (as well as yet-unaffiliated teams) present their findings about new analysis methods or client solutions. The teams with the top presentations are invited to present their work before senior directors, who determine the winners. All the presenters are considered winners, however. Participation in the finals competition (at a luxury resort) and the attention from peers and senior directors is a significant reward in itself. The competition encourages participation in practice-development activities, fosters connections between innovative individuals and groups, and reinforces the mix of collaboration and competition that characterizes the firm. This celebration of knowledge contributions at a high-profile competition, although it might breed destructive competition in other organizations, works very well at McKinsey, where it reinforces values of individual and team performance, collaboration, and contributing to the firm's knowledge base.

Rewarding "voluntary" behavior presents a dilemma: How do we encourage behavior through extrinsic means when the intrinsic motivation for such behavior is considered a matter of pride and identity? People often value the satisfaction derived from giving for reasons of professional affiliation or commitment to a larger cause, not because they are rewarded with a "carrot." Xerox technicians, for example, were put off by a proposal to create small financial incentives for contributing to the Eureka knowledge base. They told Xerox managers, "This is what gives us meaning; don't try to pay us for it. That would cheapen the whole thing." The real reward for contributing a tip to the Eureka system is to have your name posted as the author of the tip—to have your name "in lights" before thousands of your peers. At their annual conference, technicians will stop and thank or congratulate someone they recognize as the author of a tip they have used or seen on the system.[11] While it is worth exploring ways to reward knowledge as well as productivity contributions, recognition by peers, not financial rewards, is the primary motivator for community participation.[12] However, people who contribute regularly to a community often want that contribution to be recognized by the organization. Incorporating community contributions into performance reviews is a way of acknowledging the community's importance and "making it count" in the overall scheme of things in the organization.

Funding

Funding is crucial to allow community members to dedicate time to learning and innovation activities.[13] Such investments also make a strong symbolic statement about the organization's commitment to its knowledge initiative. The most common funding approaches focus at three different levels:

- *Individual participation.* This includes time and travel for members to participate in community activities. McKinsey consultants are expected to use discretionary nonclient time for professional growth or practice-development activities. At Hill's Pet Nutrition's Richmond Plant, line technicians have the option on Friday afternoons (while still on the clock) to join regular community sessions regarding topics such as packaging or food processing. IBM provides dedicated funds for core group members to participate on a regular basis, with a commitment of time that ranges between 5 and 20 percent.

- *Budgets for projects.* The organization may choose to fund communities partly or fully through specific projects that they lead. Some organizations have a pot of money that communities can access when they need to fund specific projects. At McKinsey, communities can apply for such funds by writing a formal proposal, and considerable prestige is associated with such specially funded projects. The World Bank uses projects as the primary way to fund communities. Communities use a portion of the project funds to cover their infrastructure costs. As a primary funding mechanism, this approach is reliable only when sponsors and community leaders agree on criteria and minimize the extent to which politics influence funding decisions.

- *Blanket funding for community infrastructure.* Some firms choose to provide blanket funding that covers a variety of community activities. Most common is funding for community coordinators. Depending on the community's size and level of activity, organizations generally fund 20 to 100 percent of the coordinator's time so he or she can focus attention on the development of the community and its practice.

Many organizations distinguish between more formal, well-funded communities with dedicated staff (called "practices" at McKinsey) and emergent, informal communities (called "special interest groups" at an IT consulting firm) that receive no dedicated funds. The funded communities are accountable for knowledge products or services, while unfunded communities get less scrutiny regarding the value they generate.

The source of funding is also significant. In some cases, it makes sense to fund community development and coordinator roles at the corporate level. This is appropriate, for example, when the community initiative is still establishing its legitimacy, or when communities span multiple business units and their value will show up at the corporate level but not predictably in any given business unit. Over time, it is good to have business units recognize the business value of communities by contributing some of the funding.

Conclusion

MEASURING AND MANAGING communities become more important as they become prevalent, gain influence, and garner control over resources in the organization. Although measurement and management methods may be more intuitive and ad hoc in the early stages of a community-based knowledge initiative, they become more rigorous over time as investments increase. Even in the early phases, companies have found that measures reinforce the support of executive sponsors and accelerate the legitimacy of communities in the eyes of teams, business units, and members.

The management functions described here—including measures, goal setting, performance management, and funding—are not unfamiliar, and yet there are nuances involved when learning to apply them to foster community health and value. For each task, executives and communities need to determine at what level to focus and negotiate the right balance of inside-outside responsibility. A solid measurement system enables executive and community leaders to negotiate more explicit, fact-based agreements on how to share management responsibilities.

Communities cannot be measured and managed in conventional ways. Traditional methods are not likely to appreciate the creativity, sharing, and self-initiative that are the core elements of how a community creates value. Still, we have only begun to understand the challenges of measuring and managing these informal phenomena in organizations. There are many pitfalls along the way—including the dangers of both under- and overmanagement. We cannot treat knowledge resources as if they were simple quantities, for example, nor can we treat them as too complex or tacit to measure at all. We cannot unilaterally prescribe community goals and activities, nor can we ignore communities that control a significant budget yet fail to meet expectations.

The question, we argue, is not *whether* to measure and manage communities, but *how*. This is the point of our emphasis on "cultivating" communities. Communities need attention—from inside and outside—to reach their potential. We believe that unless communities become integrated into the management context—and this means both managing them and letting them manage—then they will not gain the competence, legitimacy, and influence that they could achieve. We argue here, of course, that the very notion of "management" must be reframed to include both informal and formal phenomena. But how do you effectively combine informal elements such as passion, trust, and instinct with the traditional management emphasis on effort, focus, and efficiency? Developing communities intentionally and systematically poses this challenge more explicitly and concretely than ever before—and promises many rewards to those who can learn to address it successfully.

nine

Community-Based
Knowledge Initiatives

T HE ATRIUM OF THE WORLD BANK IN WASHINGTON, D.C., *is a vast and stately space of glass, steel, and concrete. The architectural grandeur befits a major financial institution—no sign anywhere of a knowledge initiative. But if you happen to visit on the day of a "knowledge fair," you will see something quite different. Between pillars, you will find booths run by the Bank's communities of practice. What these booths display are not financial spreadsheets, but information about the community's knowledge of development issues and the projects they are pursuing: biodiversity, information systems in agriculture, gender in rural development, inequality and socioeconomic performance, and land policy and administration. The brouhaha of animated conversations with visitors adds a buzz to the decorum of the place. Some booths attract your attention with a catchy exhibit. There is a papier-mâché pig on a pedestal. Stop by, look at the displays, and ask questions of the members running the booths. They will be glad to discuss their latest achievements, describe their upcoming initiatives, and hear what you have to say. Perhaps, from the encounter of your knowledge and theirs, a new idea will take flight.*

The atrium is a perfect location for a knowledge fair. You can't miss it. It is for everyone to see—visitors as well as employees scurrying to their offices. At first, there was some resistance to using this dignified area for something seemingly as disorderly as a fair, but the support team did not let this initial reticence get in the way. Since the success of their first attempt in the spring of 1998, knowledge fairs have become a regular addition to important events at the Bank, including the annual meeting attended by 12,000 visitors and dignitaries from around the world. Many visitors as well as employees have commented that this was their first opportunity to get a comprehensive look at the Bank's many projects. They had learned more at the fair than through the plethora of publications and formal presentations.

Indeed, a fair presents an ideal opportunity for people from different communities to interact, exchange views, and gain a concrete awareness of what others are doing. Over time, the booths have become quite sophisticated. Good ideas have spread from one booth to another. Many communities have become experts at describing their practice in understandable ways. These knowledge fairs have been instrumental in establishing the key role of knowledge and communities of practice. They help to reinforce the Bank's commitment to communities and to the knowledge initiative while helping individual communities communicate the value of their knowledge assets.

This highly visible sign of a community-based knowledge initiative was a substantial achievement. The support team had worked extremely hard to convince traditional bankers of the importance of managing knowledge, not just money, and even worse, of using communities to do so. It turned out to be a real struggle. However, many were eventually persuaded by simple but telling stories from the field that revealed real problems and pointed to possible solutions. For example, a health worker in Kamana, Zambia, was confronted with serious problems diagnosing and treating malaria. Zambia is one of the poorest countries in Africa and Kamana is a remote city, 600 kilometers from the capital. Yet, the health worker had been able to get crucial information from the Web site of the Centers for Disease Control in Atlanta. This story showed clearly the potential of information technology to make knowledge accessible, even to people in the remotest areas of the world. The Bank's wealth of development knowledge, however, was not organized in a way that was accessible to a health worker in Zambia. That story and others like it did what neither financial statistics nor logical reasoning alone could do: help executives understand what was needed and commit to an investment of millions of dollars to launch a knowledge initiative.

The knowledge initiative had received its official blessing in 1996, when the Bank's president declared at their annual meeting that the World Bank would become the "knowledge bank." The idea was to "eradicate poverty through knowledge." The Bank should become the place in the world to access knowledge about development—garnered from its own internal experience as well as that of partners, including governments, universities, foundations, and other nongovernmental organizations. By the summer of 1997, the support team (by now a director and five staff members) had thoroughly benchmarked leading organizations, surveyed internal practices, and developed plans to help sector- and country-based lines of business develop and share knowledge. A substantial budget was set aside for knowledge-management activities across the organization, and a sponsoring board was established to oversee the Bank's activities in the area.

By the fall of 1997, however, it became clear that an essential element was missing from the overall plan. Early initiatives had focused on the Bank's informational infrastructure. These included developing a classification system for types of knowledge resources in the Bank, establishing centralized help desks to respond to inquiries, and building a better technology platform to link members worldwide. But the support team discovered that this focus on collecting information had to be supplemented with a focus on connecting people.[1] The areas where the knowledge-sharing system worked best were those in which a group of practitioners interacted on a regular basis, with a tradition of sharing knowledge and collaborating to solve problems. A team leader from Yemen, for example, had contacted the education help desk because a client wanted to know how to design an information system for its education services. The help desk was able to plug into an existing community whose members decided that the most relevant experience was from Kenya. They gathered the documents and sent them to the team leader in Yemen, along with a set of comments on the strengths and weaknesses of the Kenyan approach. Within forty-eight hours, the team leader was sitting with the client discussing how to tackle the problem.

The support team started to focus on these informal groups. They found about twenty-five of them functioning across the organization, plus an unknown number of local ones. They decided that the best way to strengthen knowledge sharing at the Bank was to support these groups, which came to be known as "Thematic Groups" because they were focused on development themes such as community-based rural development, roads and highways, public health, urban upgrading, nutrition, or water resource management. In January 1998, a special executive board that was sponsoring the knowledge initiative decided to redirect a part of the budget and offer direct financial support to Thematic Groups who came forward with a plan of action. They invited thought leaders in emerging areas to form a Thematic Group if they could find constituencies of practitioners and clients who were interested in their domain of expertise. This approach helped to ensure the groups would have strategic value as well as member enthusiasm. This highly visible invitation for proposals elicited a groundswell of grassroots initiative by groups throughout the Bank. The initiative was further strengthened when the team organized its first knowledge fair. By the summer of 1998, more than one hundred Thematic Groups had come forward.

In early 1999, the executive board commissioned a task force of external experts to join its internal support team in conducting a systematic review of its early community efforts as preparation for making significant enhancements to its knowledge system. Based on these results, a number of changes were made, including coaching for community leaders, creating dedicated community-support functions, and systematizing the Web-based repositories and Web sites. The report concluded that Thematic Groups were the "heart and soul" of the initiative.

Design Principles for a Community-Based Knowledge Initiative

C ULTIVATING COMMUNITIES TAKES place in an organizational or interorganizational context. They are much influenced by context and achieve full value only when well integrated. The challenge of cultivating communities, therefore, is not only about organizing groups but also about transforming organizations. The point, after all, is not to launch communities for their own sake, but to build the organization's overall capacity to learn and innovate. An organizational context provides funding for community activities as well as challenging opportunities to apply new methods and expertise. It also provides a continuous stream of contacts with innovative suppliers and new recruits. But partnering with the organization cuts both ways. On the one hand, it magnifies a community's influence and increases opportunities for members. On the other hand, it introduces new requirements and constraints—such as policies that limit members' flexibility, systems that don't support knowledge-sharing activities, or managers who won't allocate time for innovation projects. The "aliveness" of a community, no matter how passionate and active its members, will be severely limited unless it finds ways to integrate itself with the surrounding organization.

The idea is to design organizational knowledge initiatives that leverage the inherent aliveness of communities, rather than trying to engineer or manufacture it from the outside in. Community-based knowledge initiatives are most likely to succeed when they build on the same design philosophy that operates at the community level. In both cases you are "designing for aliveness." At the community level, the design philosophy is about eliciting the passion and participation of members. At the organization level, it is about combining this passion with the resources and power of the organization to create value far beyond what a community could achieve otherwise. Therefore, it is no surprise that principles of aliveness at the organization level reflect those at the community level. Before describing how to run a community-based knowledge initiative, we briefly revisit the "principles of aliveness" articulated in chapter 3, this time to highlight their applicability to the organizational level. Organizational initiatives should be designed to evolve naturally, encourage new leaders, seek ambitious value objectives, choreograph formal and informal elements, elicit widespread participation, build on the culture, and create momentum.

> *Evolutionary design.* The best way to develop a knowledge organization is through a guided evolutionary process that tests multiple approaches and builds on experience over time. The right combination of design elements is discovered through iterative action-reflection cycles, not by executing a detailed blueprint, however logical and comprehensive. The motto we use is: "Design a little,

implement a lot." You are seeding the organization with a variety of prototypes to fit different purposes and situations, letting the natural action of the organization show which are most likely to be effective. The structure you are creating needs to "find itself." It cannot be described in detail or mandated at the outset because community boundaries are often hard to define. Over time, domains may merge or split, communities may go global or develop fractal structures that align with regions or business units. The important thing is to start something, see what energy it elicits, and build from there. You treat the organization as an organism to find out how it will react to your interventions. This evolutionary approach means that you can start small, building on local pockets of energy that already exist, rather than trying to orchestrate a company-wide lockstep process. It is efficient in terms of time and resources because you make fewer unnecessary, speculative design changes, and because designs can be customized to local needs.[2]

Distributed leadership. Communities thrive on internal leadership. Similarly, a knowledge organization depends on a distributed cadre of formal and informal leaders—both inside and outside communities—who have the vision and ability to help them reach their potential. The more visible communities' value and influence become, the more power community leaders and sponsors can wield in the organization. A knowledge initiative thus generates a new power base in the organization. Because such leadership is critical to success, design efforts should engage and leverage this new constituency, not ignore it or dampen its emergence. You do this by encouraging leaders—people who have the skills and vision to align community initiatives with the business strategy—to emerge in strategic domains.

Participation across multiple structures. At the community level, you look for a range of perspectives and participants to help cover the diverse elements of a community's domain, membership, and practice. At the organization level, you must recruit the participation and support of constituencies in various roles throughout the organization. These include senior executives, team leaders, staff managers, research centers, members of operational and project teams, community leaders and members, and external agents such as suppliers, customers, and "free-agent" contractors. Communities are most effective when they connect teams across divisions to catalyze ideas and solutions that would not be discovered otherwise. Wherever there are gaps or discontinuities—for example, where community members have little access to important operational teams that apply their expertise—these should be addressed. The principle here is not only to encourage participation, but also to help weave connections among these diverse constituents. This is done both by encouraging informal relationships and by designing formal systems and policies that foster coordination and alignment.

Dance of formal and informal. Communities create aliveness through a mix of public and private spaces that encourage diverse forms of participation. For a knowledge initiative at the organization level, the comparable principle is to combine formal and informal dimensions. Aliveness results from choreographing the dance between the informal professional passions and aspirations of practitioners and the organization's formal operational requirements; between feelings of identity and belonging at the community level and goals and objectives at the organization level. At the World Bank, for instance, there is a tension between the members' desire to take charge of their communities and the organization's traditional budget process, which is associated with lists of deliverables. The tension between the members' "informal" desire to learn and build relationships and the organization's "formal" demands to get results is inevitable and even desirable. The point is not to avoid or eliminate this tension, but to work with it to align passions and opportunities whenever possible, and to acknowledge the pull from both sides as a source of potential options.

Value. The responsibility of stewarding a community includes showing how it creates value for members, the teams they support, and the organization. At the organization level, the value focus is not only on what single communities contribute, but also how constellations of communities, teams, and business units combine to build and execute strategic capabilities. It is especially important to make the corporate value of communities (and combinations of communities) both transparent and compelling to division leaders, because they are committing valuable staff to activities whose benefits often manifest outside their business units. Engineering communities at National Semiconductor Corporation, for example, not only reduced the cycle time for chip designs, but also developed a constellation of communities that could help them build a world-class mixed-signal design capability that was strategically important for the firm as a whole. The value they sought was at the level of the organization, not just at the level of communities or business units.

Building on the existing culture. We've mentioned that communities must try to offer a balance of familiar and exciting events. Similarly, the knowledge initiative must balance its need to both build on and change the organization's culture. In many organizations, it may be tempting to say that a cultural transformation is necessary for communities to flourish. But taking on an entire company culture is usually not the best way to start a knowledge initiative. In fact, an APQC study found that community-based knowledge initiatives were most successful when they leveraged one or more core values of the organization.[3] For example, communities at Ford drew on a risk-averse engineering culture where codifying "proven practices" and spreading them through a programmatic software system worked very well. By contrast, the knowledge-sharing initiative at Lotus built on the company's core value of collaboration. It was managed in a much more decentralized way that relied heavily on the collaborative norms shared by software developers. Over time, communities develop their own culture, and they can transform an organization's culture through their collective influence on members and on the teams and other units with whom they interact. The advantage of a community-based approach lies precisely in the ability to begin building a more robust learning culture on a small scale, without taking on the entire organization. Communities are themselves instrumental to the cultural transformation that they require.

Pacing the initiative. Serious organization-level initiatives take time. It can take five years or more to accomplish a significant cultural change in an organization—and yet more-targeted initiatives can achieve results in months. An important part of launching an organization knowledge initiative is to set expectations that will allow a natural rhythm to unfold, a pace that matches the scale and complexity of the various dimensions of the initiative. For example, it may take only a few months to launch a number of communities, but the development of new strategic capabilities that require combining expertise across communities and business units may take much longer. Therefore, it is important to find a pace—what we called rhythm at the community level—for introducing new communities and changes in systems and policies that will keep the momentum without overloading community members or their managers and sponsors. For example, six to nine months after several communities have been launched, you might conduct a visible "renewal" survey to assess what has been accomplished and what needs to be done, and to position senior managers to voice their support for the initiative. After operating as pilots for a year, the organization might establish formal budget allocations for communities, redesign the appraisal or reward system to recognize knowledge contributions, or reinforce communities' legitimacy by including links to their Web sites on the company's official home page.

One way to view a community-based knowledge initiative is as a "social movement" at the organization level. Ideally, it builds momentum over time, and the momentum creates a sense of "pull" where it does not feel forced. Rather, it should coincide with the growing interest to participate among people at different levels of readiness, including early adopters, middle majorities, and skeptics.[4] This action-oriented change approach does not offer a conveniently codified, programmatic plan for implementing an effective knowledge organization. The issues that must be addressed along the way—including core values, identity, relationships, and formal and informal structures—simply cannot be abstractly prescribed from outside the action. The advantage of this participative, emergent approach is that it opens up a wide range of development options and enables the organization to adapt methodologies and insights learned from others to fit its own particular (and changing) conditions.

Get an Initiative Under Way

B UILDING A KNOWLEDGE system is a complex undertaking. You may have extant communities at more or less mature stages, but the point is to launch and cultivate several representative communities in an intentional way in order to establish them more systematically in the organization. Like any change initiative, a community-based knowledge initiative goes through phases. These phases are not unlike those of traditional organizational initiatives, but they place the emphasis on fostering the development of communities. They reflect the dynamic nature of communities that evolve through life-cycle stages as they mature, and indeed the phases of the initiative—prepare, launch, expand, consolidate, and transform—recall the developmental phases of communities introduced in chapter 4.

Phase 1: Prepare

Before you can start, you must lay a foundation. This includes assessing the current condition and preparing the way for possible development paths. You will need to identify strategic capability gaps, areas where learning activities are uncoordinated, and measurement system requirements. Most important, this is the time to establish a strong connection to the business strategy, either by analyzing competencies and business processes or by interviewing managers and practitioners to gain their insights regarding the knowledge implications of the business strategy. Depending on the organization, you will also need to have an initial action plan, gain preliminary support from a sponsor, or convince stakeholders of the value of what you are planning. You may also need to form alliances with line or staff groups—for instance, a business unit with a specific knowledge challenge or the corporate university.

Organizations differ to the extent that they explicitly link communities to the business strategy, but this point deserves emphasis nonetheless. After all, the cases we feature here—including product development engineers at DaimlerChrysler, geologists at Shell, strategy consultants at

McKinsey, and economic-development advisors at the World Bank—are all communities working in areas that represent distinctive competencies in their respective firms. Their organizations count on them to steward those capabilities and to spawn new ones for the future.

Therefore, it makes sense to begin the knowledge initiative by creating a shared map that explicitly describes the capabilities required to achieve the firm's strategic goals. Kao, a leading household and chemical products maker in Japan, uses an extensive map that comprehensively outlines the range of sub-specialties, physical characteristics, marketable products, and societal outcomes that derive from its five core scientific disciplines.[5] Senior executives and community leaders alike can use such a map to orient themselves strategically and to help focus attention and investments during start-up. The strength of the approach is that it builds on the strategic imperative felt by most firms today to define and manage their core competencies more consciously and systematically. The knowledge initiative helps firms to act on this imperative. It builds the organization's institutional capacity—via communities of practice—by enabling members to take the lead in stewarding strategic capabilities and putting them to work.

Another aspect of the preparation phase that bears special mention is the technological infrastructure. For many organizations, IT tools have provided the focus for knowledge-management initiatives, and yet we argued in chapter 1 that even the best technology applications fail unless practitioners adapt them to reflect their practice.[6] Given this caveat, communities, like everyone else, are becoming increasingly dependent on technologies to manage resource libraries, support learning activities, connect with colleagues, and build their reputation and presence in the organization. This is especially true when a community is geographically distributed, but even a colocated community will need some technology to keep in touch between meetings and build a knowledge base. The following online facilities are among the most useful to communities.

- A home page to assert their existence and describe their domain and activities.
- A conversation space for online discussions.

- A repository for their documents, including research reports, best practices, and standards.

- A good search engine to find things in their knowledge base.

- A directory of membership with some information about members' areas of expertise in the domain.

- In some cases, a shared workspace for synchronous electronic collaboration, or to enhance teleconferences with visuals.

- Community management tools, mostly for the coordinator but sometimes also for the community at large. These might include the ability to know who is participating actively, which documents are downloaded, how much traffic there is, which documents need updating, and so forth.

Although a technological infrastructure is not an essential precondition for launching communities of practice, in most organizations it is necessary to address IT issues early in the initiative, even if the strategy is to start with existing facilities and decide on a permanent platform later. In any case, it is important to adopt technological solutions that integrate well with the systems that people already use for their work. If they have to switch platforms or learn to use an entirely new system, they are less likely to participate in the online activities of their communities.[7]

Phase 2: Launch

Now you are ready to start launching communities in key domains. You will need to find places where there is energy on the part of potential members and enough organizational significance to draw some attention. There are several tactical choices for launching communities, and the right approach for any organization depends on a number of factors, including strategic urgency, culture, and current levels of expertise in community development.

High-visibility versus low-visibility. A high-visibility approach works best in a culture where a highly visible promotional effort is likely to be treated more seriously. Otherwise, a lower-visibility approach is generally better, because it gives the initiative leaders time to learn from experience and to build momentum and interest through early results and word of mouth—without the pressure to succeed across the board. Schlumberger launched a number of communities in a large two-day workshop that featured outside speakers and was kicked off by senior management. The launch was featured in the company's internal press. This high-visibility launch made it clear that management took communities very seriously.

Top-down versus bottom-up. A top-down approach—where senior managers identify communities based on the strategic goals of the organization—makes sense when market opportunities are clear and urgent and when visible top-management involvement is a cultural prerequisite for credibility, attention, and resources. For example, top executives at Mercedes-Benz and Schlumberger defined the focus of community domains. This worked because it was consistent with the culture and because the domain defini- tions were relatively straightforward. The advantage of a bottom- up approach—where the organization provides tailored levels of support to any viable community that shows initiative—is that it leverages the energy and aspirations of grassroots leaders. The risk of the bottom-up approach is that voluntary leaders may not nec- essarily be aligned with strategic priorities or cover the full spec- trum of issues. The World Bank used a bottom-up approach that encouraged communities to nominate themselves and combined this with a high-visibility announcement of the launch in order to get the attention of practitioners across its worldwide operations. A top-down approach was not likely to succeed at the Bank, where many of the domains were less clearly defined and where the professional culture would have resisted such direction. This invitational bottom-up initiative might not have worked so well, however, but for the fact that practitioners were familiar with the informal communities that had existed for years and felt confident that a call to convene colleagues with similar interests would be welcomed and understood.

Parallel versus sequential. You can launch a number of communi- ties in parallel or launch them sequentially in order to capitalize on lessons learned from each new community. The downside of a sequential approach is that you lose the advantage of learning from multiple cases running simultaneously and the chance to leverage collective educational events and peer-to-peer coaching across communities. The advantage of a sequential launch is the opportunity to start off with a few exemplary communities and then build on what you learn from experience. Schlumberger's launch was not only top-down and highly visible, it was also a parallel launch in which eighteen communities were started at once. Airbus took a sequential approach. Managers identified four representative domains to explore how communities could improve knowledge sharing and development. One focused on new technology and one on an established technology; another crossed organizational boundaries while a fourth did not. The choice of these pilots was explicitly intended to explore the range of communities that would eventually constitute the knowledge system. What they learned from these pilots gave them enough confidence to start launching communities across the organization.

Of course, the best launch approach in practice will combine elements from each set of options. For example, domains may be defined from the top down to align with the business strategy, but this doesn't preclude cultivating grassroots initiatives. Ideally, the initiative can draw on the benefits of both approaches, even if one is predominant.

Each organization is unique, and it is useful to try out your strategy with pilots first in order to learn what works and what does not. In fact, we have found that most managers prefer to go one step at a time. Pilots serve as a training ground for support staff coordinators and give managers a chance to get used to the idea of communities. They prepare the support team, sponsors, and stakeholders for changes on a much broader scale as the number of communities grows.

A launch is not necessarily limited to a small number of pilots, however. When senior managers urgently want to improve results and when they are confident in their approach, they may see little reason to conduct a limited pilot effort. Mercedes-Benz, for example, launched nearly one hundred communities during the opening phase of its initiative. In the Mercedes-Benz case, however, they had the benefit of drawing on lessons learned from a highly successful and comparable application of communities in the Chrysler division, which reduced the uncertainties associated with such an effort. In any case, the senior managers at Mercedes-Benz did not expect that all communities would succeed equally well. They chose to launch many communities at once because they faced urgent business and market conditions, and they wanted to speed up the implementation of an approach that had a proven record. This intensive parallel approach accelerated their learning process because it increased the number and variety of communities to compare and contrast; they were able to discern both success factors and disorders more easily.

Phase 3: Expand

Once senior managers have become convinced of a community-based approach, initiative sponsors may decide to launch communities across the board to cover all of the key knowledge domains. If you have done your work well during the launch phase, you will have built a strong foundation for expanding and further integrating communities in the organization. By now you should have several viable communities that are producing value for members and stakeholders, an experienced support team, and a network of supportive sponsors and stakeholders. You should also have developed a shared vision among a critical mass of members regarding the direction of the communities and how they can become integral mechanisms for running the business.

The spread of communities of practice throughout an organization is usually not a conventional pilot-rollout process by which a successful template is applied programmatically. Rather, it is an organic diffusion that expands as people get the idea, see its potential, and develop new aspirations. The process gains momentum through various combinations of top-down directives and encouragement and bottom-up initiative and responsiveness. In some companies, such as the World Bank and HP, the process is vigorously promoted but quite open, and communities of practice are invited to take the initiative. Other firms, like Shell and Ford, have adopted a more systematic approach based on an analysis of their knowledge needs.

Expansion requires integration. Even in moderately complex organizations, the knowledge system includes multiple communities of practice as well as teams, individual practitioners, business and staff units, research centers, and external partners who are engaged in a variety of learning, innovation, and problem-solving activities throughout the organization. It is one thing to make communities pervasive, but another to integrate their disparate activities in a functioning knowledge system. As stewards of the domains that define the knowledge system, communities perform key functions to integrate activities across the organization. We see communities play these roles at firms such as McKinsey, where new client-engagement teams call practice managers to describe a client's problem and to learn what is known in their domain that could help solve it.

The introduction of communities by itself, of course, will not solve the challenge of managing the knowledge system in an integrated way. Disparate communities focused narrowly on their own domains would merely replace a haphazard assortment of activities and sponsors with a new set of silos. In order to integrate a knowledge system, it is essential to appreciate the roles that community boundaries play in that system. As we argued in chapter 7, the very notion of a community of practice implies the existence of boundaries. Yet boundaries are learning assets in their own right that need to be put to work by creating opportunities for interaction, such as the knowledge fairs described in the World Bank story. Certain people also play the role of knowledge brokers. Viant, for instance, has selected a few employees to serve as "catalysts" for project teams, connecting people and ideas across boundaries. The company views this function as critical to achieving an integrated learning system.

Phase 4: Consolidate

There are several ways to help consolidate communities as integral and generative elements of the organization. Leaders can help institutionalize communities by giving them legitimacy and status in the organizational structure. But this nominal role must be backed up by functional integration that makes knowledge and learning integral to everything that the organization does. Organizations that successfully integrate communities weave community activities into everyday functions—how teams find a better way to solve a problem, how new hires learn the ropes, or how to keep up with recent technical breakthroughs. Finally, they align communities with business strategies, measurement systems, and human resource (HR) policies designed to reinforce knowledge-development goals. At this point, knowledge development becomes integrated into the organization's culture and modus operandi.

Institutionalization. In most organizations, there is a limit to what can be achieved without some degree of institutionalization. Yet, institutionalizing communities is a delicate process both structurally and culturally. The focus should not be to institutionalize specific communities, but rather to integrate the overall function of communities in the organization. By "institutionalizing" communities, we do not mean making them a part of the organizational chart, but rather legitimizing their role as stewards of knowledge resources by integrating them with other functions, and aligning organizational systems to support them. Successful organizations have avoided wholesale institutionalization done for its own sake or as a superficial means of legitimization—such as making participation compulsory or creating reporting relationships inside communities. Instead, their efforts are designed to elicit genuine enthusiasm among members and enable them to steward knowledge resources for both professional and organizational ends. This balance is essential if organizations are to gain the benefits of communities without killing their initiative with procedural red tape and departmental constraints.

Integrate communities with other functions. Communities need to work with other functions that deal with knowledge, such as corporate universities and R&D departments. For instance, communities can support the training function by providing informal as well as formal opportunities for newcomers to develop their skills and professional identity. At DaimlerChrysler, for example, new engineers complement the basic skills that they learn in classes by participating in Tech Club meetings, where they witness regular problem-solving sessions with experienced practitioners who are wrestling with new types of design challenges. They can try out ideas, learn where to find answers, and build relationships with experts and peers. The Tech Clubs focus on areas of technical knowledge that are too complex or too new to codify in manuals or to deliver through formal training. Once an emergent area of knowledge becomes better understood and explicitly codified, it is turned over to the training department, which then takes responsibility for educating new engineers in that area. Communities are also in a good position to evaluate the competence of new recruits. Participation in organizational tasks such as recruitment and selection processes takes time, however, and organizations should be careful not to mandate community responsibility for these processes in ways that sap a community's energy and momentum. In one company, for example, the HR department asked communities to assess the technical ability of new recruits, but did not ask them to get further involved in the hiring process.

Align the organization. Organization structures and systems provide a context that coordinates and motivates action and are therefore critical elements of the overall knowledge organization. Communities are unlikely to realize their potential unless organization goals, business processes, funding mechanisms, structures, IT systems, measurements, HR policies, rewards, facilities, and other elements are aligned to support knowledge initiatives as well as they do productivity requirements. These elements generally operate more as enablers than drivers of activities in the knowledge system, although in aggregate they can have a great deal of influence on attitudes and behaviors.

In the early phases of the knowledge initiative, you will not likely have the support at the organization level to make significant changes in complex and contentious areas such as appraisal systems. The support team and sponsors can respond to issues on a case-by-case basis if they are not ready to recommend firm-wide changes right away. For example, they might meet with reluctant business unit leaders to persuade them to support members' participation in community activities, or they could ask the IT group to explore a new application by testing it with several active communities. These temporary "work-arounds" will pave the way for possible long-term solutions. As communities become more ubiquitous and as their activities and influence grow, however, it becomes necessary to address more directly the institutional systems and policies that influence their effectiveness.

Phase 5: Transform

Just as children transform their parents as they grow, communities transform the organizations in which they thrive. If knowledge becomes the central driver of an organization's business, we should expect communities to play an increasingly central role. Ultimately, focusing on communities has a transformative effect on the organization. To date, a growing number of organizations have begun intentional community-based knowledge initiatives, but most have yet to be transformed radically by their communities. However, we see early signs of transformative effects in the ways communities are starting to drive strategy at the World Bank and McKinsey.

The transformation potentially brought about by communities of practice is twofold. First, communities become more than an integral way of running the business; they become the focal structure. We have argued that in some cases they are becoming the primary vehicle for belonging to the organization, a point of stability in an organization constantly reshaping itself to match the demands of a market in flux. Second, communities do not merely transform how the business operates; they transform it *continuously*. That is, the identity of the organization has so deeply incorporated the values associated with learning and innovation that transformation has become a way of life. It must be if the organization is going to keep up with hypercompetitive markets where learning and innovation are relentless forces that call for continuous development of people, products, and even the firm itself.

In parallel with the phases of a community-based knowledge initiative, two additional development efforts are necessary to run the initiative and to sponsor its integration with the organization's strategies, processes, and systems.

1. *Develop an internal practice of community development.* Create a support team, conduct educational events, and build a community among community-development practitioners.

2. *Cultivate management sponsorship and stakeholder support.* Identify key stakeholders, find ways to involve them, and generate executive sponsorship for communities and the initiative more broadly.

The rest of this chapter addresses these issues in more detail.

Develop a Practice of Community Development

SIMPLY ESTABLISHING COMMUNITIES to cover the range of domains in a system is not enough; they must also function effectively. Communities generally need coaching and methodological support to reach their full potential. Most organizations that have launched a strategic knowledge initiative understand that they will need an internal capability to build and sustain communities. Such support is two-pronged. It features both dedicated structural units—what we call a "support team" and a "coordinating community"—and an educational process. All focus on raising awareness about communities, building the elements of a practice to support their development, and integrating them within the broader knowledge system.

Establish a Support Team

The support team is at the core of a knowledge initiative. As the World Bank story illustrates, the support-team members play key roles as evangelists and teachers who raise awareness about communities of practice. They conduct workshops, stage conferences, and meet with people—coordinators, community members, and stakeholders—to lay a foundation on which communities can build for the future.[8] The support team's function is particularly important early in the initiative because communities evolve in idiosyncratic ways—there is simply no way to program their evolution—and integrating community leadership into an organization is a new challenge for nearly all managers. Support teams help firms accelerate the natural learning and evolution processes required for communities to reach their potential. The support team usually consists of a handful of full-time members and several part-time members, ideally with backgrounds that include strategy, organization design, and IT, as well as familiarity with the business and a strong understanding of the theory and practice of knowledge management. Their ability to help communities succeed during the launch phase is crucial to the success of the organization's overall knowledge initiative. Organizations that are serious about launching a knowledge initiative should staff this function carefully and then actively support its development and legitimacy in the firm. The following are typical functions of a support team.

- *Run the knowledge initiative.* The support team usually assumes responsibility for planning the knowledge initiative and integrating the knowledge system as communities proliferate. The support team helps to benchmark best practices in other organizations as well as assess knowledge-initiative activities and results inside the organization. The support team develops the community-launch project plan to review with executive sponsors. At the World Bank, the support team conducts focus groups and surveys of community members and their constituents to find out how well Thematic Groups are working, to what extent they are meeting demand, and to identify areas for improvement.

- *Provide direct support to communities.* Communities often benefit from coaching and support to develop into a mature community. As the litany of community disorders suggests, communities can fail to perform in a number of ways for many reasons. In fact, it is not atypical for firms with many communities to find that nearly a third fail to reach their potential if left alone. The support team coaches community leaders and helps design community problem-solving sessions and innovation projects. The support team at DaimlerChrysler has been instrumental in the successful maturation of the Tech Clubs there (as described in box 9-1).

BOX 9-1 A SUPPORT-TEAM MEMBER AT DAIMLERCHRYSLER

LARRY IS A MEMBER of a team that has been working for several years to support the Tech Club initiative at DaimlerChrysler. Larry's focus has been to help coordinators like Emile (see box 4-3) develop Tech Clubs that attract participation, produce useful knowledge resources (such as completed sections of the EBoK), and get the support of senior managers. Larry sits in on both engineering and executive Tech Club meetings and coaches coordinators on how to facilitate discussion in the meetings. He confers with leaders after meetings to review factors that made the meeting more or less successful. Was the supplier's presentation sufficiently technical and advanced to pique members' interest and provide value? Should the coordinator have asked one of the community's experts to team up with a rookie to work on a difficult section of the EBoK? Why were engineers from one of the platform teams absent this time—should the coordinator follow up with them one-on-one?

Larry also conducts community launches and specialized workshops for coordinators to help them get started or to reflect on their progress. He works with DaimlerChrysler staff managers to integrate communities into broader knowledge initiatives, such as the development of a common technology platform, or to help align the appraisal system so it encourages participation and management support. He serves as a liaison between the engineering Tech Clubs and managers in the executive Tech Clubs to help them negotiate realistic knowledge-building goals and to set expectations for how the Tech Clubs can support the platform teams. He has been instrumental in transferring the Tech Club model from the Chrysler division to the Mercedes-Benz division after the merger. He flew regularly to Germany to conduct workshops for managers and coordinators on the Chrysler experience. He also worked with the support team at Mercedes-Benz to help them anticipate and respond to typical issues, such as reluctance from some engineers to share their valuable expertise with colleagues on other teams, or weak leadership skills in newly assigned coordinators.

- *Address technology issues.* The support team can help communities identify their technology needs and work with relevant groups to build the necessary infrastructure. Because IT is so salient for knowledge-management initiatives, it helps to have IT expertise in the support team—perhaps including an IT professional—to identify the right IT tools for communities and to help them apply them effectively.

- *Act as liaison with executive sponsors and stakeholders.* The support team works with communities throughout the organization and therefore can spot patterns indicating which policies or systems should be changed to support communities' development. They are also in a position to report on leadership and culture issues that hamper communities' effectiveness and to recommend corrective actions.

- *Coordinate with business lines and staff groups.* The support team works with business unit and staff managers to ensure they understand the strategic and operational challenges associated with managing knowledge. It helps these stakeholders identify strategic opportunities or address necessary changes in systems or policies that they control. For example, the support team at the World Bank worked with the HR department to draft a new appraisal system for managers that heightened the importance of supporting knowledge-development initiatives at the Bank.

The support team builds the organization's capacity to develop communities by gathering resources, including models, tools, and insights. If the organization uses external consultants to help guide the initiative, the support team is responsible for internalizing external consultants' skills and methods. Support team offerings include a straw model, a development toolkit, and access to external resources.

- *A community straw model.* Early in the initiative, it helps to build a customized vision of how communities will operate in the organization. Such a community "straw model" can draw on exemplary cases from other companies and from extant communities already operating in the organization. It provides a template that communities can then adapt to their individual situations and needs.

- *Community-development toolkit.* The support team usually puts together a toolkit that explains the detailed "how-to" activities associated with developing communities at their various stages and with designing the surrounding elements of the knowledge organization. This toolkit combines external expertise with lessons learned internally in the course of the initiative. In addition to providing guidance, such a toolkit also creates a shared language among participants to facilitate conversations about what to do, when to do it, and how to guide members' journey into unfamiliar territory.

- *Access to external resources.* Developing a practice means drawing on external as well as internal sources of expertise—including leading practitioners from other firms, consultants, and scholars—through participation in conferences, consortia, and professional networks. Such external perspectives are invaluable sources of ideas as well as a means for building credibility and confidence among knowledge practitioners inside the company.

Provide Education and Raise Awareness

The support team also educates people directly by teaching fundamentals and raising awareness, thus further legitimizing community initiatives. Education and awareness-building activities are important because evolutionary design processes depend on highly informed and educated participants—including community members, managers, and stakeholders. Typical topics for educational workshops include: What are communities of practice and what do they do? What benefits do they produce—for members, teams, customers, and the organization? What are examples of successful communities? What roles are important, and what skills and time commitments do these require? Will we need to change structures, systems, and policies to support communities? If so, how?

The Mercedes-Benz division launched a broad education effort during a management-education conference on the topic of knowledge management, which was sponsored by the DaimlerChrysler Corporate University. A senior Mercedes-Benz executive announced their initiative in an enthusiastic speech to managers across the firm. Soon after, the Mercedes-Benz division held its own conference for all managers in the division to explain the knowledge initiative in more detail. Later, they provided introductory workshops for community coordinators led by experienced coordinators and support-team members from the Chrysler division. The corporate support team complemented and reinforced these education efforts with an online resource center that provided standardized toolkits, updates on workshops, highlights of recent achievements, and news related to knowledge management from other companies.

It is particularly important to train and coach community coordinators. They influence the success of a community more than any other single factor, and yet their role is new to most people. At their best, coordinators have a combination of conventional management and interpersonal skills, plus skills in "corporate community organizing"— abilities that are generally not covered in management education and professional development programs. One way to help accelerate the development of coordinators is to conduct a series of development workshops for all coordinators who are or plan to be involved in organizing communities. These workshops provide coordinators a shared experience and language to talk about their challenges and enable them to build a foundation of trust and commitment to help each other informally. Workshops typically cover a range of issues, including start-up activities, designing a launch, facilitating effective knowledge-sharing events (both face-to-face and "virtual"), building interest and participation through both the public and private space of the community, managing a knowledge repository, and measuring value.

Form a Coordinating Community

Once communities are up and running and coordinators have experienced firsthand the challenges of community development, one way to combine education with practice development is to form a "coordinating community"—a community of practice whose domain is community development. At Montgomery Watson, for example, a group of community leaders meet every month for a one-hour teleconference. Their meetings include formal presentations on how to measure the value of communities, sharing tips on how to use technology, and informal discussions about ways to get members to participate actively.

Because community development is a practice like any other, the coordinating community has an opportunity to "walk the talk" and to model how to build a practice. They develop a learning agenda regarding how to develop communities, how to assess their health and contributions, and how to align organizational systems. They share ideas and methods during workshops, visits, and collaborative projects as would any other community. Members of the coordinating community typically include leaders from current and emergent communities in the organization as well as others with an interest in the topic. The coordinating community provides personal encouragement as well as skill-development opportunities to community coordinators. Support-team members usually lead the coordinating community, but over time, the coordinating community often shares or even assumes some of the functions of the support team.

A coordinating community helps integrate the knowledge system. It can facilitate exchanges across community boundaries. It coordinates projects where opportunities exist for synergies and cost savings. In a large company, a typical knowledge initiative includes a hundred communities or more. Multidivisional firms of the future may end up with more than a thousand. Each community is unique, and yet all of them share common methods and challenges. A large population of communities provides a terrific opportunity to track "natural experiments" on what interventions work best to develop successful communities. A coordinating community accelerates and increases the organization's ability to learn from its experience. It also provides an excellent forum for identifying where misalignments or enhancement opportunities exist—in HR policies or technology design, for example. When such an issue occurs in isolated instances, it may be written off as a core-group idiosyncrasy or a random dip in participation. If multiple communities are struggling with staffing or technology problems, however, it is easier to diagnose them as issues at the organizational level, rather than place all the blame on community deficiencies.

Cultivate Stakeholder Support and Executive Sponsorship

A COMMUNITY-BASED KNOWLEDGE strategy is a process of organizational transformation, and as such it will bring difficult (albeit not unfamiliar) issues to the surface. These include competition between business units, teams, and individual practitioners; political battles to control the learning agenda and to define what constitutes "value"; and resistance to managing yet another messy variable in the organization. Supporting the development of communities as corporate resources is particularly tricky. Members wonder: Do we really need to help those other business units? Will we have to devote our time to training newcomers? If I invest my time in this, will it help my career? Senior managers need to assess their readiness to see this initiative through the growing pains and typical organizational difficulties that arise (as described in chapter 7). They can perform a number of functions, including

- communicating a vision of the knowledge organization,
- setting knowledge-related priorities and funding levels,
- facilitating investments in communities that cross business unit boundaries,
- encouraging participation, and
- ensuring alignment of organizational systems and policies.

Cultivating management support means identifying sponsors who will fund and guide the initiative as well as key stakeholders who will influence its success. You need to find out what they expect of communities, and in turn, influence those expectations. Important stakeholders to consider include corporate executives; business unit leaders; staff executives in HR, IT, and the Corporate University; and directors of knowledge-intensive functions such as R&D, product development, and engineering.

Leaders can help launch community-based knowledge initiatives as either champions or sponsors. These terms are often used interchangeably to refer to senior managers who provide direction and support for the knowledge initiative, but it is useful to distinguish between the two roles in order to avoid setting unrealistic expectations for executive support.

- A *champion* is a senior manager who believes strongly that communities of practice should be a primary mechanism for managing knowledge in the organization. He or she aggressively supports the development of communities by providing guidance, funds, visibility, legitimacy, or other means of clearing the way for communities to thrive and achieve results.

- A *sponsor* is also willing to provide funding and some level of legitimacy or support for community initiatives. Unlike a champion, however, the sponsor is not as passionate about what communities can accomplish and does not provide the same amount of support. Sponsors are less likely than champions to push communities and the organization to innovate, and they are more likely to request early evidence that communities are worth time, attention, and resources.

Ultimately, communities benefit from both types of leaders. On the one hand, champions provide more latitude to communities and are likely to push communities as well as business units and teams to find new ways to build and apply knowledge resources. On the other hand, while sponsors are willing to provide initial support, they are more skeptical and will push communities to make their value measurable and visible. They represent many stakeholders in the organization who share this point of view. Thus, these two types of leaders provide leeway for communities to explore, and each—in distinct ways—pushes communities to manifest their value in the organization.

It also helps to educate executives about the development needs, concrete benefits, and organizational challenges associated with the knowledge initiative. One-on-one or small-group discussions with stakeholders are often the best way to understand their concerns and build a shared understanding for going forward. DaimlerChrysler's support-team leader spent a great deal of his time during the first year of their initiative cultivating stakeholder support. He made the rounds of senior executives and staff and business-line managers to find out what activities were underway, educate them about new approaches, and develop ideas for specific projects.

As the initiative progresses, it is often useful to institutionalize senior management sponsorship. Organizations manage these functions in various ways.

- *Individual sponsors.* At IBM and Schlumberger, each community has an executive sponsor who provides access to the top-management team and thus gives the community a voice in management decisions.

- *Knowledge board.* At firms such as DaimlerChrysler, McKinsey, and the World Bank, there are distinct executive bodies sponsoring the knowledge initiative. This executive group, which we call a "knowledge board," ideally includes line managers and has the senior-level perspective and influence to translate the firm's business strategy into priorities for the knowledge initiative.

- *Office of the CKO (Chief Knowledge Officer).* At Clarica Life Insurance Company, the CKO (called VP of Strategic Capabilities) sponsors the knowledge initiative. He provides a point of focus for legitimizing the work of communities. He represents the voice of knowledge on the board of directors and treats them as a de facto knowledge board.[9]

However provided, the function of institutionalized sponsorship becomes increasingly important as the initiative grows in reach and influence. It provides symbolic as well as substantive support to the knowledge initiative. The symbolic importance of sponsor and senior executive actions speaks more loudly than formal publicity efforts, so it is important for those leaders to be aware of their actions and statements on the initiative.[10] People inside and outside of communities will look for signals regarding the seriousness of the effort and the readiness of senior management to fully support it—even if that means addressing long-standing tensions or political turf wars in the process. The symbolism of these roles is only positive, however, to the extent it confirms managers' day-to-day support for knowledge development.

The foundation of leadership has always been about learning—learning about the world, others, and oneself. It has always been about passionately setting out a vision and putting together a sound strategy to support it; about developing people to take initiative and follow their bliss, while also reinforcing their commitment to performance objectives and holding them accountable. The challenges of communities, then, bring us back full circle to the central challenges of leading organizations. The only difference may be that we can now more fully appreciate the nature of the leadership challenge, and rediscover that fostering learning and innovation has always been the most sustainable route to long-term business success.[11]

Conclusion

THE VALUE OF communities of practice is not only to manage knowledge resources, but also to help organizations succeed in a transformative economy. The litany of forces transforming our economy— globalization, technological innovation, demographic shifts, and decentralization, among others—has become commonplace, and these forces show no sign of abating. Communities of practice help firms adapt to the emerging threats and opportunities of the new economy in several ways.

- *Create new business opportunities* by leveraging internal expertise and relationships with customers and competitors to convert insights into new products and services.

- *Reconstitute expertise* that gets lost when firms move to decentralized, cross-functional units, thus helping companies get the best of both worlds—accountability and market presence as well as firm-wide access to knowledge resources.

- *Enable companies to compete on talent, and for talent,* by providing a professional "home" for practitioners—a stable context for developing skills and reputation—as well as an intangible but crucial sense of identity and belonging.

- *Capitalize on the participation in multiorganization "value webs"* by making the most of the knowledge resources that are exchanged through practitioner networks that cross firm boundaries.[12]

The transformative potential of communities in organizations hinges on the paradox of "cultivating" informal structures as opposed to managing them in conventional ways. But this is not to disparage formal structures and rigorous management methods. In fact, the current salience of informal phenomena results ironically not from the failure, but rather from the success of formal structures and methods in organizations. Consequently, there is less to gain from innovations in formal structures alone. Informal phenomena—professional passion, relationships, and identity—are now the frontier of management. The point of institutionalizing the role of communities is not to formalize them by making them follow procedures or meet efficiency goals, but rather to *strengthen* them as informal entities; to give them a voice and a visible, legitimate role in the dance between formal and informal elements. In fact, informal phenomena have always been crucial to the success of formal systems and policies. Communities provide new opportunities to leverage the power of both dimensions—and their complementary dynamics—more completely.

The challenge to manage the dance between formal and informal elements has been recognized, of course, since the rise of large organizations in the early twentieth century. But the new challenge to develop communities of practice in organizations brings this issue home for managers in a very concrete way. Indeed, community participation encourages members to find their vocation, to connect with colleagues, and to find work that both builds and uses their skills. What is new about managing in the knowledge economy is the need to appreciate the tangible value of these intangible assets—passions, relationships, and skills—as much or more than the conventional assets listed on the balance sheet.[13] As communities become more pervasive and influential in organizations, managers will find they have a new wealth of resources to work with if they can learn to choreograph the interplay between the formal and the informal.

Although creating a knowledge organization hospitable to communities of practice requires organization-level initiatives, communities are nevertheless principal agents of the change process. Communities are effective instruments of organizational change for the same reasons they are powerful agents for shaping and executing company strategies. They are inherently participative, voluntary structures whose participants enact their own designs. Changes are therefore more likely to be enacted as intended—and aligned with both the purposes of the organization and the interests of members. In the long run, communities may well reframe the boundaries and even the defining characteristics of the firm itself in an economy where knowledge is the primary source of value.[14] The challenge of developing communities capable of such transformations is ultimately about developing transformative organizations—where communities, paradoxically, are the central agents of the change.

CHAPTER ten

Reweaving the World

Communities beyond Organizations

WHAT IF THIS BOOK WERE SIMPLY GIVING VOICE *to a broader groundswell? What if communities of practice transformed the ways we think about organizing? What if they became the core building blocks of organizations in the future? What if businesses started to organize their suppliers and their markets as communities? What if shared practice became the foundation of civic communities? And what if citizens started to design their world on the model of fractal communities, linking local and global practice development? In other words, if you were the CKO of the world, how would you design your knowledge initiative?*

The Extended Knowledge System

IN THIS BOOK we have concentrated primarily on the ability of communities of practice to steward knowledge inside organizations, because this is where we have found the best examples of systematic

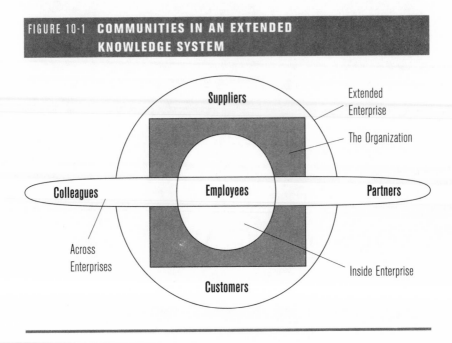

FIGURE 10-1 COMMUNITIES IN AN EXTENDED KNOWLEDGE SYSTEM

work so far. However, the complexity of markets and learning systems in the knowledge economy have sparked a trend toward communities that are not confined to the boundary of a single organization. Rather, these communities help weave broader value webs created by relationships and exchanges both within and beyond the boundaries of the firm. As illustrated in figure 10-1, this "extended knowledge system" includes suppliers, distributors, customers, and a variety of other partners and communities outside the firm.

Communities in Business-to-Business Clusters

Knowledge is increasingly an issue for relationships with suppliers at one end and with distributors and retailers at the other. As firms outsource processes, interorganizational communities of practice help to maintain internal expertise while strengthening relationships with outsourcing partners. We have seen that the Tech Clubs at Daimler-Chrysler invite suppliers to their meetings. On the downstream side, Hallmark is organizing communities of practice among its retailers and

Clarica is doing the same for the independent agents who sell its insurance products.

Indeed, manufacturers, suppliers, and distributors in common industry sectors form natural clusters that provide fertile soil for the growth of interorganizational communities of practice.[1] Firms in the automobile and chemicals industries, for example, have organized their own purchasing networks in which participants develop common standards and have access to online mechanisms for conducting business with suppliers via the Internet. These arrangements can significantly reduce transaction costs and increase the negotiating leverage of participants with regard to price, quality, and availability from suppliers.

Beyond transactional efficiency, however, is the potential for significant knowledge exchange. Toyota, for instance, has invested a great deal of effort in creating a knowledge-sharing network among its suppliers. Many large firms help their suppliers improve their operations, but these relationships are typically specific to each individual supplier. Toyota encourages mutual relationships among suppliers. It expects companies that it helps improve quality and efficiency to share their lessons with other selected suppliers. As one Toyota manager explained, "That's one of our requirements, because if we take the time and effort to transfer the know-how, we need to be able to use the suppliers' operation as a vehicle to help other suppliers." Toyota's approach is three-pronged. A supplier association creates general but weak ties among all suppliers. A consulting group provides education and direct assistance. Finally, a set of "voluntary study groups" build strong multilateral ties among specific suppliers. They include five to ten companies who work together on various themes, visit each other's facilities to offer suggestions for improvements and learn from each other, and present key insights at an annual meeting. This system has created strong norms of reciprocity among Toyota suppliers and has resulted in remarkable improvements in performance and productivity.[2]

Communities in Consumer Markets

Similar potential exists at the consumer level. Businesses need knowledgeable consumers as well as knowledge from these consumers. In turn, consumers benefit from firms that really understand their needs.[3] A growing number of consumer groups are organizing around topics such as travel, parenting, musical interests, and fitness activities. iVillage.com, for example, provides a "women's network" site that encourages women to exchange questions, resources, and ideas—as well as opinions regarding related products and services—on topics such as parenting, dieting, relationships, and work.[4]

If sufficiently organized, such consumer communities may even seek to influence the way companies serve their needs. E-commerce adds a new dimension to this potential. Companies can leverage as never before the inherent potential to define markets by *practices*, not merely by conventional customer demographics. For instance, do-it-yourselfers who share experiences, tips, and techniques are connected by the practice of home improvement. This is recognized by manufacturers that sponsor such communities on their Web sites.[5] The next step is to involve such communities in a process of product development that becomes integral to the development of the practice.

Many firms are attracted by this potential as a way to create loyalty to a brand or service. Of course, there is an inherent tension between a company's commercial interests and the dynamics of community development. Creating genuine communities among consumers (whether face-to-face or online) is not easy—and many attempts to organize market-based "communities" hardly fit the description. Such communities require something compelling to elicit member participation and bring people together—a real opportunity to share useful knowledge and to develop a valued identity. Companies that organize such communities are unlikely to attract participants unless they are committed to creating value for members, putting "community before commerce."[6]

Communities across Firms

The need to learn across company boundaries is spawning a growing number of interorganizational partnerships. These range from full mergers to joint ventures to loose learning networks. Organizations increasingly have to be ready to join forces with competitors to take advantage of market opportunities that require complex knowledge. Mergers, joint ventures, and alliances that intend to provide access to new capabilities for participating firms depend on trust between practitioners on all sides as well as high levels of "absorptive capacity"—the ability to make use of what you learn—within each firm.[7] This internal capacity as well as external trust with colleagues across firms in turn depend on communities in relevant areas of practice, both inside and across the participating firms. In these mergers, ventures, and alliances, interorganizational communities of practice are ideal vehicles for realizing the knowledge potential that exists across firms.[8]

The same is true of looser learning partnerships, which include interorganizational consortia, relationships with universities, professional associations, and learning networks of firms that collaborate on shared problems. The Northeast Indiana TQM Network, for instance, brought together a dozen firms that decided to join forces to learn about implementing quality programs. These firms were typically too small to afford the investment in total quality programs that larger companies have made. They decided to pool their resources to access outside expertise, learn from each other's experience, purchase and develop common training material, assess the merit of different practices, and build a common baseline of knowledge. Participation in the network has enabled members to "accelerate and strengthen their learning process, extend their range of TQM knowledge, learn from each other's successes and failures, and as one member put it, 'share the pain of a difficult but very necessary process.'"[9]

Civil Society

IN TRYING TO understand the potential of community-based organizing, there is no reason to limit our horizon to business. Peter Drucker argues that knowledge-economy forces will heighten the importance of developing the "social sector," because: "It is in and through the social sector that a modern developed society can again create responsible and achieving citizenship, can again give individuals (and especially knowledge people) a sphere in which they can make a difference in society."[10] Indeed, in the last several years of our organizational work, we have seen that community-based approaches can be applied more broadly to build capacity in the civil sector. The world itself has become the ultimate organization, and the challenges that it faces are increasingly related to knowledge. The principles that apply to businesses, their markets, and the broader learning systems in which they participate also apply to the challenges faced by our societies. In fact, the socioeconomic requirements for sustained prosperity in a global economy will demand that we apply these principles beyond the private sector. How could we apply a community-based approach to cultivate our worldwide learning capacity? What would a community-based approach to "world design" look like? The story of the "Boost4Kids" civic learning network in the United States illustrates this potential.

It was June 1998. Dr. Bob Ross, San Diego County Health and Human Services Director, walked on stage at then Vice President Al Gore's seventh annual "Family Reunion" and held up a hefty 800-page binder of detailed application forms. These were the forms a typical at-risk family of four—with a disabled father who had lost his job and a mother seeking employment and insurance for her kids—would need to complete in order to get the assistance they needed. Ross explained that since the 1930s, when human services programs were first created, there had been sixty years of policy and program development spurred by national change, social upheaval, and political waves. As a result, local cities and counties must now deal with an impossible tangle of unconnected, highly targeted, and restrictive programs and budget allocations in order to help children and families. This makes it difficult to treat people as whole beings in a social context, not as a "3717 kid" or "40A3 family"—known only in terms of the legislative program they qualify for. Dr. Ross asserted before the Vice President and assembled audience that the current regulations were a rat's nest—overlapping, unconnected, and burdensome—and that they wasted funds and limited the ability of local agencies and nongovernment groups to help people in need. He challenged the federal government to find a way to reduce the red tape and help local groups get results.

One of the recommendations to come out of this conference was to form a learning network of local family-service coalitions that would include federal- and state-agency participants. The purpose of the network was to enhance the ability of local coalitions to learn and to create better ways to support the healthy development of kids and families. A steering committee of "federal champions" from various agencies was convened and, along with executives operating out of Vice President Gore's "Reinventing Government" office, they began to recruit and select local family-services coalitions to join a national learning network. Ultimately, seventy-five local groups applied and thirteen were selected as core members—based on criteria that included a track record of multi-sector collaboration, partnership with state-agency officials, and a commitment to learn and innovate to achieve improved outcomes.

The network incorporates the three elements of a community of practice. Its *domain* is succinctly described as "results for children," and this includes addressing issues related to school readiness, health insurance, nutrition, healthy behaviors of youth, and child abuse. The focus is on young children, but the community members find that child-related issues are better addressed in the context of families. There is a great deal at stake in this area. At the time, California alone had one million children without health insurance. Of these, 750,000 were eligible for insurance covered by federal programs, but could not gain access to the right channels. The costs to children, their families, and to society of untreated illnesses such as lead poisoning, asthma, and other ailments far outweigh the cost of preventative treatments covered by health insurance—and easily reach hundreds of millions of dollars annually.[11]

The *community* consists of the thirteen local coalitions chosen from around the country—three in California and others in Florida, Georgia, Hawaii, Iowa, Maine, Maryland, Michigan, North Carolina, and Vermont. Typically, member coalitions include government and nonprofit agencies, citizen groups, and businesses. Each coalition has several active participants in the network. They include county health and human services directors, leaders of nonprofit organizations, social workers, educators, and state-level health and human services directors or governor's office staff. The network was convened by staff in the Vice President's office. They formed a steering committee of "federal champions" that includes managers from a variety of federal departments, including Health and Human Services, Education, Agriculture, Transportation, and others. The champions' role is to partner with local coalitions to analyze needs and opportunities, identify resources, and "bust barriers" at the state and federal levels to innovate and solve problems.

The *practice* of the community includes skills and techniques related to delivering the education, nutrition, and other basic programs that serve children and families. Their practice includes methods for increasing the enrollment of kids in health insurance and nutrition programs, improving access to quality daycare, and raising levels of kids' readiness for school. They use a variety of mechanisms for sharing ideas, methods, and information.

- They hold face-to-face conferences twice a year where they share goals and strategies, build relationships, and decide what issues and specific projects they want to explore together.

- They convene regular teleconferences that include expert speakers on specific topics and general discussion of problems and best practices.

- A listserv—moderated by the community coordinator—provides updates on issues relevant to members such as new sources of funding, upcoming legislation, news articles, and so on. Members also use it to ask and answer occasional questions.

- Their Web site publishes news and helpful information relevant to the domain—including strategies for helping kids and families in need, resources for funding, examples of measurement approaches, case studies, links to other relevant sites, innovative practices, and outcome measures from states and regions throughout the country.

- Members engage in common projects, such as learning to use graphical information systems data to analyze socioeconomic conditions in order to target outreach and intervention efforts.

- Members exchange informal phone calls, e-mails, and sched-
  uled visits to discuss new ideas, get help with implementation,
  negotiate support from state and federal agencies, and so forth.

To illustrate why coalition members are so enthusiastic about participating in the network, consider what they have done to build capacity
related to afterschool programs. One of the initiatives that members
decided to work on together was to learn more about how to implement
afterschool programs effectively to serve a whole city or county. The federal staff coordinators were familiar with a successful program managed
by the Baltimore coalition. They arranged for a recognized afterschool
expert to team up with leaders of the Baltimore initiative to speak at a
community teleconference devoted to this topic. The Palm Beach members were so impressed with Baltimore's ability to use graphical information systems to map the coverage of afterschool programs in Baltimore
that they later arranged to visit Baltimore to learn more. Subsequently,
Palm Beach was able to get support for an ambitious plan to deliver
afterschool programs throughout the county to reach under-served
areas. Another initiative of a subgroup of network members has been to
develop an electronic application form that lets families apply for multiple programs at once—rather than filling out fifteen different applications in five different offices, as is commonly the case.

Network participation has helped members get access to new kinds
of skills and support. The Boost4Kids "brand" has helped coalitions get
local press attention for their efforts and has reduced the stigma for
clients applying for insurance and nutrition programs. The involvement
of members at the state and federal level has helped local members make
headway on innovation efforts—such as the electronic application form—
that might otherwise have taken much longer. A number of members
have said that participating in the network helps them sort out which
new ideas and information to pay attention to, because as several stated,
"We always have plenty to keep us busy." The network has helped members discover learning and innovation opportunities and gain access to
the skills and support needed to successfully act on them. Finally, members are enthusiastic about the potential for such networks of local coalitions to influence social change. As one member said, "There will come a

point as this grows to scale that we will change the thinking and culture of the country about what we can do for kids and families."

The Boost4Kids network has been used as a model for two other federally sponsored networks. One is called 21st Century Skills Network, which focuses on workforce development strategies that start in high school and continue into adulthood; the other is SafeCities, which focuses on a myriad of law enforcement and social action strategies to reduce gun violence. These three networks have just begun to develop, and among their challenges has been finding new sources of federal sponsorship after the change in the presidential administration. Although their work is consistent with a bipartisan philosophy to pursue socioeconomic development through local community initiative, there are few precedents among federal agencies to support such networks. Yet these civic practitioner networks may help renew a long-standing vision for how a democracy—at any level of governance—can achieve socioeconomic ends by enabling civic groups and coalitions to take charge of their own destiny.[12] The number of such opportunities is increasing.

Recently, for example, a group called CEOs for Cities—consisting of big-city mayors, university presidents, nonprofit leaders, and business CEOs from fifteen cities nationwide—has been organized with foundation sponsorship. Their purpose is to spur economic development in cities by influencing national policy, sponsoring research, and fostering practitioner networks that will accelerate innovation and learning across cities, on topics such as workforce skills, infrastructure development, and housing.[13] Others, such as the Local Initiatives Support Corporation and the U.S. Chamber of Commerce, are developing practitioner networks on similar topics. The experience of these networks and a growing number of others shows the potential for applying the community-based approach to organizing civil society.[14]

Community-Based World Design

There is no reason to assume that civic communities of practice should remain within national borders. As the World Bank experience shows, there is much that countries can learn from one another. Nor need we assume that national governments are the best instigators of such learning systems. In the wake of the 1992 Earth Summit in Rio de Janeiro, a number of cities around the world instituted an "Agenda 21" process (for twenty-first century development). Citizens in cities organize around areas of interest—such as urban design, environmental practices, local agriculture, educational initiatives, and ecological transportation—and develop initiatives to improve conditions in their cities. Participants in Kirchheim-unter-Teck, Germany, for example, have completed initiatives in several of these areas and taken an increasingly visible and powerful role for pushing the development agenda in their city (to the consternation of some of the more entrenched local politicians, who are jealous of their power). This shows the potential of global practices developed by civic groups in their local communities.

Until now, the World Bank's community initiatives have focused mainly on connecting leading practitioners within the Bank and occasionally with outside experts. But recently, communities of practice have started to transform the strategy of the Bank by pointing to a whole new approach to world development. The Bank has begun to leverage what it knows about communities to help client countries build their own communities of practice. One initiative is developing a community of mayors from capital cities in Central America and the Caribbean, each of whom is a leader of a mayors' association in his or her own country. This community of mayors meets for several days each quarter to share ideas about ways to improve living conditions and economic results in their cities. A member of the Bank's support team acts as a consultant to the community, helping them to build on the model of successful Thematic Groups. Others from the Bank provide subject-matter expertise on specific topics. With the Bank's help, the mayors intend to form subcommunities of practitioners across their cities on topics such as urban upgrading and solid-waste management. Their vision is, over time, to spread the overall approach to additional cities in their countries through a system of related communities.[15]

If we view the world as a learning system, we can imagine a constellation of communities of practice—a "worldwide web" of interwoven communities that focus on various civic practices at different levels, including district, municipal, regional, national, and global. This broader learning system collectively provides the foundation of social capital to foster global learning and to improve socioeconomic outcomes.[16] For example, as a city mayor, you would imagine your civic development challenge not only in terms of managing departments and budgets and pushing for new legislation, but also in terms of building the strength of local, multisector coalitions that steward civic disciplines in areas such as economic development, housing, and public safety. You would assess each of these coalitions in terms of how well they represented local constituencies, fostered trust and collaboration among diverse stakeholders, and leveraged local skills as well as external expertise and resources to solve local problems. You would encourage local coalitions in each civic domain—education, housing, health care, safety, economic development, infrastructure, cultural affairs, land use, and others—to link with relevant practitioner networks that include innovators and experts from around the nation and even the world. From this perspective, the challenge of governance is to build capacity by developing a constellation of communities of practice to steward various civic disciplines that are relevant to any city or nation.[17] These practice-based communities operate at both local and global levels, and complement the function of place-based communities in the civil sector just as they do teams and business units in the private sector.

To return to our initial question, if you were the CKO of the world, you would already have a growing number of early examples to support a community-based approach to your knowledge initiative. From the experience of organizations, you would know that designing the world as a learning system requires a mixture of intentional design actions and bottom-up community building and leadership. The challenge of "world design" would seem both unreasonably ambitious and yet something you could start working on right away. It is not driven by a grand scheme, but it grows step by step, community by community. It is already happening, requiring perhaps a bit of attention and systematization.[18]

Your challenge would have compelling implications for governance and, more generally, for civic participation. It generates many more questions. How do we govern organizations and society when we rely increasingly on knowledge and therefore on social capital voluntarily created and maintained by citizens? What can formal organizations—business, government, nonprofit—do to foster communities of practice that develop members and make contributions to sponsoring organizations and society? How might city and county governance be reconceived by framing the challenge of governing civil society in terms of practices as well as places? How can local communities be linked so they learn from each other's experience? How can intercity "CEO communities" consisting of mayors and other civic leaders act to catalyze and guide intercity practitioner networks in multiple domains? What is the role of government agencies at all levels to sponsor, legitimize, fund, legislate, institutionalize, or otherwise support such initiatives? Finally, how might a practice-based approach to social innovation and governance gain influence and impact by going global? What does this model suggest for global governance questions, on any number of topics, including the economy, environment, urban development, defense, human rights, and others?[19]

Learning Leadership from Business

Community organizing has a long tradition. This book is an attempt to show in practical ways how community-based approaches can be applied to organizing for knowledge. We have focused on business because for historical reasons, business has taken the lead in exploring these issues. Companies were ready to run. The knowledge economy had prompted them to focus on knowledge, and the limitations of early technologically based attempts had drawn attention to the social and cultural dimensions of knowledge. Current socioeconomic trends and the experience of leading firms suggest that communities of practice will continue to proliferate as knowledge-based structures that support learning and knowledge in organizations. But as we gain experience developing business-based communities, it will become easier to apply such methods outside the firm and even beyond networks of firms. Civil-sector communities might organize markets—including both businesses and consumers—and organize citizens with common interests in areas such as housing, parenting, health, education, the arts, and other areas of practice associated with human society.

Hence, what we are learning in businesses about organizing for learning and knowledge has important implications for the evolution of markets and for the challenges and opportunities associated with governance in society and the world.[20] Because community-organizing methods emphasize voluntary initiative and are organized around practices rather than boundaries that are defined by place or ownership structures, they are particularly relevant to market- and society-based applications. Business organizations are a good learning laboratory for several reasons. They have the motivation and the resources to move up the learning curve quickly. They are becoming a catalyst for civic communities of practice that help attract and develop a highly skilled workforce. And what people learn at work will influence their approach to civic life: Their experience of work-related communities of practice will help them take leadership in creating similar structures in other parts of their lives.

Firms that understand how to translate the power of communities into successful knowledge organizations will be the architects of tomorrow—not only because they will be more successful in the marketplace, but also because they will serve as a learning laboratory for exploring how to design the world as a learning system.

Notes

Chapter 1

1. In fact, the term *community of practice* was coined in the context of studies of traditional apprenticeship. Apprenticeship is often thought of as a relationship between a master and a student. Yet we observed that learning took place mostly during interactions with journeymen and more advanced apprentices. *Community of practice* is the term we used to refer to this social structure. Once we had the concept, however, we started to see these communities in many other settings, where there was no official institution of apprenticeship. See J. Lave and E. Wenger, *Situated Learning: Legitimate Peripheral Participation* (New York: Cambridge University Press, 1991).

2. In 1902, in his preface to the second edition of *The Division of Labor in Society* (New York: Free Press, 1964), sociologist Emile Durkheim traced the history of professional groups from ancient times through the twentieth century. Durkheim argued that occupational communities could provide the social connections that were needed to strengthen the fabric of societal trust and mutual commitment—even as the forces of industrialization and attendant social disruptions threatened to tear apart the historical ties that bound people together in ancestral towns and villages.

3. Scott Cook and Dvora Yanow describe this cluster of flute-making companies located in Boston. "Culture and Organizational Learning," *Journal of Management Inquiry* 2, no. 4 (1993): 373–390. More generally, Michael Porter showed that various types of industries, including shipbuilding, advertising, and household furniture, tend to cluster within a particular geographic region. "Clusters and the New Economics of Competition," *Harvard Business Review*, November–December 1998, 77–90. J. C. Spender found that industries themselves make up a kind of knowledge-based cluster

that includes companies sharing a common "industry recipe." *Industry Recipes: An Enquiry into the Nature and Sources of Managerial Judgement* (Oxford: Blackwell, 1989). A number of scholars have documented the ways in which Silicon Valley operates as an industry cluster with a concentration of technical and management skills related to high technology. See A. Saxenian, *Regional Advantage: Culture and Competition in Silicon Valley and Route 128* (Cambridge, MA: Harvard University Press, 1996); S. S. Cohen and G. Fields, "Social Capital and Capital Gains in Silicon Valley," *California Management Review* 41, no. 2 (1999): 108–130; and J. S. Brown and P. Duguid, *The Social Life of Information* (Boston: Harvard Business School Press, 2000), 161–172.

4. Over the last decade it has become widely accepted that an organization's capacity to learn, innovate, and leverage knowledge-based capabilities are critical to achieving market success. Since Peter Senge's *The Fifth Discipline: The Art and Practice of the Learning Organization* (New York: Currency/Doubleday, 1990) created a broader audience for the seminal work of Chris Argyris and Donald Schön, *Organizational Learning: A Theory of Action Perspective* (Reading, MA: Addison-Wesley, 1978), and for works by others on organizational learning, a slew of books have, in recent years, addressed the topics of learning and knowledge. Some of these books include: J. L. Badaracco, *The Knowledge Link: How Firms Compete through Strategic Alliances* (Boston: Harvard Business School Press, 1991); J. B. Quinn, *Intelligent Enterprise: A Knowledge and Service Based Paradigm for Industry* (New York: Free Press, 1992); P. F. Drucker, *Post-Capitalist Society* (New York: HarperBusiness, 1993); G. Hamel and C. K. Prahalad, *Competing for the Future* (Boston: Harvard Business School Press, 1994); D. Leonard-Barton, *Wellsprings of Knowledge: Building and Sustaining the Sources of Innovation* (Boston: Harvard Business School Press, 1995); I. Nonaka and H. Takeuchi, *The Knowledge-Creating Company: How Japanese Companies Create the Dynamics of Innovation* (New York: Oxford University Press, 1995); T. A. Stewart, *Intellectual Capital: The New Wealth of Organizations* (New York: Doubleday, 1997); T. H. Davenport and L. Prusak, *Working Knowledge: How Organizations Manage What They Know* (Boston: Harvard Business School Press, 1998); and D. A. Garvin, *Learning in Action: A Guide to Putting the Learning Organization to Work* (Boston: Harvard Business School Press, 2000).

5. Quinn, *Intelligent Enterprise*, and T. J. Peters, *Liberation Management: Necessary Disorganization for the Nanosecond Nineties* (New York: Knopf, 1992), describe the trends toward both disaggregation and extended networks, which are themselves driven by the imperative to compete on the basis of knowledge assets.

6. J. L. Badaracco argues that "globalization of knowledge" is the driving force behind the changes taking place in the modern corporation as it engages in joint ventures, alliances, and networks that connect firms around the world. See *The Knowledge Link*, 9.

7. Professional relationships and social ties are important reasons why people stay with a company. See P. Cappelli, "A Market-Driven Approach to Retaining Talent," *Harvard Business Review*, January–February 2000, 103–111, and G. Dessler, "How to Earn Your Employees' Commitment," *Academy of Management Executive* 13, no. 2 (1999): 58–67. Don Cohen and Larry Prusak argue that companies can "win the war for talent" by offering employees an opportunity to build a sense of community with workplace colleagues. *In Good Company: How Social Capital Makes Organizations Work* (Boston:

Harvard Business School Press, 2001), 19. Moreover, employees have good reason to stay when their companies can offer attractive opportunities to participate in robust communities. Research undertaken at Bell Labs found that its star performers were those scientists who were members of strong networks. See R. E. Kelley and J. Caplan, "How Bell Labs Creates Star Performers," *Harvard Business Review*, July–August 1993, 128–139.

8. A number of observers have emphasized the importance of developing a "knowledge strategy" that is linked to the overall business strategy. See M. H. Zack, "Developing a Knowledge Strategy," *California Management Review* 41, no. 3 (1999): 125–145; N. Foote and B. Manville, "Strategy as If Knowledge Mattered," *Fast Company*, April 1996, 66–67; and M. T. Hansen, N. Nohria, and T. Tierney, "What's Your Strategy for Managing Knowledge?" *Harvard Business Review*, March–April 1999, 106–116. Such strategies have historically been referred to in the academic literature as "resource-based" strategies. See Nonaka and Takeuchi, *The Knowledge-Creating Company*, 46–49, and J. B. Barney, "Looking Inside for Competitive Advantage," *Academy of Management Executive* 9, no. 4 (1995): 49–61. For examples of communities that steward strategic capabilities, see J. S. Brown and E. S. Gray, "The People Are the Company," *Fast Company*, November 1995, 78–82, and J. Storck and P. A. Hill, "Knowledge Diffusion through 'Strategic Communities,'" *Sloan Management Review* 41, no. 2 (2000): 63–74. An important benefit of strategic communities is their ability to help the firm both inform and implement strategic visions, thus closing the perennial gap between strategy development and execution.

9. In his studies of professional practice, and architects in particular, Donald Schön talks about having a "conversation with the situation." This conversation is framed by the experience of the professional, but is always an interactive, improvisational, and reflective engagement with a problem. See *The Reflective Practitioner: How Professionals Think in Action* (New York: Basic Books, 1983), 76–104.

10. Peter Drucker describes surgeons as classic "knowledge workers" who must be responsible for building learning and innovation into their work, and who rely on colleagues for assessing effectiveness in their practice. "Knowledge-Worker Productivity: The Biggest Challenge," *California Management Review* 41, no. 2 (1999): 86. Cohen and Prusak describe the problems that occur when a doctor has no colleagues with whom he can confer to keep current in the field. They recount the story of FDR's doctor who, in his dedication to his one famous patient, lost contact with other patients and colleagues and ironically thus "may have failed to learn things that might have extended the president's life." *In Good Company*, 7.

11. See R. McDermott, "Why Information Technology Inspired, but Cannot Deliver Knowledge Management," *California Management Review* 41, no. 3 (1999): 103–117.

12. M. Polyani, *The Tacit Dimension* (New York: Anchor Doubleday, 1966). Nonaka and Takeuchi describe the nature of tacit knowledge in a broader treatment of epistemology that includes both Eastern and Western perspectives. *The Knowledge-Creating Company*, 20–55.

13. Nonaka and Takeuchi (*The Knowledge-Creating Company*) and D. Leonard and S. Sensiper ("The Role of Tacit Knowledge in Group Innovation," *California Management Review* 40, no. 3 [1998]: 112–132) argue that tacit knowledge is a critical source

of innovation. Executives at Chapparal Steel were never worried about competitors learning to replicate their distinctive methods while visiting their operations, because they claimed that in a visit one only sees the visible, and it is the invisible that really matters. See D. Leonard-Barton, "The Factory as a Learning Laboratory," *Sloan Management Review* 34, no. 1 (1992): 23–38. Tacit knowledge is not only about expert skill, but also about the "care why" that motivates practitioners to create and to achieve excellence in their work. J. B. Quinn, P. Anderson, and S. Finkelstein, "Managing Professional Intellect: Making the Most of the Best," *Harvard Business Review*, March–April 1996, 72. On the nature of knowledge more generally, C. W. Churchman provides an extraordinary historical review of Western epistemology and suggests implications for "the design of inquiring systems" in organizations and society. *The Design of Inquiring Systems: Basic Concepts of Systems and Organization* (New York: Basic Books, 1971).

14. See Schön, *The Reflective Practitioner*, for examples of the highly tacit nature of individual professional expertise in areas such as architecture, psychotherapy, engineering, and town planning. R. Nelson and S. Winter describe a type of tacit knowledge that is embedded in "routines" at the organizational level which no one person can understand completely. *An Evolutionary Theory of Economic Change* (Cambridge, MA: Harvard University Press, 1982), 96–136.

15. W. M. Snyder, "Organization Learning and Performance: An Exploration of the Linkages between Organization Learning, Knowledge, and Performance" (Ph.D. diss., University of Southern California, 1996), 37–43.

16. Law is a good illustration of the dance of the tacit and the explicit. Our societies have found it very useful to articulate our social norms into laws, but we also have judges and legal experts who interpret these laws. What makes laws effective is what literary theorist Stanley Fish calls the "community of interpretation" that gives them meaning in practice. You can never fully articulate how this community gives meaning to laws. In fact, the more you articulate, through briefs and precedents, the more you need a community to make sense of the new documents. You need both: the laws and the community. The explicit and the tacit always need each other to be effective. See S. Fish, *Doing What Comes Naturally: Change, Rhetoric and the Practice of Theory in Literary and Legal Studies* (Durham, NC: Duke University Press, 1989).

17. Practice is a tangled combination of tacit and explicit dimensions. The challenge of managing their interplay has been described as a "generative dance between organizational knowledge and organizational knowing" (S. D. N. Cook and J. S. Brown, "Bridging Epistemologies: The Generative Dance between Organizational Knowledge and Organizational Knowing," *Organizational Science* 10, no. 4 [1999]: 381–400) and as a "balancing act between process and practice" (J. S. Brown and P. Duguid, "Balancing Act: How to Capture Knowledge without Killing It," *Harvard Business Review*, May–June 2000, 73–80). E. Wenger refers to this interplay in his discussion of the duality of the community processes of "reification" and "participation." *Communities of Practice: Learning, Meaning, and Identity* (New York: Cambridge University Press, 1998), 51–71.

18. Bruno Latour emphasizes the importance of having colleagues with whom to debate facts and interpretations in order to establish a scientific domain. He argues that the "first principle" of technology and science (or "technoscience") is that "the

construction of facts and machines is a *collective* [Latour's italics] process." He describes the existential dilemma of a technoscience practitioner who finds himself without colleagues: "What happens to the inside of a specialty made up of only one person? This is the question that makes Joao so despondent: the inside disappears as well. Since he has no one to discuss the draft of his articles with, no one to try out the links he makes between various parts of chip architecture, no one to whom he can submit his proposals for trials of strength, no one to debug his prototypes, Joao ends up not *knowing* what is real and what is fictional in MOS technology." See *Science in Action: How to Follow Scientists and Engineers through Society* (Cambridge, MA: Harvard University Press, 1987), 29, 152.

19. For a further discussion of the collective and individual character of knowing and learning, see Wenger, *Communities of Practice*, 86–102, 134–148.

20. Badaracco offers evidence of how quickly the stocks of knowledge are growing and changing. For example, he cites studies by bibliometry and scientometry scholars who have found that the growth rates of scientific journals, books, and papers has been doubling in quantity every fifteen years for the past two centuries—a kind of Moore's Law of exponential growth in scientific insight. He explains that knowledge is becoming more specialized as it grows—there were fifty-four scientific specialties listed in the National Register of Scientific and Technical Personnel after World War II, and twenty years later there were 900. *The Knowledge Link*, 24–25. Recently, a Merrill Lynch study found that 50 percent of employee skills will become outdated within three to five years. M. Moe and H. Blodgett, "The Knowledge Web," Global Securities Research & Economics Group, Global Fundamental Equity Research Department, 2000.

21. J. P. Walsh and G. R. Ungson's review of organizational memory describes the variety of ways in which knowledge can be stored or embedded in organizations. See "Organizational Memory," *Academy of Management Review* 16, no. 1 (1991): 57–91. See also R. D. Pea, "Practices of Distributed Intelligence and Designs for Education," in *Distributed Cognitions: Psychological and Educational Considerations*, ed. G. Salomon (New York: Cambridge University Press, 1993), 47–87, on the ways knowledge is distributed in the context of practice and social relationships.

22. Peter Senge indicated that researchers as well as managers have been discovering new ways to organize for learning and managing knowledge. He was asked in a recent interview what he had learned in the last ten years about "the challenge of bringing the idea of the learning organization into reality." Senge responded, "We're finding again and again that the guiding principle is that significant innovations must be diffused through informal, self-organizing networks, through horizontal communities of practice. How you strengthen these communities is the key to how you disseminate innovation and maintain the innovators." R. Zemke, "Why Organizations Still Aren't Learning," *Training* (September 1999): 49.

23. Centers of excellence serving highly distributed practitioners are sometimes organized according to a community-like model in which a group of working practitioners—in conjunction with full-time staff—takes the initiative to steward their practice. See K. Moore and J. Birkinshaw, "Managing Knowledge in Global Service Firms: Centers of Excellence," *Academy of Management Executive* 12, no. 4 (1998): 83–86, 92.

24. Many observers have noted the challenge of managing communities of practice: "indeed, managing [them] can kill them" (T. A. Stewart, *Intellectual Capital: The New Wealth of Organizations* [New York: Doubleday, 1977], 97); or "virtually everyone who has studied them agrees that communities of practice cannot be created out of the blue by management fiat . . ." (D. Stamps, "Communities of Practice: Learning Is Social. Training Is Irrelevant?" *Training* 34, no. 2 [1997]: 39); or "communities of practice evolve, they are not created" (J. Liedtka, "Linking Competitive Advantage with Communities of Practice," *Journal of Management Inquiry* 8, no. 1 [1999]: 7).

25. D. G. Hoopes and S. Postrel found, for example, that software developers were less likely to produce "glitches" and more likely to finish projects on time when they could leverage a base of shared knowledge and cooperative relationships with colleagues. "Shared Knowledge, 'Glitches,' and Product Development Performance," *Strategic Management Journal* 20, no. 9 (1999): 837–865. Robin Teigland found that Internet consultants and programming "techies" increased their creativity and ability to solve difficult problems when they participated in both intra-firm and external (Internet-based) communities of practice. "Communities of Practice in an Internet Firm—Netovation versus On-Time Performance," in *Knowledge and Communities: Resources for the Knowledge-Based Economy*, ed. E. Lesser, M. Fontaine, and J. Slusher (Boston: Butterworth-Heinemann, 2000), 151–178.

26. A number of scholars have noted that communities of practice foster both human capital (individual skills and professional identity) and social capital (social networks that give rise to trust, reciprocity, and shared understanding). Cohen and Prusak, *In Good Company*, and J. Nahapiet and S. Ghoshal, "Social Capital, Intellectual Capital, and the Organizational Advantage," *Academy of Management Review* 23, no. 2 (1998): 242–266. For articles that focus on value to members for their own professional development or access to expertise, see M. C. Higgins and K. E. Kram, "Reconceptualizing Mentoring at Work: A Developmental Network Perspective," *Academy of Management Review* 26, no. 2 (2001): 264–288; D. Krackhardt and J. R. Hanson, "Informal Networks: The Company behind the Chart," *Harvard Business Review*, July–August 1993, 104–111; and E. Fink and L. B. Resnick, "Developing Principals as Instructional Leaders," *Phi Delta Kappan* 82, no. 8 (2001): 598–606. For articles that show how the professional peer-to-peer relationships that are characteristic of communities of practice can contribute to the success of intrafirm and interfirm networks and alliances, see W. Tsai and S. Ghoshal, "Social Capital and Value Creation: The Role of Intra-firm Networks," *Academy of Management Journal* 41, no. 4 (1998): 464–476; W. W. Powell, W. W. Koput, and L. Smith-Doerr, "Interorganizational Collaboration and the Locus of Innovation: Networks of Learning in Biotechnology," *Administrative Science Quarterly* 41, no. 1 (1996): 116–145; and J. P. Liebeskind et al., "Social Networks, Learning, and Flexibility: Sourcing Scientific Knowledge in New Biotechnology Firms," *Organizational Science* 7, no. 4 (1996): 428–443.

27. R. McDermott describes the connection between teams and communities as a "double-knit" structure. "Learning across Teams: How to Build Communities of Practice in Team Organizations," *Knowledge Management Review* 8 (May–June 1999): 32–38. Nonaka and Takeuchi describe the relationship between business units, project teams, and knowledge structures as a "hypertext organization" because project teams

and formal units draw on the knowledge structures on an as-needed basis as if clicking on hypertext to access information through a URL. *The Knowledge-Creating Company*, 160–196.

28. Various types of informal structures, of course, have always existed in organizations. There has been considerable research since the early years of management theory on the interdependence of formal and informal phenomena in organizations, including the pioneering research on work groups by F. J. Roethlisberger and W. J. Dickson (*Management and the Worker: An Account of a Research Program Conducted by the Western Electric Company, Hawthorne Works, Chicago* [Cambridge, MA: Harvard University Press, 1939]), and C. I. Barnard's reflections on "informal organizations and their relation to formal organizations" (*The Functions of the Executive* [Cambridge, MA: Harvard University Press, 1968]), 114–123. Since the 1950s, there has been a steady stream of research on how to integrate "human factors" in formal organizations—manifested in studies related to group dynamics (J. R. Hackman, "Group Influences on Individuals," in *Handbook of Industrial and Organizational Psychology*, ed. M. D. Dunnett [Chicago: Rand McNally, 1976], 1455–1518); sociotechnical systems (W. A. Pasmore, *Designing Effective Organizations: The Sociotechnical Systems Perspective* [New York: Wiley, 1988]); organizational culture (E. H. Schein, *Organizational Culture and Leadership* [San Francisco: Jossey-Bass, 1992]); "informal networks" (D. Krackhardt and J. Hanson, "Informal Networks: The Company behind the Chart"); and "self-organizing systems" (M. J. Wheatley, *Leadership and the New Science: Discovering Order in a Chaotic World* [San Francisco: Berrett-Koehler, 1994]). Recently, scholars have become more explicit about the role of personal networks in organization design. J. H. Gittell and L. M. Weiss, "Linking Intra- and Inter-organizational Networks through Organization Design: The Case of Patient Care Coordination," working paper 97-064, Harvard Business School, Boston, 2001. For a review of perspectives on the "informal organization," see also R. W. Scott, *Organizations: Rational, Natural, and Open Systems* (Englewood Cliffs, NJ: Prentice Hall, 1992).

29. Thomas Malone and Robert Laubacher argue that an increasing amount of work is done by independent freelancers who have no organizational home. "The Dawn of the e-Lance Economy," *Harvard Business Review*, September–October 1998, 144–152. They predict that these independent practitioners are likely to organize into independent "guilds" for several reasons, including socialization, professional development, and reducing health care costs and financial risks. R. Laubacher and T. W. Malone, "Retreat of the Firm and the Rise of Guilds: The Employment Relationship in an Age of Virtual Business," Twenty-First Century Initiative working paper 033, MIT Sloan School of Management, Cambridge, MA, 2000.

Chapter 2

1. Companies have used many terms to describe groups that correspond to our understanding of communities of practice, including "tech clubs," "learning networks," "thematic groups," "knowledge communities," "competency networks," "practices," "interest groups," and "knowledge centers," among others. Researchers have also used a variety of

names to describe similar phenomena, including "invisible colleges" (D. Crane, *Invisible Colleges: Diffusion of Knowledge in Scientific Communities* [Chicago: University of Chicago Press, 1972]); "occupational communities" (J. Van Maanen and S. Barley, "Occupational Communities: Culture and Control in Organizations," in *Research in Organizational Behavior*, vol. 6, ed. B. M. Staw and L. L. Cummings [Greenwich, CT: JAI Press, 1984]); "communities of practitioners" (C. Argyris, R. Putnam, and D. M. Smith, *Action Science* [San Francisco: Jossey-Bass, 1987]), and D. A. Schön, *Educating the Reflective Practitioner* [San Francisco: Jossey-Bass, 1987]); "cognitive communities" (J. F. Porac et al., "Competitive Groups as Cognitive Communities: The Case of the Scottish Knitwear Manufacturers," *Journal of Management Studies* 26 [1989]: 397–416); "epistemic communities" (P. Haas, "Introduction: Epistemic Communities and International Policy Coordination," *International Organization* 46, no. 1 [1992]: 1–36); "communities of knowing" (R. J. Boland and R. V. Tenkasi, "Perspective Making and Perspective Taking in Communities of Knowing," *Organization Science* 6, no. 4 [1995]: 350–372); "occupational cultures" (E. H. Schein, "Three Cultures of Management: The Key to Organizational Learning," *Sloan Management Review* 38, no. 1 [1996]: 9–20); "knowledge communities" (J. Botkin, *Smart Business* [New York: Free Press, 1999]); and "guilds" (D. Leonard and W. Swap, "Gurus in the Garage," *Harvard Business Review*, November–December 2000, 71–79).

2. We discuss distributed communities in more detail in chapter 6.

3. A. L. Oliver and P. Liebeskind, in "Three Levels of Networking for Sourcing Intellectual Capital in Biotechnology," *International Studies of Management and Organization* 27, no. 4 (1998): 76–103, describe interrelated intrafirm and interfirm knowledge-sharing networks in the biotechnology industry. Leonard and Swap, in "Gurus in the Garage," describe an example of an interorganizational network of venture capitalists in Silicon Valley.

4. In an article on types of "work-related learning networks," R. F. Poell et al. differentiate networks that are more formally sponsored and directed by managers and those that are more horizontal or "organic." "Strategies in Organizing Work-Related Learning Projects," *Human Resource Development Quarterly* 10, no. 1 (1999): 43–61.

5. David Whetten, in his Presidential Address at the 2000 Annual Meeting of the Academy of Management, described the "social intercourse among academics" as "a fellowship" in which "the business of academe is best accomplished when it is encompassed within a social fabric characterized by open, honest, and trusting relationships." "What Matters Most," *Academy of Management Journal* 26, no. 2 (2000): 176. Research on academic professional development supports Whetten's assertion of the importance of personal relationships for the professional development of scholars. C. J. G. Gersick et al., "Learning from Academia: The Importance of Relationships in Professional Life," *Academy of Management Journal* 43, no. 6 (2000): 1026–1044.

6. The notion of practice has a long intellectual history and has become an important way to frame the nature of knowledge in action in organizations. The American philosopher John Dewey argued that knowledge was manifested most rigorously by what you could *do*, not merely what you claimed to understand. See C. Argyris, R. Putnam, and D. M. Smith, *Action Science*, and D. A. Schön, *The Reflective Practitioner*

(New York: Basic Books, 1983). In social theory, Bourdieu's seminal work on the nature of practice has helped to establish its importance as an influential sociological framework. *Outline of a Theory of Practice* (Cambridge: Cambridge University Press, 1977). For a review of distributed practice at the organization level, see H. Tsoukas, "The Firm as a Distributed Knowledge System: A Constructionist Approach," *Strategic Management Journal* 17 (winter special issue 1996): 11–25.

7. E. Wenger, *Communities of Practice: Learning, Meaning, and Identity* (New York: Cambridge University Press), 1998. See also L. Berry et al., who noted, "An interactive community of coworkers who collaborate, overcome, and achieve together is a powerful antidote to service burn-out." "Five Imperatives for Improving Service Quality," *Sloan Management Review* 31, no. 4 (1990): 33. Cited in J. Liedtka, "Linking Competitive Advantage with Communities of Practice," *Journal of Management Inquiry* 8, no. 1 (1999): 5–16.

8. Many communities create an explicit "knowledge map" of their domain by generating issues, categorizing them, and drawing connections between them. For instance, a community focused on helping offices implement team-based structures at the Veterans Benefits Administration created a map of key issues, including team-development skills and processes, management support, levels of interest in various regional offices, availability of team-based measures, and others. The map helped the community define its learning agenda and organize projects. See also T. H. Davenport and L. Prusak, *Working Knowledge: How Organizations Manage What They Know* (Boston: Harvard Business School Press), 72–80.

9. M. Csikszentmihalyi (*Creativity: Flow and the Psychology of Discovery and Invention* [New York: HarperCollins, 1996]); T. M. Amabile ("Motivating Creativity in Organizations: On Doing What You Love and Loving What You Do," *California Management Review* 40, no. 1 [1997]: 39–58); and M. Polanyi (*The Tacit Dimension* [New York: Anchor Doubleday, 1966]), among others, have explained the importance of passion and personal investment in a domain to spur creativity and to engage the persistent effort that is required to develop expertise or create significant innovations.

10. T. Bender and S. M. Kruger's sociological definition of community is a helpful benchmark: "A community involves a limited number of people in a somewhat restricted social space or network held together by shared understandings and a sense of obligation. Relationships are close, often intimate, and usually face to face. Individuals are bound together by affective or emotional ties rather than by a perception of individual self-interest. There is a 'we-ness' in a community; one is a member." *Community and Social Change in America* (Baltimore: Johns Hopkins University Press, 1982), 7–8. K. J. Klein and T. A. D'Aunno ("Psychological Sense of Community in the Workplace," *Journal of Community Psychology* 14 [1986]: 365–377) cite S. B. Sarason's definition of the psychological sense of community as "the sense that one belongs in and is meaningfully a part of a larger collectivity" (*The Psychological Sense of Community* [San Francisco: Jossey-Bass, 1974], 1); they apply this notion to "functional subgroups" in organizations that consist of members who "work together on a common task (e.g., marketing, purchasing)." A. Etzioni notes that the term "community," like "many widely used terms [is]

not readily definable;" he then defines several key characteristics: a web of affect-laden relationships, commitment to shared values, norms, and meanings—along with a shared history and identity, and a relatively high level of responsiveness to both members and the world. "The Responsive Community. A Communitarian Perspective," *American Sociological Review* 61, no. 1 (1996): 1–11.

11. T. H. Davenport and J. C. Beck argue that in an economy with a surfeit of information, attention is increasingly at a premium. Communities help members sift through the surfeit to find out which ideas, methods, and problems to pay attention to. *The Attention Economy: Understanding the New Currency of Business* (Boston: Harvard Business School Press, 2001).

12. J. Van Manaan and S. Barley's description of "occupational communities" does not clearly specify whether ongoing mutual interaction is a defining element. "Occupational Communities: Culture and Control in Organizations," 287–365. Brown and Duguid refer to groups who share a practice but whose "relations among network members are significantly looser than those within a community of practice" as "networks of practice." They explain: "[M]ost of the people within such a network will never know, know of, or come across one another. And yet they are capable of sharing a great deal of knowledge." "Knowledge and Organization: A Social-Practice Perspective," *Organization Science* 12, no. 1 (2001): 205.

13. Dorothy Leonard and Walter Swap argue that creativity and innovation depend on "creative abrasion," the right combination of diversity and common ground that can propel iterative processes of divergence and convergence toward a creative output. *When Sparks Fly: Igniting Creativity in Groups* (Boston: Harvard Business School Press, 1999).

14. According to anthropologists, "real" communities rarely include more than 150 members because that is about the highest number of people one can know in significant emotional terms. Community feelings of mutuality and intimacy are woven from threads of interpersonal relationships, and these take time and experience to develop. M. Kochen found that while contemporary people may know over 1,000 people, they only maintain about 20 active community ties. *The Small World* (Norwood, NJ: Ablex, 1989). M. Gladwell explains that such size limits are driven by the "psychological preconditions for transactive memory," which he defines as "knowing someone well enough to know what they know, and knowing them well enough so that you can trust them to know things in their specialty. It's the re-creation, on an organizationwide level, of the kind of intimacy and trust that exists in a family." *The Tipping Point: How Little Things Can Make a Big Difference* (Boston: Little Brown, 2000), 190.

15. Historically, group studies have identified multiple types of leadership in groups including task-oriented and people-oriented leaders. R. F. Bales, "Task Roles and Social Roles in Problem-Solving Groups," in *Readings in Social Psychology*, ed. E. Maccoby et al. (New York: Holt, Rinehart and Winston, 1958), 437–447. Gladwell describes several types of leaders who are crucial to social movements and relevant for communities—connectors, mavens, and salesmen. *The Tipping Point*. Research on civic organizing efforts has identified a number of community-organizing roles, including motivator, networker, teacher, convener, integrator, driver, and mentor, each of

which plays an especially important role at particular stages of an initiative's life cycle. D. Henton et al., *Grassroots Leaders for a New Economy: How Civic Entrepreneurs Are Building Prosperous Communities* (San Francisco: Jossey-Bass, 1997), 77.

16. R. D. Putnam, *Bowling Alone: The Collapse and Revival of American Community* (New York: Simon & Schuster, 2000); Cohen and Prusak, *In Good Company* (Boston: Harvard Business School Press, 2001).

17. Putnam notes the importance of "generalized reciprocation" where one gives to others without expectation of direct quid pro quo. Such gifts are much more likely in communities with high levels of social capital where members share "mutual expectations that a benefit granted now should be repaid in the future," even if not from the direct recipient. He goes on to describe the virtuous cycle between such giving and the trust that fosters it: "In communities where people can be confident that trusting will be requited, not exploited, exchange is more likely to ensue. Conversely, repeated exchange over a period of time tends to encourage the development of a norm of generalized reciprocity." *Making Democracy Work: Civic Traditions in Modern Italy* (Princeton, NJ: Princeton University Press, 1993), 173. On a practical level, D. H. Maister explains that the first principle for fostering such collaboration in a professional services firm is to encourage "*long-term repeated interaction between the same people* [Maister's italics]. Cooperation emerges when people find it in their interest to do favors for each other, to help each other out. However these favors rarely occur simultaneously. . . . To sustain this, the future must have a large enough shadow: those who are to cooperate must have a large enough chance of interacting with, and needing, each other again." *Managing the Professional Service Firm* (New York: Simon & Schuster, 1993), 338. A community's sense of connectedness and continuity provides the "future shadow" that fosters a feeling of mutual commitment and makes such reciprocation more likely.

18. Amy Edmonson's research on team learning showed a relationship between mutual trust and members' ability to acknowledge and learn from errors as a team. "Learning from Mistakes Is Easier Said than Done: Group and Organizational Influences on the Detection and Correction of Human Error," *Journal of Applied Behavioral Science* 32, no. 1 (1996): 5–28.

19. Psychologist Mihalyi Csikszentmihalyi explains that artists and scientists rely on the foundation of a commonly shared "field" for both sources of inspiration and the practice elements needed to bring them to fruition. *Creativity*. C. Moorman and A. S. Miner have demonstrated a correlation between an organization's memory and its capacity for improvisation. "Organizational Improvisation and Organizational Memory," *Academy of Management Review* 23, no. 4 (1998): 698–723.

20. A number of studies in organizational culture have focused on occupational groups—such as engineers, marketers, and managers—as subcultures within an organization. E. H. Schein, "Three Cultures of Management"; J. Martin, *Cultures in Organizations* (New York: Oxford University Press, 1992); and S. A. Sackman, "Culture and Subcultures: An Analysis of Organizational Knowledge," *Administrative Science Quarterly* 37, no. 1 (1992): 140–161.

21. B. Jordan, "Cosmopolitan Obstetrics: Some Insights from the Training of Traditional Midwives," *Social Science and Medicine* 28 (1987), 925–944.

22. J. Orr, in *Talking about Machines: An Ethnography of a Modern Job* (Ithaca, NY: IRL Press, 1996), argues that the war stories shared by the repair technicians constitute a form of collective memory for their community. R. C. Schank and G. S. Morson (*Tell Me a Story: Narratives and Intelligence* [Chicago: Northwestern University Press, 1995]); T. H. Davenport and L. Prusak (*Working Knowledge*); and S. Denning (*The Springboard: How Storytelling Ignites Action in Knowledge-Era Organizations* [Boston: Butterworth-Heinemann, 2001]) explain that stories are often the best way to capture and transfer knowledge, because they integrate contextual information better than purely conceptual or procedural methods.

23. Nonaka and Takeuchi explain that distinct "knowledge-creating" activities—such as "externalization," or "combination"—are typically matched to corresponding types of knowledge—such as "conceptual" or "systemic" knowledge. *The Knowledge Creating Company*. W. M. Snyder describes a range of learning approaches, formal and informal, cognitive and behavioral, and how these can best be applied to discover and diffuse tacit and explicit knowledge. "Organization Learning and Performance: An Exploration of the Linkages between Organization Learning, Knowledge, and Performance" (Ph.D. diss., University of Southern California, 1996).

24. In some cases neighborhood groups do organize as communities of practice, often in response to an urgent problem. In such cases members develop a shared practice in community organizing—related to specific issues such as housing, public safety, or education. See P. Medoff and H. Sklar, *Streets of Hope* (Boston: South End Press, 1994).

25. See D. Krackardt and J. R. Hanson, "Informal Networks: The Company behind the Chart," *Harvard Business Review*, July–August 1993, 104–111, and N. Nohria and R. C. Eccles, *Networks and Organizations: Structure, Form, and Action* (Boston: Harvard Business School Press, 1992), for descriptions of informal networks in organizations. J. Lipnack and J. Stamps, *The TeamNet Factor: Bringing the Power of Boundary Crossing into the Heart of Your Business* (New York: Wiley, 1995), and *The Age of the Network* (New York: Wiley, 1994) describe intentional networks in organizations designed explicitly to connect distributed team activities for various purposes such as marketing and training. Many of the characteristics and principles of these "teamnets" also apply to communities of practice—multiple leaders, voluntary links, and integrated levels. Communities of practice, however, focus more intently on stewarding a practice, as opposed to teamnets' broader range of objectives, which include marketing, product delivery, and resource management, as well as knowledge-related goals.

26. Csikszentmihalyi's study of creativity in a multitude of disciplines, including arts and sciences, found that three analogous elements were critical: a chosen "domain," a "field of experts" who can recognize and validate innovations (i.e., "community"), and a "culture" that includes theories, rules, methods, and stories (like our notion of "practice"). Csikszentmihalyi, *Creativity*. These three dimensions are also recalled by the three elements used to describe community in one stream of the Jewish tradition: believing, belonging, and behaving; and by the three foundational elements of Buddhism: buddha (enlightenment; domain), sanga (community), and dharma (practice).

Chapter 3

1. C. Alexander, S. Ishikawa and M. Silverstein, *A Pattern Language: Towns, Buildings, Construction* (New York: Oxford University Press, 1977), and J. Jacobs, *The Death and Life of Great American Cities* (New York: Vintage, 1993).

2. Traditional approaches to organization design have generally focused on the design of formal systems and structures to address environmental demands, task uncertainty, and individual needs (J. R. Galbraith, *Organization Design* [Reading, MA: Addison-Wesley, 1977]), or to leverage the power of information technology (M. Hammer and J. Champy, *Reengineering the Corporation: A Manifesto for Business Revolution* [New York: HarperBusiness, 1993]). While these design objectives are reasonable and effectively address important problems, Cal Pava noted that they do not address the dynamic, nonlinear, boundary-spanning nature of knowledge work conducted by members of "discretionary coalitions." "Redesigning Sociotechnical Systems Design: Concepts and Methods for the 1990s," *The Journal of Applied Behavioral Science* 22, no. 3 (1986): 207. Historically, a number of scholars have argued for organic metaphors to describe organizations, including T. Burns and G. M. Stalker, who referred to innovative organizations as "organic" versus more efficiency-oriented, "mechanistic" organizations (*The Management of Innovation* [London: Tavistock, 1961]). Since then many scholars have described organizations using metaphors or frameworks that describe the "aliveness" of organizations from a variety of perspectives. F. Capra (*The Web of Life: A New Understanding of Living Systems* [New York: Doubleday, 1997]) describes organizations as biological systems; M. J. Wheatley (*Leadership and the New Science: Discovering Order in a Chaotic World* [San Francisco: Berrett-Koehler, 1994]) describes them as systems that are governed by self-organizing principles associated with complexity and chaos theory; A. P. de Geus (*The Living Company* [Boston, MA: Harvard Business School Press, 1997]) argues that learning is the key to sustaining the living organization; J. C. Collins and J. I. Porras (*Built to Last* [New York: HarperCollins, 1994]) emphasize the importance of shared values; G. M. Bellman (*The Beauty of the Beast* [San Francisco: Berrett-Koehler, 2000], 53) challenges members to develop organizations that aspire to life and "regenerate themselves" over many generations. Finally, Dexter Dunphy and Andrew Griffiths argue that corporations must, in turn, foster both a healthy environment and a vibrant "human ecosystem" to remain sustainable for the long term. Notably, they state that achieving such ends depends on a global community of practice to steward the "organizational renewal movement." *The Sustainable Corporation: Organisational* [sic] *Renewal in Australia* (St. Leonards, Australia: Allen & Unwin, 1998), 202, 204.

3. Christopher Alexander's approach to designing buildings and towns in a way that invites aliveness and vitality informs much of this approach to community design. Alexander, Ishikawa, and Silverstein, *A Pattern Language*, and Alexander, *The Timeless Way of Building*.

4. C. Alexander, *The Timeless Way of Building* (New York: Oxford University Press, 1979).

5. K. Kelley compares the design of complex machines and social systems to the process of intentionally creating a prairie. It is not a process where the design can be

defined up front and executed programmatically. Rather, it begins by establishing a living "chunk" or "whole organelle," which grows organically. *Out of Control: The New Biology of Machines, Social Systems, and the Economic World* (Reading, MA: Addison-Wesley, 1994), 45, 57–68.

6. This principle is consistent with the direction of organization theory and practice since the seminal work of McGregor, *The Human Side of Enterprise* (New York: McGraw-Hill, 1960), and Argyris, *Integrating the Individual and the Organization* (New York: Wiley, 1964). Warren Bennis and Philip Slater, among others, have emphasized design approaches that call for increased participation of members at all levels in decisions about the design and management of their work. Bennis and Slater, *The Temporary Society* (New York: Harper & Row, 1968). In later decades, Argyris and Schön have described in detail the conditions for dialogue, or "organizational learning," to address both routine issues and those that challenge basic values and beliefs. *Organizational Learning: A Theory of Action Perspective* (Reading, MA: Addison-Wesley, 1978). McLagan and Nel outline various levels of participation and how to change roles and systems to support participative management approaches. *The Age of Participation* (San Francisco: Berrett-Koehler, 1995).

7. The perspective of insiders is most powerful when it includes an understanding of outsiders. Social change, whether in an organization or society at large, is often driven by an insider who has acquired perspective on the world outside. See, for instance, R. A. Nisbet, *Social Change and History: Aspects of the Western Theory of Development* (London: Oxford University Press, 1975), and J. Campbell, *The Hero with a Thousand Faces* (Princeton, NJ: Princeton University Press, 1949).

8. J. Lave and E. Wenger found that apprentices learned a great deal through "legitimate peripheral participation"; that is, by participating peripherally in a practice where there were opportunities to learn from masters and more experienced journeymen. *Situated Learning: Legitimate Peripheral Participation* (New York: Cambridge University Press, 1991). For example, apprentice tailors in Africa gained entry to the practice at first by running errands and performing simple finishing tasks, such as sewing buttons, which involved little risk but gave them a good sense of the final product.

9. R. McDermott, "Why Information Technology Inspired, but Cannot Deliver Knowledge Management," *California Management Review* 41, no. 3 (1999): 103–117.

10. R. Oldenburg explains that informal public places such as piazzas, cafés, and hair salons provide an essential context for fostering the various interpersonal connections that weave a community together over time. *Celebrating the Third Place: Inspiring Stories about the Great Good Places at the Heart of Our Communities* (New York: Marlowe & Company, 1989). P. Katz and V. Scully describe the "new urbanism" school of city planning, which emphasizes design elements such as front porches on residential streets, to encourage spontaneous conversations between neighbors. *The New Urbanism: Toward an Architecture of Community* (New York: McGraw-Hill, 1993).

11. Oldenberg, *Celebrating the Third Place*.

12. C. J. G. Gersick found that project teams exhibited a consistent time-based pattern of behavior in which team members would predictably shift gears at the halfway point and become more self-conscious about how to use the remaining time to meet

their objective. "Time and Transition in Work Teams: Toward a New Model of Group Development," *Academy of Management Journal* 31, no. 1 (1988): 9–41.

Chapter 4

1. R. McDermott and J. Kendrick, "How Learning Communities Steward Knowledge," in *Best Practices in Knowledge Management*, ed. Lewis Carter (Boston: Linkage Press, 2000).

2. See R. McDermott, "Planned Spontaneity," *Knowledge Management Review* 3, no. 4 (2000): 5–11.

3. We see this life-cycle pattern in social systems at various levels, including in individual psychological development (R. Kegan, *The Evolving Self* [Cambridge, MA: Harvard University Press, 1982]); in groups (B. W. Tuckman, "Development Sequences in Small Groups," *Psychological Bulletin* 63 [1965]: 384–399); in organizations (L. Greiner, "Evolution and Revolution as Organizations Grow," *Harvard Business Review*, July–August 1972, 37–46); and in the rise and fall of nations (M. Olson, *The Rise and Decline of Nations: Economic Growth, Stagflation and Social Rigidities* [New Haven, CT: Yale University Press, 1982]).

4. Developmental psychologists describe the value of working through predictable challenges as instrumental to the maturing process. Kegan, *The Evolving Self*; J. Loevinger, *Ego Development* (San Francisco: Jossey-Bass, 1976); and E. H. Erikson, *Childhood and Society* (New York: Norton, 1963). Organizational studies also demonstrate the value of dealing with unexpected "jolts" as catalysts for growth. A. D. Meyer, "Adapting to Environmental Jolts," *Administrative Science Quarterly* 27, no. 4 (1982): 515–537. More recent studies show the importance of responding to "disruptive technologies" (C. M. Christensen, *The Innovator's Dilemma* [Boston: Harvard Business School Press, 1997]), or "discontinuities" (R. Foster and S. Kaplan, *Creative Destruction* [New York: Doubleday, 2001]) in order to thrive as market conditions change.

5. J. Scott (*Social Network Analysis* [London: Sage, 1991]) and R. Cross et al. ("Knowing What We Know: Supporting Knowledge Creation and Sharing in Social Networks," in *Organizational Dynamics*, forthcoming) show how network analysis can help to make informal networks visible—showing not only what strengths to build on but where there are missing links or opportunities to connect practitioners with complementary interests and skills.

6. American Productivity & Quality Center, *Building and Sustaining Communities of Practice: Continuing Success in Knowledge Management* (Houston: American Productivity & Quality Center, 2000).

7. R. D. Putnam (*Bowling Alone* [New York: Simon & Schuster, 2000]), and A. Etzioni (*The Spirit of Community: The Reinvention of American Society* [New York: Simon & Schuster, 1993]), among others, note the loss of traditional community ties and rituals in the United States. Wellman and Leighton, meanwhile, use social network analysis to show that contemporary urbanites find primary social ties in "nonneighborhood networks," thus: "'Community' need no longer necessarily be tied to 'neighborhood.'"

"Networks, Neighborhoods, and Communities: Approaches to the Study of the Community Question," *Urban Affairs Quarterly* 14, no. 3 (1979): 363–390.

8. Maria Poarch found that people rely a great deal on colleagues at work as sources of personal support and for opportunities to discuss both family and civic issues. "Ties That Bind: U.S. Suburban Residents on the Social and Civil Dimensions of Work," *Community, Work and Family* 1, no. 2 (1998): 125–148.

9. M. Gladwell states that effective informal networks depend on "connectors," people with many diverse relationships that provide mechanisms for people with shared interests to meet each other. *The Tipping Point: How Little Things Can Make a Big Difference* (Boston: Little Brown, 2000), 30–59. In the civil sector, "civic entrepreneurs" are instrumental to the development and sustenance of voluntary civic groups. D. Henton et al., *Grassroots Leaders for a New Economy: How Civic Entrepreneurs Are Building Prosperous Communities* (San Francisco: Jossey-Bass, 1997).

10. An APQC study of twelve organizations with active communities found that "the most critical success factor (there are many) is the skill of the community leader." American Productivity & Quality Center, "Creating a Knowledge-Sharing Culture" (Houston: American Productivity & Quality Center, 1999), 9. A study by the Corporate Executive Board calls the "network broker" (or community coordinator) the "most visible element of community of practice." "Building Sustainable Advantage: Community-of-Practice Network," in *Heart of the Enterprise: Core Competencies and the Renaissance of the Large Corporation* (Washington, DC: Corporate Executive Board, Corporate Leadership Council, 1996), 171–192.

11. Firms such as McKinsey have adopted a model that combines community leadership, domain expertise, and organizational sponsorship. McKinsey's "practice leaders" are senior consultants with significant status and budget authority and the ability to advance the careers of members. Their practices achieve greater impact than would be possible otherwise because practice leaders leverage the hierarchy as well as their own professional capabilities, relationships, and aspirations.

12. There is an interesting parallel between the early stages of community development and the creativity process itself. Creativity researchers generally describe an iterative sequence of activities that includes conscious efforts to discover what is known (through study or experience), letting this knowledge incubate (while taking a walk, sleeping, or turning to other projects), and looking for a new coherence to emerge, which can then be further developed and elaborated. M. Csikszentmihalyi, *Creativity: Flow and the Psychology of Discovery and Invention* (New York: HarperCollins, 1996), and T. M. Amabile, *Creativity in Context: Update to the Social Psychology of Creativity* (Boulder, CO: Westview Press, 1996).

Chapter 5

1. R. McDermott and J. Kendrick, "How Learning Communities Steward Knowledge," in *Best Practices in Knowledge Management*, ed. L. Carter (Boston: Linkage Press, 2000).

2. D. Leonard and W. Swap describe the importance of a requisite variety of perspectives to produce the "creative abrasion" that generates creative ideas and solutions. *When Sparks Fly* (Boston: Harvard Business School Press, 1999). Ned Herrmann argues that creative groups ideally combine a variety of "thinking styles," such as problem solver, planner, socializer, and conceptualizer. *The Creative Brain* (Lake Lure, NC: The Ned Herrmann Group, 1989). Studies of innovation at the organization level indicate the value of diverse perspectives through relationships with external experts and firms, for example, R. Henderson and I. Cockburn's research on the pharmaceutical industry. "Measuring Competence? Exploring Firm Effects in Pharmaceutical Research," *Strategic Management Journal* 15 (winter special issue 1994): 63–84.

3. Studies of populations of organizations (often referred to as "pop-ecology" studies) suggest that the natural death of organizations fosters the evolution of new organizations that better address market niches. H. E. Aldrich, *Organizations and Environments* (Englewood Cliffs, NJ: Prentice-Hall, 1979), and M. Hannan and J. Freeman, "The Population Ecology of Organizations," *American Journal of Sociology* 82, no. 5 (1977): 929–964. Similarly, constellations of communities are likely to be healthier when individual communities are allowed to die out, merge, or otherwise transform themselves in order to enable new or remaining communities to best utilize available resources to create value.

Chapter 6

1. R. McDermott and J. Jackson, "Designing Global Communities," under review.

2. "Distributed" is the preferred term over "virtual" or "online" because, as is the case for "distance education" initiatives, these communities generally connect in many ways—including face-to-face—although they may rely primarily on "virtual" communications. C. Dede, "Emerging Technologies and Distributed Learning," *American Journal of Distance Education* 10, no. 2 (1996): 4–36. The term "distributed" also helps to highlight the multiple dimensions of distance to bridge. A number of recent books address the topic of facilitating distributed communities online. See C. Figallo, *Hosting Web Communities: Building Relationships, Increasing Customer Loyalty, and Maintaining a Competitive Edge* (New York: Wiley, 1998); A. J. Kim, *Community Building on the Web: Secret Strategies for Successful Online Communities* (Berkeley, CA: Peachpit Press, 1999); R. M. Palloff and K. Pratt, *Building Learning Communities in Cyberspace* (San Francisco: Jossey-Bass, 1999); and J. Preece, *Online Communities: Designing Usability, Supporting Sociability* (New York: Wiley, 2000).

3. See F. Capra, *The Web of Life: A New Understanding of Living Systems* (New York: Doubleday, 1997); J. Gleick, *Chaos: Making a New Science* (New York: Penguin, 1987); and M. J. Wheatley, *Leadership and the New Science* (San Francisco: Berrett-Koehler, 1994), for explanations of fractal concepts and how they apply to organizations.

4. American Productivity & Quality Center, *Building and Sustaining Communities of Practice: Continuing Success in Knowledge Management* (Houston: American Productivity & Quality Center, 2000). The importance of face-to-face meetings is reinforced by studies of complex, unarticulated social communication that occurs only in

face-to-face interactions. See N. Nohria and R. C. Eccles, "Face-to-Face: Making Network Organizations Work," in *Networks and Organizations: Structure, Form, and Action*, eds. N. Nohria and R. C. Eccles (Boston: Harvard Business School Press, 1992), 288–308.

5. C. Dede explains the benefits of combining multiple media to foster learning in higher education contexts. "Emerging Technologies and Distributed Learning in Higher Education," in *Higher Education in an Era of Digital Competition: Choices and Challenges*, ed. D. Hanna (New York: Atwood, 2000), 71–92. See also S. Cohen and D. Payiatakis, "E-Learning: Harnessing the Hype," *Performance Improvement Quarterly* (forthcoming) on the efficacy of "blended learning" approaches that combine online, self-study, and face-to-face methods.

6. N. Nohria and S. Ghoshal, *The Differentiated Network: Organizing Multinational Corporations for Value Creation* (San Francisco: Jossey-Bass, 1997).

7. J. L. Badaracco argues that truly global firms must learn to leverage knowledge assets and capabilities across business unit and country-market boundaries. *The Knowledge Link: How Firms Compete through Strategic Alliances* (Boston: Harvard Business School Press, 1991).

Chapter 7

1. More generally speaking, social capital in communities or in society at large can have negative as well as positive effects when insular communities discourage the aspirations of members. For example, unplanned adolescent pregnancies are reputed to be common in some areas due to social norms that discourage teens from preventing them. A. Portes and P. Landolt, "The Downside of Social Capital," *The American Prospect*, May–June 1996, 18–21, 94. American Indian boys with high academic and athletic achievements often do not apply to elite colleges for fear of retribution or shunning by tribal members. S. Roberts, "In the Shadows: A Special Report, Off-Field Hurdles Stymie Indian Athletes," *New York Times*, 17 June 2001. D. Cohen and L. Prusak describe two kinds of social capital: the beneficial kind that provides resources and flexibility through rich network relationships, and the restrictive or toxic kind that insulates and isolates members from new perspectives and opportunities. *In Good Company: How Social Capital Makes Organizations Work* (Boston: Harvard Business School Press, 2001). Paul Adler argues that trust "has its own dark side. . . . Trust-based institutions are often exclusivistic and elitist, particularly when the source of trust is shared norms or familiarity. These institutions are poorly equipped to deal with the knowledge management challenge." "Market, Hierarchy, and Trust: The Knowledge Economy and the Future of Capitalism," *Organizational Science* 12, no. 2 (2000): 214–234.

2. All the stories in this chapter have been disguised to hide the identities of real companies and participants.

3. M. P. Fiorina describes an example in the civic sphere of an environmental association outside Boston that held up the construction of a new school soccer field on land abutting a conservation area for six years. They did so against the judgment of state

natural resources officials as well as the great majority of town residents—who unfortunately were not well organized enough to assert their own collective political will. "Extreme Voices: A Dark Side of Civic Engagement," in *Civic Engagement in American Democracy*, ed. T. Skocpol (Washington, DC: Brookings Institution, 1999), 395–425.

4. In the example of the imperialist environmental group cited above, Fiorina states that it is only when a representative base of citizens actively participate in civic associations that a city, region, or country can protect itself from the negative consequences of well-organized, extremist groups.

5. I. L. Janis's well-known concept of "groupthink" results from such insularity—a condition that he describes as a primary reason the Kennedy administration blundered so badly in the Bay of Pigs fiasco. See *Victims of Groupthink: A Psychological Study of Foreign-Policy Decisions and Fiascoes* (Boston: Houghton Mifflin, 1972).

6. Documentism is correlated to an exaggerated faith in the value of explicit knowledge that is captured in isolation from the practice environment and the people who use it. Explicit knowledge—reports, manuals, conceptual models, and analytical tools—depends on tacit judgment and skills to be applied effectively. S. D. N. Cook and J. S. Brown, "Bridging Epistemologies: The Generative Dance between Organizational Knowledge and Organizational Knowing," *Organizational Science* 10, no. 4 (1999): 381–400.

7. We adopt the terminology proposed by J. S. Brown and P. Duguid (and others), who discuss this paradox of knowledge in organizations. "Knowledge and Organization: A Social-Practice Perspective," *Organization Science* 12, no. 2 (2001): 198–213.

8. See E. H. Schein's discussion of the communication and coordination difficulties experienced by practitioners across three typical subcultures in organizations—management, engineering, and sales. "Three Cultures of Management: The Key to Organizational Learning," *Sloan Management Review* 38, no. 1 (1996): 9–20.

9. These are the results of a study by Gabriel Szulanski, who analyzed 122 best-practice transfers across eight companies. "Exploring Internal Stickiness: Impediments to the Transfer of Best Practice within the Firm," *Strategic Management Journal* 17 (winter special issue 1996): 27–43.

10. The tendency for practitioners to stick to their own kind—and the resulting "stickiness" of knowledge itself—explains why knowledge "brokers" are so important in organizations that depend on combining knowledge from different domains to create distinctive products and services. See A. Hargadon and R. I. Sutton, "Technology Brokering and Innovation in a Product Development Firm," *Administrative Science Quarterly* 42, no. 4 (1997): 716–749.

11. J. S. Brown and P. Duguid say that knowledge runs on "rails" created by broad "networks of practice" that make it easy for knowledge to flow between organizations. "Knowledge and Organization: A Social-Practice Perspective," 204.

12. These combinations of domains often yield distinctive, inimitable competencies that create exceptional market value. See R. M. Grant, "Prospering in Dynamically Competitive Environments: Organizational Capability as Knowledge Integration," *Organization Science* 7, no. 4 (1996): 375–387.

13. For example, von Hippel found that such exchanges were routine in the steel industry and a critical component of innovation processes. "Collaboration between Rivals: Informal Know-How Trading," *Research Policy* 16, no. 6 (1987): 303–315. Large consulting firms have developed sophisticated methods of protecting client confidentiality and proprietary knowledge, while facilitating knowledge diffusion in the industry.

14. The concept of boundary object was originally proposed by Leigh Star and James Griesemer, "Institutional Ecology, 'Translations' and Boundary Objects: Amateurs and Professionals in Berkeley's Museum of Vertebrate Zoology, 1907–1939," *Social Studies of Science* 19, (1989): 387–420. A. Hargadon and R. I. Sutton describe the value of both artifacts and people to help broker knowledge across boundaries to spur innovation. "Technology Brokering and Innovation in a Product Development Firm"; and "Building an Innovation Factory," *Harvard Business Review*, May–June 2000, 157–166.

15. W. M. Snyder and T. G. Cummings describe a number of typical organizational learning disorders that are relevant to communities. "Organization Learning Disorders: Conceptual Model and Intervention Hypotheses," *Human Relations* 51, no. 7 (1998): 873–895.

16. See T. Kuhn's famous description of the transformation of scientific communities, *The Structure of Scientific Revolutions*, 3d ed. (Chicago: University of Chicago Press, 1996), and L. Laudan's account of scientific transformations in terms of the problem-solving abilities of theories, *Progress and Its Problems* (Berkeley, CA: University of California Press, 1981).

17. Skills and knowledge (and related systems and values) are constituent elements of what D. Leonard-Barton describes as an organization's "core rigidities." These are the "flip side" of a firm's core capabilities, which can become liabilities in changing times. *Wellsprings of Knowledge: Building and Sustaining the Sources of Innovation* (Boston: Harvard Business School Press, 1995), 29–56.

18. K. E. Weick, *The Social Psychology of Organizing*, 2d ed. (New York: Random House, 1979).

Chapter 8

1. Analogously, David Garvin argues that if organizations are going to manage themselves intentionally as learning organizations, they must learn to measure learning processes. "Building a Learning Organization," *Harvard Business Review*, July–August 1993, 78–91.

2. Indeed, we should not underestimate the challenges of measuring the value of knowledge. J. L. Badaracco cites a well-known economist who, "after considering the difficulties of defining, categorizing, and measuring knowledge, felt that the effort led into a philosophical morass from which, as David Hume suggested, the only escape was to climb out, clean oneself off, go home, have a good dinner, and forget all about philosophy." *The Knowledge Link: How Firms Compete through Strategic Alliances* (Boston: Harvard Business School Press, 1991), 19. Tom Davenport and Larry Prusak recommend much caution when accounting for knowledge assets. They cite a Microsoft CFO who

argued against changing accounting systems to reflect intellectual capital—despite Microsoft's considerable strength in this area. *Working Knowledge: How Organizations Manage What They Know* (Boston: Harvard Business School Press, 1998), 172, 187.

3. K. Sveiby, L. Edvinsson, and M. S. Malone propose a variety of methods for measuring "intellectual capital." *Intellectual Capital: Realizing Your Company's True Value by Finding Its Hidden Roots* (New York: HarperBusiness, 1997). T. A. Stewart also presents a range of possible measures, but recommends healthy skepticism and continued experimentation and study in order to increase the usefulness and validity of such measures. *Intellectual Capital: The New Wealth of Organizations* (New York: Doubleday, 1997), 222–246.

4. See R. Glazer, "Measuring the Knower: Towards a Theory of Knowledge Equity," *California Management Review* 40, no. 3 (1998): 175–194, and D. Cohen, "Toward a Knowledge Context: Report on the First Annual U.C. Berkeley Forum on Knowledge and the Firm," *California Management Review* 40, no. 3 (1998): 22–39, for discussions of the dynamic and contextual nature of knowledge and the challenges of measuring this phenomenon.

5. Researchers in the fields of R&D and innovation have found that a combination of qualitative case-based methods and quantitative approaches is most effective. See B. M. Werner and W. Souder, "Measuring R&D Performance—State of the Art," *Research-Technology Management*, March–April 1997, 34–42, and R. M. Kanter, *The Change Masters: Innovation and Entrepreneurship in the American Corporation* (New York: Simon & Schuster, 1985), 371–393. Qualitative research on organizations has gained in terms of both rigor and reputation in recent years. It is especially useful for identifying causal links between independent and dependent variables—such as learning, knowledge, and performance. See K. M. Eisenhardt, "Building Theories from Case Study Research," *Academy of Management Review* 14, no. 4 (1989): 532–550; M. B. Miles and A. M. Huberman, *Qualitative Data Analysis: An Expanded Sourcebook*, 2d ed. (Thousand Oaks, CA: Sage Publications, 1994); and R. K. Yin, *Case Study Research: Design and Methods* (Newbury Park, CA: Sage Publications, 1989).

6. S. Denning, *The Springboard: How Storytelling Ignites Action in Knowledge-Era Organizations* (Boston: Butterworth-Heinemann, 2001); H. M. Trice and J. M. Beyer, *The Cultures of Work Organizations* (Englewood Cliffs, NJ: Prentice Hall, 1993).

7. Stories can be notoriously misleading when they are unrepresentative or inaccurate or gloss over key features of the case. Frederick Taylor's famous case study about reengineering methods that radically reduced the costs of pig iron production, for example, was recently invalidated by research that relied almost exclusively on primary sources. C. D. Wrege and R. M. Hodgetts, "Frederick Taylor's 1899 Iron Observations: Examining Fact, Fiction, and Lessons for the New Millennium," *Academy of Management Journal* 43, no. 6 (2000): 1283–1291. Stories can also be misrepresentative when they inaccurately consolidate diverse experiences and interpretations in organizations. A story becomes "hegemonic" when it "totalizes" fragmentary accounts into an "experts" story that gives undue privilege to elites in the organization. D. M. Boje et al., "Hegemonic Stories and Encounters between Storytelling Organizations," *Journal of Management Inquiry* 8, no. 4 (1999): 340–360.

8. Miles and Huberman show how to aggregate displays of data to support case study evidence in ways that make information easier to comprehend and address data validity and reliability issues. *Qualitative Data Analysis*.

9. This phase builds on expressions used by T. H. Davenport, personal communications with authors.

10. T. M. Ruddy and R. Cheslow, "Eureka II" (presentation at the Communities of Practice conference, San Diego, CA, April 2000). Brown and Duguid note that the 24,000 technicians at Xerox who share repair tips are better understood as a "network of practice" than as a single community. They acknowledge, however, that such a network "may comprise several communities of practice which together form part of a larger network." "Knowledge and Organization: A Social-Practice Perspective," *Organization Science* 12, no. 2 (2001): 206.

11. J. S. Brown, "Social Networks and Learning, Work, and Innovation" (speech at the Community: The Social Side of the New Economy conference, Washington, DC, 14 November 2000). This story is also recounted in Cohen and Prusak, *In Good Company: How Social Capital Makes Organizations Work* (Boston: Harvard Business School Press, 2001), 10.

12. Rewards are a highly charged design element in organizations because they can easily create a sense of unfairness and injustice among members. Rewards given to "outstanding" individuals can backfire when there are no reliable or credible measures for contributions in the organization. Moreover, studies of intrinsically motivated behavior, such as sharing knowledge with one's peers, have shown that extrinsic efforts to reinforce this behavior can dampen rather than heighten members' efforts. See F. Luthans and A. D. Stajkovic, "Reinforce for Performance: The Need to Go beyond Pay and Even Rewards," *Academy of Management Executive* 13, no. 2 (1999): 49–57, and G. Heil, W. Bennis, and D. C. Stephens, *Douglas McGregor, Revisited: Managing the Human Side of the Enterprise* (New York: Wiley, 2000), 81–105. T. M. Amabile formally states what she calls the "Intrinsic Motivation Principle of Creativity" as follows: "Intrinsic motivation is conducive to creativity. Controlling extrinsic motivation is detrimental to creativity, but informational or enabling extrinsic motivation can be conducive, particularly if initial levels of intrinsic motivation are high." "Motivating Creativity in Organizations: On Doing What You Love and Loving What You Do," *California Management Review* 40, no. 1 (1997): 46. Carla O'Dell and Jackson Grayson provide several brief examples of rewards used to encourage best-practice sharing in a passage they title "To reward or not to reward, that is the question." "If We Only Knew What We Know: Identification and Transfer of Internal Best Practices," *California Management Review* 40, no. 3 (1998): 168–169.

13. T. B. Lawrence, for example, found that government authorities and external resources were instrumental to the viability of a community of forensic accountants. "Examining Resources in an Occupational Community: Reputation in Canadian Forensic Accounting," *Human Relations* 51, no. 9 (1998): 1103–1131. Similarly, Theda Skocpol argues that "voluntary membership associations" in the civil sector depend on considerable external resources to initiate and sustain themselves. "How Americans Became Civic," in *Civic Engagement in American Democracy*, ed. T. Skocpol (Washington, DC: Brookings Institution, 1999).

Chapter 9

1. Leigh Weiss elaborates on these two interrelated processes in "Collection and Connection: The Anatomy of Knowledge Sharing in Professional Services Firms," *Organization Development Journal* 17, no. 4 (1999): 61–77.

2. We use the expression "design a little, implement a lot" (coined by Vivian Wright and Richard McDermott in the context of their work at HP) in part to correct for what Bill McKelvey argues is a widespread failing in organization researchers and managers who overestimate the extent to which intentional (versus "natural") forces govern the evolution of organizations. He says, "If the self-organizing emergent properties of microstate systems did not exist we would be hard pressed to explain the failure of complex firms to perform at levels reasonably expected if employees were smart, rational, perceptive, and flexible." "Quasi-natural Organization Science," *Organization Science* 8, no. 4 (1997): 373. In other words, life is messy, and while our rational intentions have influence, it's wise not to overestimate our capacity to control complex social phenomena. This is especially true when trying to foster innovation and knowledge sharing, because these are particularly dependent on "microstate" phenomena, including people's emotions, motivations, and interpersonal relationships.

3. American Productivity & Quality Center, "Creating a Knowledge-Sharing Culture" (Houston: American Productivity & Quality Center, 1999). See also R. McDermott and C. O'Dell, "Overcoming Cultural Barriers to Sharing Knowledge," *Journal of Knowledge Management* 5, no. 1 (2001): 76–85.

4. M. Gladwell recounts the results of research on another kind of social movement related to knowledge, the diffusion of farmers' use of hybrid seed corn in the 1930s. The study identified five types of participants in the innovation-diffusion process: Innovators, Early Adopters, the Early Majority, the Late Majority, and Laggards. *The Tipping Point: How Little Things Can Make a Big Difference* (Boston: Little, Brown, 2000), 196–197.

5. I. Nonaka and H. Takeuchi, *The Knowledge-Creating Company: How Japanese Companies Create the Dynamics of Innovation* (New York: Oxford University Press, 1995), 175–177.

6. Wanda Orlikowski and Debra Gash describe early enterprise-wide efforts to introduce collaboration software (Lotus Notes). They found that many consultants in one large firm described the software as a new word-processing or spreadsheet program or used it primarily as an e-mail application—ignorant of or uninterested in learning to leverage the software's capacity for virtual collaboration. "Technological Frames: Making Sense of Information Technology in Organizations," *ACM Transactions on Information Systems* 12, no. 2 (1994): 174–207.

7. While this book is not focused on technology, technology-related issues are important, and the market for community-oriented systems is growing rapidly. See E. Wenger, "Supporting Communities of Practice: A Survey of Community-Oriented Technologies," March 2001, <http://www.ewenger.com/tech>, for an outline of various approaches to establishing a technological platform for communities of practice. The report analyzes features required to support various aspects of community development and describes the different types of systems currently available on the market.

8. J. S. Brown and E. Solomon-Gray describe a support team at National Semiconductor (called a "community-of-practice council"). The support team provides advice on communities, offers technology support, develops toolkits, organizes mechanisms to connect with other communities and teams, and lobbies for funding to invest in community-related projects. "The People Are the Company," *Fast Company*, November 1995, 78–82.

9. These arguments also apply to CLOs (Chief Learning Officers). Currently, companies tend to have one or the other, although some firms do have both. CKOs tend to focus more on using technology to capture and disseminate codifiable knowledge assets. CLOs generally focus more on learning and training activities, especially at the corporate level, and often head up the corporate university. We believe the strategic and operational issues related to managing knowledge assets deserve dedicated executive attention, under whatever guise. See N. W. Foote, E. Matson, and N. Rudd, "Managing the Knowledge Manager," *The McKinsey Quarterly*, no. 3 (2001): 120–129; T. H. Davenport and L. Prusak, *Working Knowledge: How Organizations Manage What They Know* (Boston: Harvard Business School Press, 1998), 114–122; and M. J. Earl and I. A. Scott, "Opinion: What Is a Chief Knowledge Officer?" *Sloan Management Review*, no. 2 (winter 1999): 29–38.

10. M. Beer et al. found that informal yet genuine senior management support had a more positive impact on ultimate results than change efforts dominated by formal, programmatic structures and initiatives. *The Critical Path to Corporate Renewal* (Boston: Harvard Business School Press, 1990).

11. Warren Bennis argues that leaders are "made, not born" and become leaders through a lifelong commitment to learning about themselves and the world. *On Becoming a Leader* (Reading, MA: Addison-Wesley, 1989), 5. M. McCall, M. Lombardo, and A. Morrison conclude from years of research and practice related to leadership development at the Center for Creative Leadership in Greensboro, NC that the capacity to learn from experiences—both good and bad—is a distinguishing characteristic of strong leaders. *The Lessons of Experience* (Lexington, MA: Lexington Books, 1988). More recently, Bennis and Biederman have explored the distinctive quality of leaders of "great groups" of creative knowledge workers (or "sapient circles," as Margaret Mead called them). *Organizing Genius: The Secrets of Creative Collaboration* (Reading, MA: Addison-Wesley, 1997), xv.

12. Verna Allee uses the term "value web" to describe transorganizational networks where firms trade in several dimensions: goods and services, knowledge, and "intangibles" (loyalty, reputation, and so on). "Knowledge Networks and Communities of Practice," *Journal of the Organization Development Network* 32, no. 4 (2000): 4–13.

13. Tobin's q, the ratio of a firm's market value to the replacement value of its booked assets, is one way to gauge the value of a firm's intangible assets. T. A. Stewart, *Intellectual Capital: The New Wealth of Organizations* (New York: Doubleday, 1997), 225–226.

14. For more on the implications of knowledge-based structures for the theory of the firm, see B. Kogut and U. Zander, "Knowledge of the Firm, Combinative Capabilities, and the Replication of Technology," *Organization Science* 3, no. 3 (1992): 383–397,

and "What Firms Do? Coordination, Identity, and Learning," *Organization Science* 7, no. 5 (1996): 502–518; and W. M. Snyder, "Communities of Practice: Combining Organization Learning and Strategy Insights to Create a Bridge to the Twenty-First Century" (paper presented at Academy of Management Annual Meeting, Boston, August 1997).

Chapter 10

1. The film and television industries are well-known for their project-based, networked structure in which guilds of writers, directors, actors, cameramen, and other professional communities supply, develop, and accredit talent within the industry through an informal system of apprenticeship. See R. J. DeFillippi and M. B. Arthur, "Paradox in Project-Based Enterprise: The Case of Film Making," *California Management Review* 40, no. 2 (1998): 125–139, and K. Starkey et al., "Beyond Networks and Hierarchies: Latent Organizations in the U.K. Television Industry," *Organization Science* 11, no. 3 (2000): 299–305.

2. J. H. Dyer and K. Nobeoka, "Creating and Managing a High-Performance Knowledge-Sharing Network: The Toyota Case," *Strategic Management Journal* 21, no. 3 (2000): 345–367. See also I. Stuart, et al., "Case Study: A Leveraged Learning Network," *Sloan Management Review* 39, no. 4 (1998): 81–93. Adler argues that such interfirm cooperative relationships are becoming more common in the "knowledge-intensive" economy: "A burgeoning body of research shows that when firms need innovation and knowledge inputs from suppliers rather than just standardized commodities, no combination of strong hierarchical control and market discipline can assure as high a level of performance as trust-based community." "Market, Hierarchy, and Trust: The Knowledge Economy and the Future of Capitalism," *Organization Science* 12, no. 2 (2001): 224.

3. J. Hagel and A. G. Armstrong, *Net Gain: Expanding Markets through Virtual Communities* (Boston: Harvard Business School Press, 1997); R. L. Williams and J. Cothrel, "Four Smart Ways to Run Online Communities," *Sloan Management Review* 41, no. 4 (2000): 81–91; G. McWilliam, "Building Stronger Brands through Online Communities," *Sloan Management Review* 41, no. 3 (2000): 43–54; and W. M. Snyder, "Organization and World Design: The Gaia's Hypotheses" (paper presented at the Academy of Management Annual Meeting, San Diego, CA, August 1998).

4. McWilliam cites a recent study of consumer community Web sites that counted 300,000 online, topic-based discussion boards, some 85 percent of which were operated by commercial organizations. "Building Stronger Brands through Online Communities," 44.

5. McWilliam describes an example of such a community: "Bosch, a manufacturer of power tools, hosts a forum for tradespeople and do-it-yourself enthusiasts to swap information and suggestions, including prices, which brand of power tool to buy, and how to fix cracks between walls and ceilings (see the tools forum on www.boschtools.com)." Ibid., 48.

6. Hagel and Armstrong, *Net Gain*. They note that the "value of communities will rest largely on their capacity to attract the passions of their members," and then leverage their collective contributions in ways that benefit both members and sponsors.

Ibid., 33. But this hasn't been easy to do. Hagel was cited in an article remarking that "almost none of the community-based Web sites made the leap from a social forum to a profitable one, which disappointed clients." Quoted in Amy Harmon, "Getting 'Amazoned,' and other Fantasies; Eek! What have E-Consultants Wrought?" *New York Times*, 13 May 2001.

7. W. M. Cohen and D. A. Levinthal, "Absorptive Capacity: A New Perspective on Learning and Innovation," *Administrative Sciences Quarterly* 35, no. 1 (1990): 128–152.

8. M. Sawhney and E. Prandelli describe several models for managing innovation across a firm's boundaries. They argue that "communities of creation," when properly managed, are preferable to strictly proprietary or open-source alternatives: "By combining benefits of the proprietary licensing model and the open source model, the community model allows the co-participation of community members to self-maintain over time." "Communities of Creation: Managing Distributed Innovation in Turbulent Markets," *California Management Review* 42, no. 4 (2000): 42. There has been an explosion of research in recent years on alliance and network forms of organizing and an increased appreciation for the influence of social networks among members in participating firms. Practitioners are instrumental to firms' ability to develop and leverage these interfirm links. See R. Gulati, "Alliances and Networks," *Strategic Management Journal* 19, no. 4 (1998): 293–317.

9. J. Topolsky, "The Northeast Indiana TQM Network," *Firm Connections: Advancing Collaboration to Build Competitive Firms* 1, no. 2 (1993): 3, 8.

10. P. Drucker, *Managing in a Time of Great Change* (New York: Truman Talley Books/Dutton, 1995), 258–259.

11. W. M. Snyder, "Boost4Kids: Building and Sharing Knowledge to Get Results for Kids" (Special Report to the Office of the Vice President, National Partnership for Reinventing Government, Washington, DC, November 2000). See also <http://www.boost4kids.gov>.

12. Such a vision of governance, which relies heavily on voluntary "associations" (A. de Tocqueville, *Democracy in America*, ed. J. P. Mayer, translated by G. Lawrence [New York: Harper Perennial Library, 2000]); "secondary groups" (E. Durkheim, *The Division of Labor in Society*, 1933 [New York: Free Press, 1964]); "intermediate relationships and authorities" (R. A. Nisbet, *The Quest for Community: A Study in the Ethics of Order and Freedom* [London: Oxford University Press, 1953]); "mediating structures" (E. J. Dionne, ed., *Community Works: The Revival of Civil Society in America* [Washington, DC: Brookings Institution Press, 2000]); and "networks of civic engagement" (R. D. Putnam, "Bowling Alone: America's Declining Social Capital," *Journal of Democracy* 6, no. 1 [1995]: 65–78), has been voiced by researchers and social commentators for more than 100 years as the key to our sustained capacity for democratic governance and a thriving economy. Yet we are continually faced with the challenge to renew this capacity, as Robert Putnam argues in his recent book, *Bowling Alone: The Collapse and Revival of American Community* (New York: Simon & Schuster, 2000), by finding new ways to organize within the civil sector in order to renew our social capital and to govern in an increasingly complex world.

13. B. Herbert, "Championing Cities," *New York Times*, 26 April 2001.

14. D. Henton, J. Melville, and K. Walesh propose creating a "Civic Entrepreneur Network" that sounds remarkably like the various civil-sector communities of practice that we now see emerging. The "learning network" they describe would "provide an ongoing opportunity for civic entrepreneurs from diverse regions to share experience and benchmark best practices," and it would "build rapport and relationships" through face-to-face meetings, videoconferences, benchmarking visits, and computer conferences. *Grassroots Leaders for a New Economy: How Civic Entrepreneurs Are Building Prosperous Communities* (San Francisco: Jossey-Bass, 1997), 213. See the Alliance for Regional Stewardship at <http://www.regionalstewardship.org> for an example of such a network. They also see opportunities to extend such networks globally and describe a group called the Global Fellowship Network, which consists of more than 600 "public entrepreneurs" from thirty developing countries and is sponsored by the Ashoka Foundation (216).

15. See <http://www.ayudaurbana.com>.

16. M. E. Keck and K. Sikkink ("Transnational Advocacy Networks in International Politics: Introduction," in *Activists beyond Borders: Advocacy Networks in International Politics*, ed. M. E. Keck and K. Sikkink [Ithaca, NY: Cornell University Press, 1988], 1–38) describe "transnational advocacy networks" organized by (among others) "networks of scientists and experts whose professional ties and shared ideas underpin their efforts to influence policy." These networks "are characterized by voluntary, reciprocal, and horizontal patterns of communication and exchange" (8). The strong interpersonal relationships and collective knowledge that exist in such networks enable them to advocate for changes in the "practices of states" (36), as well as their policies toward enacting a "global civil society" that would improve conditions in a variety of areas, such as human rights and the environment.

17. A recent Brookings Institution publication describes a range of civic practices that must be developed in order to sustain healthy communities. R. F. Ferguson and W. T. Dickens, "Introduction," in *Urban Problems and Community Development*, ed. R. F. Ferguson and W. T. Dickens (Washington, DC: Brookings Institution Press, 1999), 1–31. Paul Grogan and Tony Proscio's report on "comeback cities" describes successful initiatives related to several of these practices, including economic development, housing, education, and public safety. *Comeback Cities: A Blueprint for Urban Neighborhood Revival* (Boulder, CO: Westview Press, 2000).

18. Sociologists and political scientists argue that civic groups are more successful when they have strong sponsors who can provide access to technical assistance, resources, and a broad base of support. See T. Skocpol, "The Tocqueville Problem: Civic Engagement in American Democracy," *Social Science History* 21, no. 4 (1997): 455–477, and M. Walzer, "Social Breakdown: The Idea of Civil Society," *Dissent* 38, no. 2, (1991): 293–304.

19. The global applicability of this community-based approach to governance suggests a view of the world as a "community of communities." Along these lines, the well-known Buddhist writer and teacher, Thich Nhat Hanh, discusses the universal, spiritual meaning that it is inherent in healthy forms of community participation. He refers to the "sangha"—the Buddhist forum in which members interrelate and pray together—as a "community of practice." *Living Buddha, Living Christ* (New York:

Berkley Publishing Group, 1995), 22. Similarly, the Catholic theologian Francis Schussler Fiorenza argues that the mission of the Church is to be a "community of interpretation" in which members continuously reflect on the theory and practice of the religious tradition—as well as on perspectives from the arts, sciences, and social experience—to discover their "ideal potential" in the world. "The Church as a Community of Interpretation: Between Discourse Ethics and Hermeneutical Reconstruction," in *Habermas, Modernity, and Public Theology*, ed. D. Browning and F. S. Fiorenza (New York: Crossroads, 1991), 66–91.

20. A number of writers have warned of dire consequences when commercial interests and multinational corporations "rule the world." D. Korten, *When Corporations Rule the World* (San Francisco: Berrett-Koehler, 1995); C. Derber, *Corporation Nation: How Corporations Are Taking Over Our Lives and What We Can Do about It* (New York: St. Martin's Press, 1998); J. Rifkin, *The Age of Access: The New Culture of Hypercapitalism, Where All of Life Is a Paid-For Experience* (New York: Jeremy P. Tarcher/Putnam, 2000). Paradoxically, people working in these same multinationals are pioneering the development of social structures and methods for learning and innovation that may provide the basis for sustainable health and prosperity in the world. This turn of events recalls Durkheim's proposition that the "professional groups" engendered by industrialization and the division of labor might one day become "the chief source of social solidarity [and] . . . the foundation of the moral order." *The Division of Labor in Society*, 333.

Bibliography

Adler, P. S. "Market, Hierarchy, and Trust: The Knowledge Economy and the Future of Capitalism." *Organizational Science* 12, no. 2 (2000): 214–234.

Adler, P., and S. Kwon. "Social Capital: The Good, the Bad, and the Ugly." In *Knowledge and Social Capital: Foundations and Applications*, edited by E. Lesser, 89–115. Boston: Butterworth-Heinemann, 2000.

Aldrich, H. E. *Organizations and Environments*. Englewood Cliffs, NJ: Prentice-Hall, 1979.

Alexander, C. *The Timeless Way of Building*. New York: Oxford University Press, 1979.

Alexander, C., S. Ishikawa, and M. Silverstein. *A Pattern Language: Towns, Buildings, Construction*. New York: Oxford University Press, 1977.

Allee, V. "Knowledge Networks and Communities of Practice." *Journal of the Organization Development Network* 32, no. 4 (2000): 4–13.

Amabile, T. M. *Creativity in Context: Update to the Social Psychology of Creativity*. Boulder, CO: Westview Press, 1996.

———. "Motivating Creativity in Organizations: On Doing What You Love and Loving What You Do." *California Management Review* 40, no. 1 (1997): 39–58.

American Productivity & Quality Center. *Building and Sustaining Communities of Practice: Continuing Success in Knowledge Management*. Houston: American Productivity & Quality Center, 2000.

———. "Creating a Knowledge-Sharing Culture." Houston: American Productivity & Quality Center, 1999.

Argyris, C. *Integrating the Individual and the Organization*. New York: Wiley, 1964.

Argyris, C., R. Putnam, and D. M. Smith. *Action Science*. San Francisco: Jossey-Bass, 1987.

Argyris, C., and D. A. Schön. *Organizational Learning: A Theory of Action Perspective*. Reading, MA: Addison-Wesley, 1978.

Badaracco, J. L. *The Knowledge Link: How Firms Compete through Strategic Alliances*. Boston: Harvard Business School Press, 1991.

Bales, R. F. "Task Roles and Social Roles in Problem-Solving Groups." In *Readings in Social Psychology*, edited by E. Maccoby, T. M. Newcomb, and E. L. Hartley, 437–447. New York: Holt, Rinehart and Winston, 1958.

Barnard, C. I. *The Functions of the Executive*. 1938. Cambridge, MA: Harvard University Press, 1968.

Barney, J. B. "Firm Resources and Sustained Competitive Advantage." *Journal of Management* 17 (1991): 121–154.

———. "Looking Inside for Competitive Advantage." *Academy of Management Executive* 9, no. 4 (1995): 49–61.

Beer, M., B. A. Spector, and R. A. Eisenstat. *The Critical Path to Corporate Renewal*. Boston: Harvard Business School Press, 1990.

Bellman, G. M. *The Beauty of the Beast*. San Francisco: Berrett-Koehler, 2000.

Bender, T., and S. M. Kruger. *Community and Social Change in America*. Baltimore: Johns Hopkins University Press, 1982.

Bennis, W. G. *On Becoming a Leader*. Reading, MA: Addison-Wesley, 1989.

Bennis, W. G., and P. E. Slater. *The Temporary Society*. New York: Harper & Row, 1968.

Bennis, W. G., and P. W. Biederman. *Organizing Genius: The Secrets of Creative Collaboration*. Reading, MA: Addison-Wesley, 1997.

Berry, L., V. Zeithaml, and A. Parasuraman. "Five Imperatives for Improving Service Quality." *Sloan Management Review* 31, no. 4 (1990): 29–38.

Boje, D. M., J. T. Luhman, and D. E. Baack. "Hegemonic Stories and Encounters Between Storytelling Organizations." *Journal of Management Inquiry* 8, no. 4 (1999): 340–360.

Boland, R. J., and R. V. Tenkasi. "Perspective Making and Perspective Taking in Communities of Knowing." *Organization Science* 6, no. 4 (1995): 350–372.

Botkin, J. *Smart Business*. New York: Free Press, 1999.

Bourdieu, P. *Outline of a Theory of Practice*. Cambridge: Cambridge University Press, 1977.

Brown, J. S. "Social Networks and Learning, Work, and Innovation." Speech to the Community: The Social Side of the New Economy conference, Washington, DC, 14 November 2000.

Brown, J. S., and P. Duguid. "Balancing Act: How to Capture Knowledge without Killing It." *Harvard Business Review*, May–June 2000, 73–80.

———. "Knowledge and Organization: A Social Practice Perspective." *Organization Science* 12, no. 2 (2001): 198–213.

———. "Organizational Learning and Communities-of-Practice: Toward a Unified View of Working, Learning, and Innovation." *Organization Science* 2, no. 1 (1991): 40–57.

———. *The Social Life of Information*. Boston: Harvard Business School Press, 2000.

Brown, J. S., and E. Solomon-Gray. "The People Are the Company." *Fast Company*, November 1995, 78–82.

Burns, T., and G. M. Stalker. *The Management of Innovation*. London: Tavistock, 1961.

Campbell, J. *The Hero with a Thousand Faces*. Princeton, NJ: Princeton University Press, 1949.

Cappelli, P. "A Market-Driven Approach to Retaining Talent." *Harvard Business Review*, January–February 2000, 103–111.

Capra, F. *The Web of Life: A New Understanding of Living Systems*. New York: Doubleday, 1997.

Christensen, C. M. *The Innovator's Dilemma*. Boston: Harvard Business School Press, 1997.

Churchman, C. W. *The Design of Inquiring Systems: Basic Concepts of Systems and Organization*. New York: Basic Books, 1971.

Cohen, D. "Toward a Knowledge Context: Report on the First Annual U.C. Berkeley Forum on Knowledge and the Firm." *California Management Review* 40, no. 3 (1998): 22–39.

Cohen, D., and L. Prusak. *In Good Company: How Social Capital Makes Organizations Work*. Boston: Harvard Business School Press, 2001.

Cohen, S. S., and G. Fields. "Social Capital and Capital Gains in Silicon Valley." *California Management Review* 41, no. 2 (1999): 108–130.

Cohen, S., and D. Payiatakis, "E-Learning: Harnessing the Hype," *Performance Improvement Quarterly* (forthcoming).

Cohen, W. M., and D. A. Levinthal. "Absorptive Capacity: A New Perspective on Learning and Innovation," *Administrative Sciences Quarterly* 35, no. 1 (1990): 128–152.

Collins, J. C., and J. I. Porras. *Built to Last*. New York: HarperCollins, 1994.

Cook, S. D. N., and J. S. Brown. "Bridging Epistemologies: The Generative Dance between Organizational Knowledge and Organizational Knowing." *Organizational Science* 10, no. 4 (1999): 381–400.

Cook, S. D. N., and D. Yanow. "Culture and Organizational Learning." *Journal of Management Inquiry* 2, no. 4 (1993): 373–390.

Corporate Leadership Council. "Building Sustainable Advantage: Community-of-Practice Network." In *Heart of the Enterprise: Core Competencies and the Renaissance of the Large Corporation,* 171–192. Washington, DC: Corporate Executive Board, 1996.

Crane, D. *Invisible Colleges: Diffusion of Knowledge in Scientific Communities*. Chicago: University of Chicago Press, 1972.

Cross, R., A. Parker, L. Prusak, and S. P. Borgatti. "Knowing What We Know: Supporting Knowledge Creation and Sharing in Social Networks." In *Organizational Dynamics*, forthcoming.

Csikszentmihalyi, M. *Creativity: Flow and the Psychology of Discovery and Invention*. New York: HarperCollins, 1996.

Davenport, T. H., and J. C. Beck. *The Attention Economy: Understanding the New Currency of Business*. Boston: Harvard Business School Press, 2001.

Davenport, T. H., and L. Prusak. *Working Knowledge: How Organizations Manage What They Know*. Boston: Harvard Business School Press, 1998.

Dede, C. "Emerging Technologies and Distributed Learning." *American Journal of Distance Education* 10, no. 2 (1996): 4–36.

———. "Emerging Technologies and Distributed Learning in Higher Education." In *Higher Education in an Era of Digital Competition: Choices and Challenges*, edited by D. Hanna, 71–92. New York: Atwood, 2000.

DeFillippi, R. J., and M. B. Arthur. "Paradox in Project-Based Enterprise: The Case of Film Making." *California Management Review* 40, no. 2 (1998): 125–139.

de Geus, A. P. *The Living Company*. Boston: Harvard Business School Press, 1997.

Denning, S. *The Springboard: How Storytelling Ignites Action in Knowledge-Era Organizations*. Boston: Butterworth-Heinemann, 2001.

Derber, C. *Corporation Nation: How Corporations Are Taking Over Our Lives and What We Can Do about It*. New York: St. Martin's Press, 1998.

Dessler, G. "How to Earn Your Employees' Commitment." *Academy of Management Executive* 13, no. 2 (1999): 58–67.

de Tocqueville, A. *Democracy in America*. Edited by J. P. Mayer, translated by G. Lawrence. New York: Harper Perennial Library, 2000.

Dionne, E. J., ed. *Community Works: The Revival of Civil Society in America*. Washington, DC: Brookings Institution Press, 2000.

Drucker, P. F. "Knowledge-Worker Productivity: The Biggest Challenge." *California Management Review* 41, no. 2 (1999): 79–94.

———. *Managing in a Time of Great Change*. New York: Truman Talley Books/Dutton, 1995.

———. *Post-Capitalist Society*. New York: HarperBusiness, 1993.

Dunphy, D., and A. Griffiths. *The Sustainable Corporation: Organisational Renewal in Australia*. St. Leonards, Australia: Allen & Unwin, 1998.

Durkheim, E. *The Division of Labor in Society*. 1933. New York: Free Press, 1964.

Dyer, J. H., and K. Nobeoka. "Creating and Managing a High-Performance Knowledge-Sharing Network: The Toyota Case." *Strategic Management Journal* 21, no. 3 (2000): 345–367.

Earl, M. J., and I. A. Scott. "Opinion: What Is a Chief Knowledge Officer?" *Sloan Management Review* no. 2 (Winter 1999): 29–38.

Edmondson, A. C. "Learning from Mistakes Is Easier Said than Done: Group and Organizational Influences on the Detection and Correction of Human Error." *Journal of Applied Behavioral Science* 32, no. 1 (1996): 5–28.

Edvinsson, L., and M. S. Malone. *Intellectual Capital: Realizing Your Company's True Value by Finding Its Hidden Roots*. New York: HarperBusiness, 1997.

Eisenhardt, K. M. "Building Theories from Case Study Research." *Academy of Management Review* 14, no. 4 (1989): 532–550.

Erikson, E. H. *Childhood and Society*. New York: Norton, 1963.

Etzioni, A. "The Responsive Community. A Communitarian Perspective." *American Sociological Review* 61, no. 1 (1996): 1–11.

———. *The Spirit of Community: The Reinvention of American Society*. New York: Simon & Schuster, 1993.

Ferguson, R. F., and W. T. Dickens. "Introduction." In *Urban Problems and Community Development*, edited by R. F. Ferguson and W. T. Dickens. Washington, DC: Brookings Institution Press, 1999.

Figallo, C. *Hosting Web Communities: Building Relationships, Increasing Customer Loyalty, and Maintaining a Competitive Edge*. New York: Wiley, 1998.

Fink, E., and L. B. Resnick. "Developing Principals as Instructional Leaders." *Phi Delta Kappan* 82, no. 8 (2001): 598–606.

Fiorenza, F. S. "The Church as a Community of Interpretation: Between Discourse Ethics and Hermeneutical Reconstruction." In *Habermas, Modernity, and Public Theology*, edited by D. Browning and F. S. Fiorenza, 66–91. New York: Crossroads, 1991.

Fiorina, M. P. "Extreme Voices: A Dark Side of Civic Engagement." In *Civic Engagement in American Democracy*, edited by T. Skocpol, 395–425. Washington, DC: Brookings Institution Press, 1999.

Fish, S. *Doing What Comes Naturally: Change, Rhetoric and the Practice of Theory in Literary and Legal Studies*. Durham, NC: Duke University Press, 1989.

Foote, N. W., and B. Manville. "Strategy as If Knowledge Mattered." *Fast Company*, April 1996, 66–67.

Foote, N. W., E. Matson, and N. Rudd. "Managing the Knowledge Manager." *The McKinsey Quarterly* no. 3 (2001): 120–129.

Foster, R., and S. Kaplan. *Creative Destruction*. New York: Doubleday, 2001.

Fukuyama, F. *Trust: The Social Virtues and the Creation of Prosperity*. New York: Free Press, 1995.

Galbraith, J. R. *Organization Design*. Reading, MA: Addison-Wesley, 1977.

Garvin, D. A. "Building a Learning Organization." *Harvard Business Review*, July–August 1993, 78–91.

———. *Learning in Action: A Guide to Putting the Learning Organization to Work*. Boston: Harvard Business School Press, 2000.

Gersick, C. J. G. "Time and Transition in Work Teams: Toward a New Model of Group Development." *Academy of Management Journal* 31, no. 1 (1988): 9–41.

Gersick, C. J. G., J. M. Bartunek, and J. E. Dutton. "Learning from Academia: The Importance of Relationships in Professional Life." *Academy of Management Journal* 43, no. 6 (2000): 1026–1044.

Gittell, J. H., and L. M. Weiss. "Linking Intra- and Inter-organizational Networks through Organization Design: The Case of Patient Care Coordination." Working paper 97-064, Harvard Business School, Boston, 2001.

Gladwell, M. *The Tipping Point: How Little Things Can Make a Big Difference*. Boston: Little, Brown, 2000.

Glazer, R. "Measuring the Knower: Towards a Theory of Knowledge Equity." *California Management Review* 40, no. 3 (1998): 175–194.

Gleick, J. *Chaos: Making a New Science*. New York: Penguin, 1987.

Grant, R. M. "Prospering in Dynamically Competitive Environments: Organizational Capability as Knowledge Integration." *Organization Science* 7, no. 4 (1996): 375–387.

Greiner, L. "Evolution and Revolution as Organizations Grow." *Harvard Business Review*, July–August 1972, 37–46.

Grogan, P. S., and T. Proscio. *Comeback Cities: A Blueprint for Urban Neighborhood Revival*. Boulder, CO: Westview Press, 2000.

Gulati, R. "Alliances and Networks." *Strategic Management Journal* 19, no. 4 (1998): 293–317.

Haas, P. "Introduction: Epistemic Communities and International Policy Coordination." *International Organization* 46, no. 1 (1992): 1–36.

Hackman, J. R. "Group Influences on Individuals." In *Handbook of Industrial and Organizational Psychology*, edited by M. D. Dunnett, 1455–1518. Chicago: Rand McNally, 1976.

Hagel, J., and A. G. Armstrong. *Net Gain: Expanding Markets through Virtual Communities*. Boston: Harvard Business School Press, 1997.

Hamel, G., and C. K. Prahalad. *Competing for the Future*. Boston: Harvard Business School Press, 1994.

Hammer, M. and J. Champy. *Reengineering the Corporation: A Manifesto for Business Revolution*. New York: HarperBusiness, 1993.

Hanh, T. N. *Living Buddha, Living Christ*. New York: Berkley Publishing Group, 1995.

Hannan, M., and J. Freeman. "The Population Ecology of Organizations." *American Journal of Sociology* 82, no. 5 (1977): 929–964.

Hansen, M. T., N. Nohria, and T. Tierney. "What's Your Strategy for Managing Knowledge?" *Harvard Business Review*, March–April 1999, 106–116.

Hargadon, A., and R. I. Sutton. "Building an Innovation Factory." *Harvard Business Review*, May–June 2000, 157–166.

———. "Technology Brokering and Innovation in a Product Development Firm." *Administrative Science Quarterly* 42, no. 4 (1997): 716–749.

Harmon, A. "Getting 'Amazoned' and other Fantasies; Eek! What have E-Consultants Wrought?" *New York Times*, 13 May 2001.

Heil, G., W. Bennis, and D. C. Stephens. *Douglas McGregor, Revisited: Managing the Human Side of the Enterprise*. New York: Wiley, 2000.

Henderson, R., and I. Cockburn. "Measuring Competence? Exploring Firm Effects in Pharmaceutical Research." *Strategic Management Journal* 15 (winter special issue 1994): 63–84.

Henton, D., J. Melville, and K. Walesh. *Grassroots Leaders for a New Economy: How Civic Entrepreneurs Are Building Prosperous Communities*. San Francisco: Jossey-Bass, 1997.

Herbert, B. "Championing Cities." *New York Times*, 26 April 2001.

Herrmann, N. *The Creative Brain*. Lake Lure, NC: The Ned Herrmann Group, 1989.

Higgins, M. C., and K. E. Kram. "Reconceptualizing Mentoring at Work: A Developmental Network Perspective." *Academy of Management Review* 26, no. 2 (2001): 264–288.

Hoopes, D. G., and S. Postrel. "Shared Knowledge, 'Glitches,' and Product Development Performance." *Strategic Management Journal* 20, no. 9 (1999): 837–865.

Jacobs, J. *The Death and Life of Great American Cities*. New York: Vintage, 1993.

Janis, I. L. *Victims of Groupthink: A Psychological Study of Foreign-Policy Decisions and Fiascoes*. Boston: Houghton Mifflin, 1972.

Jordan, B. "Cosmopolitan Obstetrics: Some Insights from the Training of Traditional Midwives." *Social Science and Medicine* 28 (1987): 925–944.

Kanter, R. M. *The Change Masters: Innovation and Entrepreneurship in the American Corporation*. New York: Simon & Schuster, 1985.

Katz, P., and V. Scully. *The New Urbanism: Toward an Architecture of Community*. New York: McGraw-Hill, 1993.

Keck, M. E., and K. Sikkink. "Transnational Advocacy Networks in International Politics: Introduction." In *Activists beyond Borders: Advocacy Networks in International Politics*, edited by M. E. Keck and K. Sikkink, 1–38. Ithaca, NY: Cornell University Press, 1998.

Kegan, R. *The Evolving Self*. Cambridge, MA: Harvard University Press, 1982.

Kelley, K. *Out of Control: The New Biology of Machines, Social Systems, and the Economic World*. Reading, MA: Addison-Wesley, 1994.

Kelley, R. E., and J. Caplan. "How Bell Labs Creates Star Performers." *Harvard Business Review*, July–August 1993, 128–139.

Kim, A. J. *Community Building on the Web: Secret Strategies for Successful Online Communities*. Berkeley, CA: Peachpit Press, 1999.

Klein, K. J., and T. A. D'Aunno. "Psychological Sense of Community in the Workplace." *Journal of Community Psychology* 14 (1986): 365–377.

Knorr-Cetina, K. D. *The Manufacture of Knowledge*. Elmsford, NY: Pergamon Press, 1981.

Kochen, M. *The Small World*. Norwood, NJ: Ablex, 1989.

Kogut, B., and U. Zander. "Knowledge of the Firm, Combinative Capabilities, and the Replication of Technology." *Organization Science* 3, no. 3 (1992): 383–397.

———. "What Firms Do? Coordination, Identity, and Learning." *Organization Science* 7, no. 5 (1996): 502–518.

Korten, D. C. *When Corporations Rule the World*. San Francisco: Berrett-Koehler, 1995.

Krackhardt, D., and J. R. Hanson. "Informal Networks: The Company behind the Chart." *Harvard Business Review*, July–August 1993, 104–111.

Kuhn, T. *The Structure of Scientific Revolutions*. 3d ed. Chicago: University of Chicago Press, 1996.

Latour, B. *Science in Action: How to Follow Scientists and Engineers through Society*. Cambridge, MA: Harvard University Press, 1987.

Laubacher, R., and T. W. Malone. "Retreat of the Firm and the Rise of Guilds: The Employment Relationship in an Age of Virtual Business." Twenty-First Century Initiative working paper 033, MIT Sloan School of Management, Cambridge, MA, 2000.

Laudan, L. *Progress and Its Problems*. Berkeley, CA: University of California Press, 1981.

Lave, J., and E. Wenger. *Situated Learning: Legitimate Peripheral Participation*. New York: Cambridge University Press, 1991.

Lawrence, T. B. "Examining Resources in an Occupational Community: Reputation in Canadian Forensic Accounting." *Human Relations* 51, no. 9 (1998): 1103–1131.

Leonard-Barton, D. "Core Capabilities and Core Rigidities: A Paradox in Managing New Product Development." *Strategic Management Journal* 13 (summer 1992): 111–125.

———. "The Factory as a Learning Laboratory." *Sloan Management Review* 34, no. 1 (1992): 23–38.

————. *Wellsprings of Knowledge: Building and Sustaining the Sources of Innovation.* Boston: Harvard Business School Press, 1995.

Leonard, D., and S. Sensiper. "The Role of Tacit Knowledge in Group Innovation." *California Management Review* 40, no. 3 (1998): 112–132.

Leonard, D., and S. Straus. "Putting Your Company's Whole Brain to Work." *Harvard Business Review*, July–August 1997, 111–121.

Leonard, D., and W. Swap. "Gurus in the Garage." *Harvard Business Review*, November–December 2000, 71–79.

————. *When Sparks Fly: Igniting Creativity in Groups.* Boston: Harvard Business School Press, 1999.

Liebeskind, J. P., A. L. Oliver, L. Zucker, and M. Brewer. "Social Networks, Learning, and Flexibility: Sourcing Scientific Knowledge in New Biotechnology Firms." *Organizational Science* 7, no. 4 (1996): 428–443.

Liedtka, J. "Linking Competitive Advantage with Communities of Practice." *Journal of Management Inquiry* 8, no. 1 (1999): 5–16.

Liedtka, J., M. E. Haskins, J. Rosenblum, and J. Weber. "The Generative Cycle: Linking Knowledge and Relationships." *Sloan Management Review* 39, no. 1 (1997): 47–58.

Lipnack, J., and J. Stamps. *The Age of the Network.* New York: Wiley, 1994.

————. *The Teamnet Factor: Bringing the Power of Boundary Crossing into the Heart of Your Business.* New York: Wiley, 1995.

Loevinger, J. *Ego Development.* San Francisco: Jossey-Bass, 1976.

Luthans, F., and A. D. Stajkovic. "Reinforce for Performance: The Need to Go beyond Pay and Even Rewards." *Academy of Management Executive* 13, no. 2 (1999): 49–57.

Madhok, A. "The Organization of Economic Activity: Transaction Costs, Firm Capabilities, and the Nature of Governance." *Organization Science* 7, no. 5 (1996): 577–590.

Maister, D. H. *Managing the Professional Service Firm.* New York: Simon & Schuster, 1993.

Malone, T. W., and R. Laubacher. "The Dawn of the e-Lance Economy." *Harvard Business Review*, September–October 1998, 144–152.

————. "The Rebirth of the Guild." *Boston Globe*, 24 August 2000.

Marsick, V. J., and K. E. Watkins. *Informal and Incidental Learning in the Workplace.* London: Routledge, 1990.

Martin, J. *Cultures in Organizations.* New York: Oxford University Press, 1992.

McCall, M., M. Lombardo, and A. Morrison. *The Lessons of Experience.* Lexington, MA: Lexington Books, 1988.

McDermott, R. "Learning across Teams: How to Build Communities of Practice in Team Organizations." *Knowledge Management Review* 8 (May–June 1999): 32–28.

————. "Planned Spontaneity." *Knowledge Management Review* 3, no. 4 (2000): 5–11.

————. "Why Information Technology Inspired, but Cannot Deliver Knowledge Management." *California Management Review* 41, no. 3 (1999): 103–117.

McDermott, R., and J. Jackson. "Designing Global Communities." Under review.

McDermott, R., and J. Kendrick. "How Learning Communities Steward Knowledge." In *Best Practices in Knowledge Management*, edited by Lewis Carter. Boston: Linkage Press, 2000.

McDermott, R., and C. O'Dell. "Overcoming Cultural Barriers to Sharing Knowledge." *Journal of Knowledge Management* 5, no. 1 (2001): 76–85.

McGregor, D. *The Human Side of Enterprise*. New York: McGraw-Hill, 1960.

McKelvey, B. "Quasi-natural Organization Science." *Organization Science* 8, no. 4 (1997): 352–380.

McLagan, P., and C. Nel. *The Age of Participation*. San Francisco: Berrett-Koehler, 1995.

McWilliam, G. "Building Stronger Brands through Online Communities." *Sloan Management Review* 41, no. 3 (2000): 43–54.

Medoff, P., and H. Sklar. *Streets of Hope*. Boston: South End Press, 1994.

Meyer, A. D. "Adapting to Environmental Jolts." *Administrative Science Quarterly* 27, no. 4 (1982): 515–537.

Miles, M. B., and A. M. Huberman. *Qualitative Data Analysis: An Expanded Sourcebook*. 2d ed. Thousand Oaks, CA: Sage Publications, 1994.

Mintzberg, H., and J. A. Waters. "Of Strategies, Deliberate and Emergent." *Strategic Management Journal* 6, no. 3 (1985): 257–272.

Moe, M., and H. Blodgett. "The Knowledge Web." Global Securities Research & Economics Group, Global Fundamental Equity Research Department, 2000.

Moore, K., and J. Birkinshaw. "Managing Knowledge in Global Service Firms: Centers of Excellence." *Academy of Management Executive* 12, no. 4 (1998): 81–92.

Moorman, C., and A. S. Miner. "Organizational Improvisation and Organizational Memory." *Academy of Management Review* 23, no. 4 (1998): 698–723.

Mowery, D. C., J. E. Oxley, and B. S. Silverman. "Strategic Alliances and Interfirm Knowledge Transfer." *Strategic Management Journal* 17 (winter 1996): 77–91.

Nahapiet, J., and S. Ghoshal. "Social Capital, Intellectual Capital, and the Organizational Advantage." *Academy of Management Review* 23, no. 2 (1998): 242–266.

Nelson, R., and S. Winter. *An Evolutionary Theory of Economic Change*. Cambridge, MA: Harvard University Press, 1982.

Nisbet, R. A. *The Quest for Community: A Study in the Ethics of Order and Freedom*. London: Oxford University Press, 1953.

———. *Social Change and History: Aspects of the Western Theory of Development*. London: Oxford University Press, 1975.

Nohria, N., and R. C. Eccles. "Face-to-Face: Making Network Organizations Work." In *Networks and Organizations: Structure, Form, and Action*, edited by N. Nohria and R. C. Eccles, 288–308. Boston: Harvard Business School Press, 1992.

———. *Networks and Organizations: Structure, Form, and Action*. Boston: Harvard Business School Press, 1992.

Nohria, N., and S. Ghoshal. *The Differentiated Network: Organizing Multinational Corporations for Value Creation*. San Francisco: Jossey-Bass, 1997.

Nonaka, I., and H. Takeuchi. *The Knowledge-Creating Company: How Japanese Companies Create the Dynamics of Innovation*. New York: Oxford University Press, 1995.

O'Dell, C., and C. J. Grayson. "If We Only Knew What We Know: Identification and Transfer of Internal Best Practices." *California Management Review* 40, no. 3 (1998): 154–174.

Oldenburg, R. *Celebrating the Third Place: Inspiring Stories about the Great Good Places at the Heart of Our Communities*. New York: Marlowe & Company, 1989.

Oliver, A. L., and P. Liebeskind. "Three Levels of Networking for Sourcing Intellectual Capital in Biotechnology." *International Studies of Management and Organization* 27, no. 4 (1998): 76–103.

Olson, M. *The Rise and Decline of Nations: Economic Growth, Stagflation and Social Rigidities*. New Haven, CT: Yale University Press, 1982.

Orlikowski, W. J., and D. C. Gash. "Technological Frames: Making Sense of Information Technology in Organizations." *ACM Transactions on Information Systems* 12, no. 2 (1994): 174–207.

Orr, J. *Talking about Machines: An Ethnography of a Modern Job*. Ithaca, NY: IRL Press, 1996.

Paloff, R. M., and K. Pratt. *Building Learning Communities in Cyberspace*. San Francisco: Jossey-Bass, 1999.

Pasmore, W. A. *Designing Effective Organizations: The Sociotechnical Systems Perspective*. New York: Wiley, 1988.

Pava, C. "Redesigning Sociotechnical Systems Design: Concepts and Methods for the 1990s," *The Journal of Applied Behavorial Science* 22, no. 3 (1986): 207.

Pea, R. D. "Practices of Distributed Intelligence and Designs for Education." In *Distributed Cognitions: Psychological and Educational Considerations*, edited by G. Solomon, 47–87. New York: Cambridge University Press, 1993.

Peters, T. J. *Liberation Management: Necessary Disorganization for the Nanosecond Nineties*. New York: Knopf, 1992.

Poarch, M. "Ties That Bind: U.S. Suburban Residents on the Social and Civil Dimensions of Work." *Community, Work and Family* 1, no. 2 (1998): 125–148.

Poell, R. F., F. J. Van der Krogt, and D. Wildemeersch. "Strategies in Organizing Work-Related Learning Projects." *Human Resource Development Quarterly* 10, no. 1 (1999): 43–61.

Polanyi, M. *The Tacit Dimension*. New York: Anchor Doubleday, 1966.

Porac, J. F., H. Thomas, and C. Baden-Fuller. "Competitive Groups as Cognitive Communities: The Case of the Scottish Knitwear Manufacturers." *Journal of Management Studies* 26 (1989): 397–416.

Porter, M. "Clusters and the New Economics of Competition." *Harvard Business Review*, November–December 1998, 77–90.

Portes, A., and P. Landolt. "The Downside of Social Capital." *The American Prospect*, May–June 1996, 18–21, 94.

Powell, W. W., W. W. Koput, and L. Smith-Doerr. "Interorganizational Collaboration and the Locus of Innovation: Networks of Learning in Biotechnology." *Administrative Science Quarterly* 41, no. 1 (1996): 116–145.

Preece, J. *Online Communities: Designing Usability, Supporting Sociability*. New York: Wiley, 2000.

Pucik, V. "Strategic Alliances, Organizational Learning, and Competitive Advantage: The HRM Agenda." *Human Resource Management* 27, no. 1 (1988): 77–93.

Putnam, R. D. "Bowling Alone: America's Declining Social Capital." *Journal of Democracy* 6, no. 1 (1995): 65–78.

———. *Bowling Alone: The Collapse and Revival of American Community*. New York: Simon & Schuster, 2000.

———. *Making Democracy Work: Civic Traditions in Modern Italy*. Princeton, NJ: Princeton University Press, 1993.

Quinn, J. B. *Intelligent Enterprise: A Knowledge and Service Based Paradigm for Industry*. New York: Free Press, 1992.

Quinn, J. B., P. Anderson, and S. Finkelstein. "Managing Professional Intellect: Making the Most of the Best." *Harvard Business Review*, March–April 1996, 71–80.

Rifkin, J. *The Age of Access: The New Culture of Hypercapitalism, Where All of Life Is a Paid-For Experience*. New York: Jeremy P. Tarcher/Putnam, 2000.

Roberts, S. "In the Shadows: A Special Report, Off-Field Hurdles Stymie Indian Athletes," *New York Times*, 17 June 2001.

Roethlisberger, F. J., and W. J. Dickson. *Management and the Worker: An Account of a Research Program Conducted by the Western Electric Company, Hawthorne Works, Chicago*. Cambridge, MA: Harvard University Press, 1939.

Ruddy, T. M., and R. Cheslow. "Eureka II." Presentation at the Communities of Practice conference, San Diego, April 2000.

Sackman, S. A. "Culture and Subcultures: An Analysis of Organizational Knowledge." *Administrative Science Quarterly* 37, no. 1 (1992): 140–161.

Sarason, S. B. *The Psychological Sense of Community*. San Francisco: Jossey-Bass, 1974.

Sawhney, M., and E. Prandelli. "Communities of Creation: Managing Distributed Innovation in Turbulent Markets." *California Management Review* 42, no. 4 (2000): 24–54.

Saxenian, A. *Regional Advantage: Culture and Competition in Silicon Valley and Route 128*. Cambridge, MA: Harvard University Press, 1996.

Schank, R. C., and G. S. Morson. *Tell Me a Story: Narratives and Intelligence*. Chicago: Northwestern University Press, 1995.

Schein, E. H. *Organizational Culture and Leadership*. San Francisco: Jossey-Bass, 1992.

———. "Three Cultures of Management: The Key to Organizational Learning." *Sloan Management Review* 38, no. 1 (1996): 9–20.

Schön, D. A. *Educating the Reflective Practitioner*. San Francisco: Jossey-Bass, 1987.

———. *The Reflective Practitioner: How Professionals Think in Action*. New York: Basic Books, 1983.

Scott, J. *Social Network Analysis*. London: Sage, 1991.

Scott, R. W. *Organizations: Rational, Natural, and Open Systems*. Englewood Cliffs, NJ: Prentice Hall, 1992.

Senge, P. M. *The Fifth Discipline: The Art and Practice of the Learning Organization*. New York: Currency/Doubleday, 1990.

Skocpol, T. "How Americans Became Civic." In *Civic Engagement in American Democracy*, edited by T. Skocpol, 27–80. Washington, DC: Brookings Institution Press, 1999.

————. "The Tocqueville Problem: Civic Engagement in American Democracy." *Social Science History* 21, no. 4 (1997): 455–477.

Snyder, W. M. "Boost4Kids: Building and Sharing Knowledge to Get Results for Kids." Special Report to the Office of the Vice President, National Partnership for Reinventing Government, Washington, DC, November 2000.

————. "Communities of Practice: Combining Organization Learning and Strategy Insights to Create a Bridge to the Twenty-First Century." Paper presented at the Academy of Management Annual Meeting, Boston, August 1997.

————. "Organization and World Design: The Gaia's Hypotheses." Paper presented at the Academy of Management Annual Meeting, San Diego, CA, August 1998.

————. "Organization Learning and Performance: An Exploration of the Linkages between Organization Learning, Knowledge, and Performance." Ph.D. diss., University of Southern California, 1996.

Snyder, W. M., and T. G. Cummings. "Organization Learning Disorders: Conceptual Model and Intervention Hypotheses." *Human Relations* 51, no. 7 (1998): 873–895.

Spender, J. C. *Industry Recipes: An Enquiry into the Nature and Sources of Managerial Judgement.* Oxford: Blackwell, 1989.

Stamps, D. "Communities of Practice: Learning Is Social. Training Is Irrelevant?" *Training* 34, no. 2 (1997): 35–42.

Star, S. L., and J. Griesemer. "Institutional Ecology, 'Translations' and Boundary Objects: Amateurs and Professionals in Berkeley's Museum of Vertebrate Zoology, 1907–1939." In *Social Studies of Science*, vol. 19. London: Sage, 1989.

Starkey, K., C. Barnatt, and S. Tempest. "Beyond Networks and Hierarchies: Latent Organizations in the U.K. Television Industry." *Organization Science* 11, no. 3 (2000): 299–305.

Stewart, T. A. *Intellectual Capital: The New Wealth of Organizations.* New York: Doubleday, 1997.

Storck, J., and P. A. Hill. "Knowledge Diffusion through 'Strategic Communities.'" *Sloan Management Review* 41, no. 2 (2000): 63–74.

Stuart, I., P. Deckert, D. McCutcheo, and R. Kunst. "Case Study: A Leveraged Learning Network." *Sloan Management Review* 39, no. 4 (1998): 81–93.

Sveiby, K., L. Edvinsson, and M. S. Malone. *Intellectual Capital: Realizing Your Company's True Value by Finding Its Hidden Roots.* New York: HarperBusiness, 1997.

Szulanski, G. "Exploring Internal Stickiness: Impediments to the Transfer of Best Practice within the Firm." *Strategic Management Journal* 17 (Winter Special Issue 1996): 27–43.

Teigland, R. "Communities of Practice in an Internet Firm—Netovation versus On-Time Performance." In *Knowledge and Communities: Resources for the Knowledge-Based Economy,* edited by E. Lesser, M. Fontaine, and J. Slusher, 151–178. Boston: Butterworth-Heinemann, 2000.

Topolsky, J. "The Northeast Indiana TQM Network." *Firm Connections: Advancing Collaboration to Build Competitive Firms* 1, no. 2 (1993): 3, 8.

Trice, H. M., and J. M. Beyer. *The Cultures of Work Organizations.* Englewood Cliffs, NJ: Prentice Hall, 1993.

Tsai, W., and S. Ghoshal. "Social Capital and Value Creation: The Role of Intra-firm Networks." *Academy of Management Journal* 41, no. 4 (1998): 464–476.

Tsoukas, H. "The Firm as a Distributed Knowledge System: A Constructionist Approach." *Strategic Management Journal* 17 (winter special issue 1996): 11–25.

Tuckman, B. W. "Development Sequences in Small Groups." *Psychological Bulletin* 63 (1965): 384–399.

Van Maanen, J., and S. Barley. "Occupational Communities: Culture and Control in Organizations." In *Research in Organizational Behavior*, vol. 6, edited by B. M. Staw and L. L. Cummings, 287–365. Greenwich, CT: JAI Press, 1984.

von Hippel, E. "Cooperation between Rivals: Informal Know-How Trading." *Research Policy* 16, no. 6 (1987): 303–315.

———. *Sources of Innovation*. London: Oxford University Press, 1988.

Walsh, J. P., and G. R. Ungson. "Organizational Memory." *Academy of Management Review* 16, no. 1 (1991): 57–91.

Walzer, M. "Social Breakdown: The Idea of Civil Society." *Dissent* 38, no. 2 (1991): 293–304.

Weick, K. E. *The Social Psychology of Organizing*. 2d ed. New York: Random House, 1979.

Weisbord, M. R. *Discovering Common Ground*. San Francisco: Berrett-Koehler, 1992.

Weiss, L. M. "Collection and Connection: The Anatomy of Knowledge Sharing in Professional Services Firms." *Organization Development Journal* 17, no. 4 (1999): 61–77.

Wellman, B., and B. Leighton. "Networks, Neighborhoods, and Communities: Approaches to the Study of the Community Question." *Urban Affairs Quarterly* 14, no. 3 (1979): 363–390.

Wenger, E. *Communities of Practice: Learning, Meaning, and Identity*. New York: Cambridge University Press, 1998.

———. "Supporting Communities of Practice: A Survey of Community-Oriented Technologies." <http://www.ewenger.com/tech>, March 2001.

Wenger, E., and W. M. Snyder. "Communities of Practice: The Organizational Frontier." *Harvard Business Review*, January–February 2000, 139–145.

Werner, B. M., and W. Souder. "Measuring R&D Performance—State of the Art." *Research-Technology Management*, March–April 1997, 34–42.

Wheatley, M. J. *Leadership and the New Science: Discovering Order in a Chaotic World*. San Francisco: Berrett-Koehler, 1994.

Whetten, D. A. "What Matters Most." *Academy of Management Journal* 26, no. 2 (2000): 175–178.

Williams, R. L., and J. Cothrel. "Four Smart Ways to Run Online Communities." *Sloan Management Review* 41, no. 4 (2000): 81–91.

Winter, S. G. "Knowledge and Competence as Strategic Assets." In *The Competitive Challenge: Strategies for Industrial Innovation and Renewal*, edited by D. Teece, 159–184. Cambridge, MA: Ballinger, 1987.

Wrege, C. D., and R. M. Hodgetts. "Frederick W. Taylor's 1899 Iron Observations: Examining Fact, Fiction, and Lessons for the New Millennium." *Academy of Management Journal* 43, no. 6 (2000): 1283–1291.

Yeung, A. K., D. Ulrich, S. Nason, and M. A. Von Glinow. *Organizational Learning Capability*. London: Oxford University Press, 1998.

Yin, R. K. *Case Study Research: Design and Methods*. Newbury Park, CA: Sage Publications, 1989.

Zack, M. H. "Developing a Knowledge Strategy." *California Management Review* 41, no. 3 (1999): 125–145.

Zemke, R. "Why Organizations Still Aren't Learning." *Training* (September 1999), 49.

Index

About the Authors

ETIENNE WENGER is as an independent consultant, researcher, author, and speaker. He was a pioneer of "communities of practice" research and is now a globally recognized thought leader in the field. He was featured by *Training Magazine* in its "A New Breed of Visionary" series. He was the coauthor, with Jean Lave, of *Situated Learning*, in which the term "community of practice" was coined. More recently, he wrote *Communities of Practice: Learning, Meaning, and Identity*, a book that lays down the theory of communities of practice. His work is not merely theoretical, however. As a consultant, he helps organizations to cultivate communities of practice and develop knowledge systems that leverage the synergy between learning and community. He also teaches online courses on communities of practice.

RICHARD McDERMOTT, President of McDermott Consulting, has been designing knowledge organizations for nearly two decades. As a hands-on consultant, he has extensive practical experience in designing companywide community development initiatives and has personally helped to start and maintain many communities of practice. His articles on communities of practice and knowledge management have appeared in the *California Management Review*, the *Knowledge Management*

Review, Journal of Knowledge Management, IHRIM Journal, Journal for Quality and Participation, Management & Innovation, Knowledge Management Magazine, Advances in Interdisciplinary Studies of Work Teams, and *Info Ressources Humaines.* He also serves on the editorial board of the *Knowledge Management Review* and is a frequent speaker at knowledge management and organizational design conferences. He was recently the content expert on two national benchmark studies: one on building a knowledge-sharing culture, the other on communities of practice.

WILLIAM M. SNYDER, PH.D., has consulted in the area of organization development for almost twenty years and has worked at McKinsey & Company on strategic knowledge initiatives for the firm and its clients. His work now focuses on the civil sector, and he advises initiatives led by civic groups, foundations, and government agencies. He worked with Vice President Gore's National Partnership for Reinventing Government to help launch several national communities of practice that focus on civic issues, including family health, public safety, and workforce development. His action-research interests lie in ways to build civil-sector institutional capacity for learning and innovation—at the local, state, federal, and global levels.

You can contact the authors online at <www.cultivatingcommunities.com>.